Publication Number 32

Duke University Commonwealth-Studies Center

Contemporary Canada

Contemporary Canada

Nathan Keyfitz   J. Murray Beck
Hubert Guindon   Claude T. Bissell
William C. Hood   Irving J. Goffman
H. E. English   James Eayrs
Gérard Dion   Richard A. Preston
John Meisel   Richard H. Leach

Edited by Richard H. Leach

Published for the
Duke University Commonwealth-Studies Center
Duke University Press, Durham, N.C.
1967

Printed in the United States of America
by Kingsport Press, Inc., Kingsport, Tenn.

Preface

The Committee on Commonwealth Studies of Duke University
sponsored a Seminar on Contemporary Canada during 1966, the
fifth seminar on Canada the committee had held since its establishment in 1956.[1] The Seminar on Contemporary Canada sought
to explore various aspects of the recent Canadian scene and to
attempt to provide an understanding of the major problems and
prospects which Canada faces as it enters its second century of
Confederation. Eleven experts on Canada were invited to come
to the Duke campus between May and October, 1966, to present
and discuss their papers with advanced graduate students and
faculty in the several social science disciplines represented on the
Committee on Commonwealth Studies. Each contributor subsequently had an opportunity to revise his paper, and they are now
collected and presented in printed form. Data on each of the contributors are listed in alphabetical order on the following pages.
It is the committee's hope that this volume will provide new insights into Canada and that it will be a useful addition to the
literature on a nation that is in the process of rapid growth and
development.

The editor, on behalf of the committee, wishes to thank the
contributors to the seminar, as well as Calvin B. Hoover, James B.
Duke Professor of Economics, and Craufurd Goodwin, Associate
Professor of Economics, both of Duke University, for their help

1. The papers contributed to the earlier seminar have been published in the
following volumes in the Duke Commonwealth-Studies series: A. R. M. Lower,
et al., Evolving Canadian Federalism (1958); Hugh G. J. Aitken, et al., The
American Economic Impact on Canada (1959); Hugh L. Keenleyside, et al.,
The Growth of Canadian Policies in External Affairs (1960); and David R. Deener,
ed., Canada–United States Treaty Relations (1963).

in planning the seminar. Special thanks are due to Richard A. Preston, William K. Boyd Professor of History, and John McKinney, Professor of Sociology, Duke University, for their help in editing the manuscript for publication in this volume.

RICHARD H. LEACH

Contributors

J. Murray Beck, Professor of Political Science, Dalhousie University. Born in Nova Scotia in 1914 and a graduate of Acadia University, Mr. Beck received both his M.A. and Ph.D. degrees in political science from the University of Toronto. A public school teacher prior to World War II, he taught political science at Acadia University and the Royal Military College of Canada before going to Dalhousie in 1963. Among his writings are *The Government of Nova Scotia* (Toronto, 1957) and *Joseph Howe: Voice of Nova Scotia* (Toronto, 1964).

Claude T. Bissell, President, University of Toronto. Born in Ontario in 1916 and a graduate of the University of Toronto, Mr. Bissell's field is English. He received his Ph.D. from Cornell University and taught there briefly before returning to the University of Toronto where he served in the Department of English and as Assistant to the President and Vice President until he assumed the presidency of Carleton College (now Carleton University) in 1956. He became President of the University of Toronto in 1958. He has written both in the fields of education and literature. In 1967 he was appointed to the first chair of Canadian studies at Harvard University.

Abbé Gérard Dion, Professor of Industrial Relations, Université Laval. A native of Quebec, born in 1912, Abbé Dion graduated from the College de Levis and did his graduate work at Université Laval. He has served on the Faculty of Social Sciences at Université Laval since 1944 and was Director, Department of Industrial Relations, from 1957 to 1964. He is the editor of the bilingual quarterly, *Industrial Relations (Relations industrielles)* and has written extensively in his field.

James Eayrs, Professor of Political Economy, University of Toronto. Born in England in 1926, Professor Eayrs was educated at the University of Toronto, Columbia University, and the London School of Economics. He joined the Department of Political Economy at the

University of Toronto in 1952. His special field is international politics and he has written a number of books on Canadian, Commonwealth, and international affairs. He is co-editor of the *International Journal*, official quarterly publication of the Canadian Institute of International Affairs, and a Fellow of the Royal Society of Canada. His books include *In Defence of Canada*, 2 vols. (Toronto, 1964 and 1965), which was awarded the Governor-General's prize for non-fiction in 1966, and *Fate and Will in Foreign Policy* (Ottawa, 1967). He was named a John Simon Guggenheim Memorial Fellow in 1967.

H. E. English, Director of the School of Commerce and Professor of Economics, Carleton University. A native of British Columbia, born in 1924, and a graduate of the University of British Columbia, Professor English received his Ph.D. in Economics from the University of California, Berkeley. From 1949 to 1962 he served in the Department of Economics at Carleton University and from 1962 to 1966 as Director of Research, Canadian Trade Committee, and Secretary of the Planning Association of Canada in Montreal. He returned to Carleton in 1966. His publications and research have been chiefly in the areas of international trade, industrial structure, and Canadian commercial and economic policy.

Irving J. Goffman, Associate Professor of Economics, University of Florida. Born in Montreal in 1933, Professor Goffman attended McGill University and received his graduate degrees from Duke University. He served as research economist for the government of Canada in 1958–59 and joined the Department of Economics at the University of Florida in 1959. He has contributed a number of articles to economic journals and is the author of *The Burden of Canadian Taxation* (Canadian Tax Foundation, 1962) and *Some Fiscal Aspects of Public Welfare in Canada* (Canadian Tax Foundation, 1962). He is presently engaged in research on Canadian expenditures.

Hubert Guindon, Associate Professor of Sociology, Sir George Williams University. Born in Quebec in 1929, Professor Guindon attended the University of Ottawa and did graduate work at the Universities of Ottawa, Montreal, and Chicago. He served on the faculty of the Université de Montréal from 1954 to 1960 and came to Sir George Williams in 1962, where since 1966 he has been chairman of the Department of Sociology and Anthropology. He has been involved in a number of community studies and has published in several scholarly journals. His article, "The Social Evolution of Quebec Reconsidered," in the *Canadian Journal of Economics and Political Science* (vol.

XXVI, November, 1960) was awarded the President's Medal by the University of Western Ontario as the best scholarly article published in 1960.

William C. Hood, Adviser, Bank of Canada. Born in Nova Scotia in 1921, Dr. Hood graduated from Mount Allison University and did graduate work in economics and econometrics at the University of Toronto (M.A. and Ph.D.) and the University of Chicago. A member of the Department of Political Economy at the University of Toronto from 1946 to 1964, he served as assistant director of research, Royal Commission on Canada's Economic Prospects, 1955–56, and director of research, Royal Commission on Banking and Finance, 1961–63. He joined the staff of the Bank of Canada in 1964. Among his publications are *Output, Labour and Capital in the Canadian Economy* (Ottawa, 1957), and *Financing of Economic Activity in Canada* (Ottawa, 1958).

Nathan Keyfitz, Professor of Sociology, University of Chicago. Born in Montreal in 1913, Professor Keyfitz graduated from McGill University and earned his doctorate from the University of Chicago. He served in the Dominion Bureau of Statistics from 1936 to 1959, when he went to the University of Toronto as Professor of Sociology. He became professor in the Department of Sociology at the University of Chicago in 1963 and chairman in 1965. He has contributed to professional journals and has served on a number of technical assistance projects for the United Nations.

Richard H. Leach, Professor of Political Science, Duke University. A native of Colorado, born in 1922, Professor Leach attended Colorado College and received his graduate degrees from Princeton University. He taught at the Georgia Institute of Technology and served as a member of the staff of the Southern Regional Education Board before joining the Department of Political Science at Duke University in 1955. His special fields of interest are intergovernmental relations and political theory, and his books include *In Quest of Freedom: American Political Thought and Practice* (Englewood Cliffs, N. J., 1959) and *Interstate Relations in Australia* (Lexington, Ky., 1965).

John Meisel, Professor of Political Studies, Queen's University. Born in Vienna in 1923, Professor Meisel attended the University of Toronto and received his Ph.D. from the University of London. He assumed his present position as Professor and Head of the Department of Political Studies at Queen's University in 1965. His special field of interest is political parties and elections. He served as research supervisor for political behavioral studies for the Royal Commission on Bilingualism and Biculturalism and is the author of *Canadian General Election of 1957* (Toronto, 1962).

Richard A. Preston, William K. Boyd Professor of History, Duke University. A native of England, born in 1910, Professor Preston received his B.A. and M.A. degrees at Leeds University and his Ph.D. degree at Yale. He was lecturer at the University of Toronto and at University College, Cardiff, and during World War II served in the Royal Air Force. He then served as an assistant professor at the University of Toronto before becoming a professor at the Royal Military College of Canada. He came to Duke University in 1965. He is a Fellow in the Royal Historical Society and a former president of the Canadian Historical Association. Professor Preston's publications include *Gorges of Plymouth Fort: A Life of Sir Ferdinando Gorges* (Toronto, 1953), *Men in Arms: A History of Warfare and Its Interrelationships with Western Society* (New York, 1956 and 1962) with S. F. Wise and H. O. Werner, *Canada in World Affairs, 1959–1961* (Toronto, 1965), and *Canada and "Imperial Defense"* (Durham, N. C., 1966).

Contents

Contemporary Canada

It is my hope that our centennial year celebrations will increase our legitimate pride in our country and help us all to see Canada whole—not in its parts, in its divisions, in its difficulties, but whole, as a great and fortunate country with an honourable past of high achievement, a present of exciting and worthy effort, and a future, if we have the will and the goodwill, which promises a destiny beyond the dreams of those who made our Confederation 100 years ago.

PRIME MINISTER LESTER B. PEARSON
Year's End Message
December 30, 1966

Introduction

Richard H. Leach

A nation's one-hundredth anniversary is generally regarded as an occasion for celebration and special recognition. Canada's centennial is especially worth celebrating because Canada demonstrates in many ways man's ability to triumph over difficulties. Thus, although Confederation took place in 1867, it was not until 1885 that the long-term success of the Canadian national enterprise was assured. For until the Canadian Pacific Railway was completed in that year, it was problematical that a Canadian nation could develop. Since then, however, Canada has gone on, not only to maturity as a nation, but also to an important position on the world stage, and as each year has passed she has demonstrated her talents and her capabilities. The fascinating story of her rapid progress from four separated and underdeveloped colonies to one of the leading members of the international community in the course of a bare hundred years has fortunately been told and told well.[1]

But if Canada's past is worth recalling, its present and its future are worth even greater attention. Therefore, a more meaningful way in which Canada's centennial can be honored is by attempting an assessment of her present circumstances with some effort to suggest the direction of future development. This book aims to do just that. Through the eyes of careful students of the Canadian scene today, certain questions that seem to be most significant in

1. See, for example, D. G. Creighton, *Dominion of the North* (Boston, 1944) and *The Story of Canada* (Toronto, 1959); A. R. M. Lower, *Colony to Nation: A History of Canada* (Don Mills, Ont., 1964); and Edgar McInnis, *Canada, A Political and Social History* (New York, 1947).

terms of Canada's future have been chosen for analysis. No claim is made that *all* the portentous aspects of Canadian life today are analyzed herein; the obvious limits of time and space apply to this project as they do to all such endeavors. Hopefully, however, those aspects which are covered will serve to give the reader a feeling of contemporary Canada and of its problems and prospects as it enters its second century of national life.

❋ ❋ ❋

The Canadian achievement has been built upon a very small population base. Even now, Canada is a nation of only 20 million, and a good proportion of that number arrived as immigrants after World War II. Population thus remains a primary problem of Canada today. Nor does that problem seem to be diminishing. On the contrary, Canada is plagued by a shortage of skilled manpower, and the steady decline of the birth rate—the 1966 birth rate was the lowest in Canadian history—does not suggest that this will be alleviated in the foreseeable future. Nor can any discussion of the Canadian people avoid consideration of the many differences between the English- and the French-speaking parts of the population, differences which will have a profound effect on future Canadian development as they have had on Canadian development in the past. The first essay among those that follow is addressed appropriately enough to questions concerning population and includes some interesting comparisons of the Canadian situation with that in the United States.

As has already been pointed out, an important element in Canada's population problem is the contrast between the two historic ethnic groups that comprise the bulk of the Canadian people, each of which has a different language and religion as well as its own traditions and customs. Much of Canadian history, of Canada's present-day politics and government, and of her future course as a nation can be related to the continual adjustment necessary to accommodate these two ethnic groups. Thus the second essay in this book is devoted to the two Canadian cultures. The problem that the contest between them poses for Canada is also touched upon in a number of the other essays. But to overemphasize the Anglo-French differences, tempting though that may be because they have so many ramifications and so much human interest, is to make too much of them. The truly remarkable thing about Canada surely is that despite this basic contrast and the resultant friction, the country has not only survived as a nation but has managed also to thrive during a hundred years of confederation. Moreover, the two cultures have not only kept their identities but have also achieved a rare form of coexistence. In the process, each has made its own contribution to Canada's growth and development.

Indeed, the most remarkable aspect of the Canadian achievement is not triumph over a potentially disruptive ethnic antipathy but amazing economic development. By far a more impressive contrast in the Canadian story is thus that between the largely exploitive and agricultural economy of 1867 and the sophisticated, substantially industrial economy of 1967. Another marked contrast may be seen between the massive unemployment and severe depression of the thirties and the remarkably widespread prosperity of the sixties. Since World War II, Canada has become an affluent nation, with one of the highest material standards of living in the world. In Canada's centennial year, by every yardstick used to measure such affluence—average annual income, automobile ownership, home ownership, use of mechanical appliances, amount of leisure time, etc.—Canadians rank at or near the top of the list of nations. The third essay is devoted to the Canadian economy. It gives particulars of the country's remarkable growth, and it poses some of the problems which that growth has inevitably brought in its wake.

A good many of those problems arise from the fact that Canada has become so highly industrialized in so short a span of time. The bulk of the country's productive effort is now directed to manufacturing and construction. The presence in Canadian soil of huge reserves of minerals and recent discoveries of vast supplies of oil, natural gas, and uranium, together with the continued development of hydroelectric power, have made Canadian industrialization possible. As a result, the old conflict of interests between primary resource industries and secondary manufacturing industries is no longer relevant. The fourth essay suggests that as soon as the Canadian economy adjusts to the new situation, the future holds great promise for further development.

Accompanying the remarkable progress in Canadian industry has been the parallel development of organized labor in Canada. There are about 1.5 million union members in Canada today, and they have played an important part in shaping public policy, especially in the area of social welfare. Canadian labor organization is perhaps unique in that Canadian labor unions operate in the image and shadow of American unions. Seven out of every ten Canadian union members belong to "international" unions whose leadership is in the United States, a fact which has understandably produced a number of problems. As also in the United States, the union situation is undergoing change. The fifth essay, which is devoted to labor unions, explores several aspects of these changes and of their implications for the future of the labor movement in Canada.

In Canada as elsewhere in the twentieth century, national growth and development have to a large extent been factors of political and governmental action. Canada has used government as a tool for national economic and social advancement from the beginning because Canadians may have understood from the outset the necessity for a good deal of state action in making an inhospitable wilderness a satisfactory place to live and an easy place to exploit in face of a potentially hostile United States. At the same time, as it did in the United States, private enterprise flourished simultaneously, with the result that, especially in the Canadian West, the same rugged individualism that became a hallmark of life below the border seemed also to become the Canadian ideal. This ambiguity provides part of the climate within which Canadian political parties have had to operate, a climate which is described in the sixth essay in this volume. The same essay goes on to suggest some of the other difficulties Canadian parties have encountered and to make the point that parties, like every other aspect of Canadian life, must make a number of changes in both their nature and their *modus operandi* if they are to be effective tools for making the adjustment to the new Canada of tomorrow.

Canadian parties in turn contribute to the climate within which the Canadian governmental system functions. That system is partly in the British pattern in that Canada has a parliamentary form of government. But Canada utilized the example and experience of the United States as well and adopted a federal system of government. Federalism, as has often been pointed out, might have been made necessary by the mere facts of geographic necessity and of the presence of Quebec among the confederating colonies. In the Canadian federal system, power is divided between the provinces and the central government by the terms of the British North America Act of 1867, which serves as Canada's constitution. Perhaps it is in the nature of federalism to be constantly in flux and to demand continuous attention and adjustment to keep it operable. At any rate, that has been the case in Canada. The seventh essay is addressed to changing Canadian federalism. It summarizes current issues in that area and points to possible avenues of development in the future.

Nothing was more conspicuous in the early development of Canadian society than the attention paid to education, and education has remained a central concern of the provinces, which have responsibility for education in Canada under the British North America Act. By the centennial year, however, the national government had come to play an important role as well. Education is compulsory through high school, some forty universities and over three hundred colleges affiliated with them or independently organized have been established, and an extensive program of adult education is in operation. As a result of these efforts, the Canadian population has become over 97 per cent literate, and Canada is renowned for her scientific and cultural advances. Even so, problems of quantity and quality in education have been exposed, and the nation is currently engaged in a process of reassessment. The chief focal points of that reassessment are discussed in the eighth essay in the volume.

Quite as impressive as Canada's educational achievements are those she has made in the field of social welfare. Canadians today are healthier than at any period in history and are among the healthiest peoples of the world, a fact which is attributable in part at least to the initiation of a wide variety of governmental and private social benefits. Today, public hospitalization plans are in operation in all Canadian provinces, and virtually all the population is included in the coverage they offer. Saskatchewan has adopted a full medical-care plan (not without considerable opposition, to be sure), and a nationwide "medicare" plan has been proposed by the federal government. Moreover, there is an extensive federal family allowance and old-age pension scheme. The ninth essay is concerned with the development of Canadian social welfare policy and with some of the problems, economic and otherwise, which that policy presents for the future.

Canada was fortunate in that it could develop and grow to maturity largely at peace with the other nations in the world. It was not until the twentieth century that a sizable amount of the national budget had to be devoted to the maintenance of a military force and a good share of national concern and attention had to be devoted to defense. Given Canada's location, population size and density, and her intimate relationship as far as defense and economic growth and development are concerned with the United States, Canada does not have the range and freedom of choice with regard to defense and military preparation that other nations enjoy. The tenth essay deals with the alternatives Canada does have and the choices it has made and comes to some interesting conclusions as to the problems and prospects arising from those alternatives and choices.

No consideration of contemporary Canada could be concerned solely with the problems and prospects arising from internal growth and development. For Canada never cut her ties with the old world; concurrently with internal development, she remained concerned with her place among the sovereign nations of the world. As early as 1880 Canada sent a representative to Paris and in 1909 added a Department of External Affairs to its governmental structure. During World War II, which Canada entered through her own declaration of war, Canada was a major source of war goods for the allies, and Canadian troops fought on land, in the air, and at sea on all the major fronts. Since then, Canada has played an important role in the United Nations, in NATO, and in providing aid to underdeveloped nations overseas. Much of the Canadian role in international relations is conditioned by her close alliance with the United States. Many of the issues and problems arising in the area of Canada's international relations are dealt with in the eleventh essay in this volume.

The final essay is devoted to presenting an overall view of Canada today and of the prospects for the future.

＊　　＊　　＊

No single volume could hope to do justice to a topic as broad as that encompassed in the title of this volume. In its first hundred years Canada has developed in ways that no one in 1867 could have foreseen. Surely the unexpected will determine development in the second century of Canada's national life. Contemporary Canada represents a triumph over a great many difficulties. Future progress will demand that other difficulties be overcome. Some of them are suggested in the pages that follow. Others are not yet clearly discernible. But if the past and present are trustworthy guides to Canada's future, those difficulties will be surmounted, and Canada's second century will be one of continued national development.

1

Human Resources in Canada: Population problems and prospects

Nathan Keyfitz

Before World War II Canada was thought to be overpopulated. Immigration was restricted to such a point that in some years the number of those returning to Europe exceeded the number of new immigrants coming in. High unemployment was interpreted as an excess of people, and the skilled were not much more in demand than the unskilled. Today, in the same physical territory, the excess has given way to a shortage. Educated immigrants are much desired and not easily obtained. Some immigration did take place during the fifties, when Europe's recovery from the war was incomplete, but this stream has tended to dry up. With advancing technology the unskilled are useless, and the skilled are chronically scarce. The Second Annual Review of the Economic Council of Canada observes somewhat sadly:

Of course, we should continue to try to encourage the inflow of skilled manpower from abroad. However, in a world of great and apparently growing shortages of more highly skilled and educated manpower, we must move energetically towards a more self-reliant development of our domestic manpower resources to meet our pressing needs.[1]

The change in values by which a shortage of people, rather than an excess, has become a problem tells us how differently Canadians see their country now than they did thirty years ago. To exaggerate only slightly, the Canada of the first half of the

1. Economic Council of Canada, *Second Annual Review: Towards Sustained and Balanced Economic Growth* (Ottawa, 1965), p. 95.

century saw itself as living by the export of certain staples—
wheat, newsprint, and minerals especially. It needed enough people to cut the forests, to till the prairies, and to dig for nickel and
gold. Once these ecological niches were filled, once the wheat
fields, gold mines, and sawmills were manned, either up to the
level of the resources available or to the level of the markets that
were in sight, whichever was lower, the country felt itself adequately populated. This population size seems to have been
reached during the twenties. If there was really just so much gold
to be mined and wheat to be sold, if the proceeds were to be
divided like booty among the existing population, then to bring in
more people would simply mean more claims on the fixed product
and hence a lower per capita share. To appreciate the strength of
this argument, which today sounds absurd, one needs to have
lived in Canada during the thirties.

This somber outlook of the public at large expressed itself
specifically in population studies. One aspect was thoroughly
worked out in the writings of Murdoch C. MacLean and Robert
H. Coats. They examined in detail the census populations of the
various rural counties of Canada, many of which were declining
with the movement to the cities during the twenties. The interpretation of the census figures was that each rural county had a
"natural" level of population, and when an attempt was made
through immigration to put more people in, they simply flowed
out—back to Europe, to the United States, or worst of all, to cities
in Canada where they either joined the unemployed or forced
others into unemployment. That cities could draw men from the
countryside to create industry was recognized, but this need for
people was seen as temporary; the people so drawn were a kind of
scaffolding, to be removed and discarded once the building was
in place.

Quite different themes animate social analysis in Canada today,
perhaps the dominant one being the question why Canadian
income per capita is lower than that of the United States. The
points at which the answer to this is sought include the sparsity of
population and the difference in the availability of higher education. Rather than thinking of more people as dividing further a

fixed natural resources pie, Canadians regard them as adding a greater than proportional increment to income—provided only that they are competent.

Another theme which has been stressed in the Duke studies of Canada and which takes a very different form today than it did before World War II is biculturalism—the fact that Canada has not one but two charter peoples, English and French. The picture of French-Canadian culture as essentially rural, based on the family farm, with its tradition and organization, as well as its piety and otherworldly aspiration, taken from seventeenth-century Brittany (as presented by a scholar like Gérin[2] or a novelist like Hémon[3]), was probably always something of a caricature, or let us say an ideal. It was the residue of this attitude that Horace Miner studied,[4] and whose disappearance he documented.[5] An intense aura of values clustered around it: "The countryside is the laboratory in which the forces of good are created," said Edmond de Nevers.[6]

For Philippe Garigue, French Canadians ceased being traditional and pre-Revolutionary a very long time ago. To consider them as essentially rural and agricultural during the nineteenth century is to neglect the cities of Quebec, Trois-Rivières, and Montreal, which, as fur-trading and later commercial and industrial centers, gave the young society a cosmopolitan imprint almost from the beginning. The lively intellectual life of Montreal goes back to pioneer times; its young intellectuals were discussing Voltaire back in the 1840's.[7] Especially incorrect is the contrast with the urban English. As Everett C. Hughes says, "Urbanity and sophistication are perhaps more characteristic of the French than of the English in Montreal."[8]

2. Léon Gérin, *Le Type economique et social des Canadiens* (Montreal, 1938).
3. Louis Hémon, *Maria Chapdelaine* (London, 1946).
4. *St. Denis: A French-Canadian Parish* (Chicago, 1963).
5. Miner, "A New Epoch in Rural Quebec," *American Journal of Sociology*, LVI (1950), 1–10.
6. *L'avenir du peuple canadien-français* (Paris, 1896), p. 301, cited by Albert Faucher, "L'émigration des Canadiens français au XIX° siècle," *Recherches Sociographiques*, V (1964), 277.
7. Séraphin Marion, *Les lettres canadiennes d'autrefois*, 5 vols. (Ottawa, 1939–46).
8. *French Canada in Transition* (Chicago, 1963), p. 209.

Nevertheless, there was enough of the rural and pious for a visiting Frenchman to suggest a kind of implicit agreement between English industrialists and French-speaking clerics whereby religion and language, churches and schools, were to be under the control of the latter, and in return a docile labor force would be guaranteed to the former. When I was a youth some thirty-five years ago, this was indeed whispered in English Montreal and was capable of sending shudders through decent French society. Today it is implicit in the thinking of most urban French Canadians.

By its own *aggiornamento* the Church is adapting its temporal and institutional condition to the contemporary environment. French Canada is recapitulating that aspect of European history by which religion has ceased to dominate economic and political relations. From being an affair of the whole community it has become a private relation of individuals to God. Thus, the students at the University of Montreal are, on the whole, practicing Catholics, but they think of religion as a private matter, not to be brought into politics, and to be restricted in education.

With the advent of nationalism, all structures that might rival the state are diminished—the church and the family, in particular, give over their functions, or else are privileged to retain them as long as they remain subordinate to the state. I am not enough of an admirer of the state to see its victory as wholly good, but that victory seems to be everywhere assured. I suggest that the last Quebec election, in which the rural constituencies were mobilized in favor of traditionalism, was only a small jog in the long trend.

Canadian history includes French aspiration to outbreed the English to secure a *victoire des berceaux* and the English counteroffensive through immigration where the immigrants would assimilate to the English. That both of these weapons are in disuse is made clear by current figures of births and immigrants.

Just as it is a problem for Canadians in general that Canada is not as rich as the United States, so it is a problem for the French Canadians, that they are not as rich and powerful as the English

Canadians. Why does the French Canadian sit at the wheel of the taxi while the English Canadian rides in the passenger's seat? Such comparisons are the order of the day among developing peoples everywhere, and though outsiders tend to see the question as economic, the participants seek answers as much in the political as in the economic sphere. The already industrialized peoples—Americans and English Canadians—have the advantage of having arrived first. Are they to be allowed to keep this advantage forever? Newcomers to industry—the English Canadians and the French Canadians vis-à-vis their respective opponents—do not merely say, "We must work harder; we must compete more efficiently." They say rather that they must exclude the competitor by political action. Canadians in general must have a tariff against American goods (which incidentally helps attract American investment). Quebecers must take over the electric company run by "les trusts anglais" and show that French-Canadian engineers are as good as any. (The company has been taken over, and the engineers *are* as good.)

French Canadians have become tired of knocking on English doors; they want their own economic structures. Political and educational autonomy were granted them by the constitution; now they will use this autonomy in their own economic interest. Instead of learning to speak better English so that he can compete in Ottawa and in English banks and other corporations, the French Canadian now wants to speak better French so as to insure full and creative membership in an international French community. It is even conceivable that knowledge of English will diminish among French Canadians in the years ahead. With some characteristic differences the story is that of developing countries everywhere.

One aspect of the freedom of French Canada is its orientation to a multiplicity of outside societies. "From the point of view of a global society, Quebec is related to France by her culture, to Canada and England by her political institutions, and to the United States by her industry."[9] Specifically, the processes of

9. Jacques Dofny and Hélène David, "Les aspirations des travailleurs de la métallurgie à Montréal," *Recherches Sociographiques*, VI (1965), 61.

social change are more likely to be engaged by contact with American than with English-Canadian industry. "The need for raw materials oriented American industrialism towards the Laurentian plateau. In agreeing to take part in this industrialism the province of Quebec was assured of a sustained market, capital investment, and technical cooperation. At the same time, however, she entered on a course of development which was to have a deeply disturbing effect on her social structures."[10]

These are broad issues. My task is the narrower one of illuminating the condition of Canadian society with data on population. I shall discuss the statistical facts of birth, death, and migration. But to tie demography into society one must look beyond these austere vital statistics to education and participation in the labor force, and this I shall attempt to do at least superficially.

Birth Rates

Table 1, compiled by Jacques Henripin,[11] shows the crude birth rates of Canada and the United States over a fifty-year period. Of

Table 1. *Birth rates, United States and Canada, 1911–64 (Births per thousand inhabitants)*

	United States		Canada
Year	Total	White	Canada
1911	29.9	29.1	33.6
1921	28.1	27.3	29.3
1933	18.4	17.6	21.0
1937	18.7	17.9	20.1
1946	24.1	23.6	27.2
1954	25.3	24.2	28.5
1957	25.3	24.1	28.2
1962	22.7	21.6	25.3
1963	21.7	20.7	24.6
1964	21.2	20.3	23.8

10. Albert Faucher, "Le caractère continental de l'industrialisation au Québec," *Recherches Sociographiques*, VI (1965), 236.

11. Jacques Henripin and Nathan Keyfitz, "Les tendances démographiques au Canada et aux Etats-Unis," *Canadian Review of Sociology and Anthropology*, II (1965), 80.

the several facts which appear in this table, the most remarkable is the parallelism of the two curves. For the fifty years shown the Canadian crude birth rate has been about 3 per thousand higher than that of the United States. The fluctuations of the two are similar, down to the recent drop from the postwar plateau since 1957. One might have thought that the United States would dip deeper in depression than does Canada, but this is not perceptible.

For the most recent period the parallelism appears even more sharply in the percentage changes between certain peaks and troughs (Table 2). This parallelism between the United States

Table 2. *Percentage changes in the birth rates over certain periods, United States and Canada, 1921–64*

Period	United States (Total)	Canada
1921–33	−34.5	−28.3
1933–37	+ 1.6	− 4.3
1937–46	+28.9	+35.3
1946–54	+ 5.0	+ 4.8
1954–57	0.0	− 1.1
1957–64	−16.2	−15.6

Note: The data in Tables 2–15 are derived from official figures and were computed by the author.

and Canada as a whole contrasts with a convergence among the several regions within each country. Quebec showed a crude birth rate of 35 per thousand population in 1921–25 to British Columbia's 18; by 1961 Quebec was 26 and British Columbia was 24.[12] The tendency to uniformity appears in ratios of children to women as they are shown in censuses at twenty-year intervals. Confining ourselves to the present century, the ratio of children under 10 years of age to women 15–45 in Quebec goes down from 1.24 in 1901 (after a sharp dip for which the fall in births during the thirties was responsible) to 1.15 in 1961. For the remaining provinces a net rise was shown over the same period, from 0.96 to 1.17, so that now the ratios are virtually identical. The results are

12. *Canada Year Book 1963–64* (Ottawa, 1964), p. 220.

Table 3. *Children under 10 years of age and women 15–45 years, Quebec and Canada other than Quebec, 1901–61*

	Quebec			Canada except Quebec		
	Children under 10	Women 15–45	Ratio	Children under 10	Women 15–45	Ratio
1901	448,000	361,000	1.24	811,000	842,000	0.96
1921	624,000	521,000	1.20	1,483,000	1,417,000	1.04
1941	701,000	796,000	0.88	1,396,000	1,855,000	0.75
1961	1,295,000	1,126,000	1.15	3,041,000	2,596,000	1.17

somewhat affected by the number of immigrants in the country, and they include a large component of infant mortality as well, so that they somewhat underestimate the differences in pure fertility at the beginning of the century. Nonetheless, it is fair to say that the excess of Quebec over the remainder of Canada diminished from about one-third to about zero during the sixty years.

Age at Marriage

The Canadian birth rate is higher than that of the United States despite a marriage age that is higher in Canada by almost two years on the average for both males and females. Table 4 shows the percentage married at each age from the last census; the most striking differences are under the age of 25. Nearly 90 per cent of the women of both countries ultimately marry, a remarkably high

Table 4. *Percentage of women married by five-year age groups, United States (White), 1960, and Canada, 1961*

Age group	United States 1960	Canada 1961
15–19	15.7	8.6
20–24	70.5	59.2
25–29	87.2	83.7
30–34	89.6	88.0
35–39	88.9	88.5

figure in comparison with Europe. The marrying tendency characteristic of the New World since pioneer days shows in both countries, but it takes effect at younger ages in the United States.

Ages of Childbearing

Besides marrying later, the Canadian wife has her children later in marriage. Table 5 shows children born per thousand married women in the two countries; the rate is higher for the United States only at ages under 20; at 40–44 the Canadian wife is 86 per cent more likely to have a child.

Table 5. *Fertility rate per thousand married women, by five-year age groups, United States and Canada, 1961*

Age group	United States	Canada	Canadian excess (+) as percentage of United States
15–19	545.8	541.2	−0.9
20–24	352.8	374.4	+6.1
25–29	223.5	255.6	+14.3
30–34	126.1	161.4	+28.0
35–39	61.9	89.9	+45.2
40–44	17.3	32.1	+86.0

The American wife not only has her children earlier on the average than the Canadian, but she has them less widely spaced. Another measure of this difference is the variance of ages of women at the birth of their children in the two countries. For 1963 the variance for the United States was 35.85; for Canada 38.21. The square roots of these figures give the standard deviations: 5.987 years for the United States and 6.181 for Canada, a small difference, but one which has persisted through a number of years. That difference is tied to labor force participation: the American housewife evidently wants to get her childbearing over so that she can resume her interrupted career as soon as possible. A similar trend appears in Canada, but in less advanced form; in a situation of labor scarcity like the present one, this is one of the factors which hold down Canadian income, a point which is worth examining in some detail.

Labor Force Participation

The labor force participation of men differs only slightly between countries, the principal difference being that where college attendance is more widespread fewer workers will be found at ages below about 21. But the difference in participation of women between Canada and the United States deserves careful study. Table 6 shows that 1965 participation rates for the United States

Table 6. *Percentage labor force participation of United States and Canadian women*

Age group	United States March, 1965[a]	Canada 1955[b]	Canada 1965[b]
−20	24.4	32.9	30.2
20–24	49.5	46.3	52.6
25–34	37.5	24.2	31.1
35–44	44.8	23.2	34.1
45–54	51.5	22.2	37.0
55–64	40.6	14.7	27.0
65+	10.5	3.9	6.0

a. United States, Department of Labor, *Monthly Report on the Labor Force,* March, 1965 (Washington, D.C., 1965), p. 23.
b. Canada, Department of Labour, *Facts and Figures about Women in the Labour Force, 1965* (Ottawa, 1965), Table 5.

are higher at all ages over 25, and strikingly higher at that. The greatest difference is between 45 and 64, representing most likely the return of married women to paid employment after their children are launched, or when they are nearly independent.

Yet comparison of the Canadian figures for 1955 and 1965 shows how rapidly the situation is changing; the increase in the Canadian rates in the ten years was about equal to the gap between Canada and the United States in 1965. Projections to

1970[13] show continuation of the trend with 37.0 per cent for ages 35–44, 43.5 per cent for 45–54, and 32.0 per cent for 55–64. The projections show about the same rate per year in change of the participation rates as have held in the past; they imply that by about 1975 Canada will have caught up to where the United States was in 1965.

Mortality

Canadian mortality rates are somewhat lower than those of the United States. In 1963 the Canadian expectation of life at age zero was over one and one half years higher than that of the United States for males, and about one year for females (Table 7). Both

Table 7. *Life expectation at age zero, United States and Canada, 1940–63*

	Males			Females		
	United States			United States		
	Total	White	Canada	Total	White	Canada
1940/41	61.46	n.a.	62.48	65.80	n.a.	66.00
1962	66.93	n.a.	68.83	73.58	n.a.	74.30
1963	66.61	67.51	68.31	73.39	74.38	74.31

countries show a slight deterioration in mortality in the most recent period, as though medicine is pushing against a ceiling; once everyone lives to age seventy further progress will await new discoveries for handling the ailments of old age. The comparison is about the same at age five as at age zero. However, if the comparison is confined to the white population, the United States comes off better; the advantage of Canada is eliminated for females and reduced to 0.8 year for males.

If Canadian mortality rates are more favorable on the whole, they are worse at the youngest ages; in the early 1920's they were higher than American rates by about one third. The rates in both

13. Frank T. Denton, Yoshiko Kasahara, and Sylvia Ostry, *Population and Labour Force Projections to 1970*, Staff Study No. 1, Economic Council of Canada (Ottawa, 1965), p. 42.

Table 8. *Infant mortality rate per thousand births, United States and Canada, 1920–64*

Year	United States	Canada
1920–24	76.7	104.7
1925–29	69.0	94.3
1932	57.6	73.3
1937	54.4	75.8
1942	40.4	53.8
1947	32.0	45.5
1952	28.4	38.0
1957	26.4	30.9
1960	26.0	27.3
1961	25.3	27.2
1962	25.3	27.6
1963	25.2	26.3
1964	24.6	25.0

Sources: United Nations, *Demographic Yearbook,* 1948, p. 404; 1961, p. 227; and 1964, p. 552.

countries have moved downward, and in 1963 the difference was small, with Canada at 26.3 deaths under one year of age per thousand births, and the United States at 25.2. The convergence is evidently due to the continentwide spread of sanitation, the increasing proportion of births which take place in the city and in hospitals, the increasing ability of the poor in both countries to command health services, and the advent of antibiotics.

Net Result of Birth and Death Differences

From one point of view the net reproduction rate (NRR) is a fair comparison of net demographic performance in two countries. The United States NRR for 1963 was 1.563; thus at the age-specific rates of birth and death prevailing in that year a girl child just born would be replaced by 1.563 girl children. In other words, it provides an estimate, based on 1963 rates, of the ratio of numbers in two successive generations. The corresponding Canadian figure is 1.717, which is 9.9 per cent higher.

But this is not the whole story. The tendency of Canadians to marry later and have their children later acts on the net population performance. The Canadian NRR may be 10 per cent higher than the American, which means that the Canadian increase is 10 per cent more per generation, but the generation is also longer.

Table 9 shows Lotka's T, the length of generation, defined as $T = (\ln R_o)\, r$, where R_o is the NRR and r the intrinsic rate. The intrinsic rate of natural increase on the female side for Canada was 20.0 per thousand in 1963 and for the United States, 17.1 per thousand. During the course of a fixed period of twenty-five years at these rates, the United States population would multiply in the ratio 1.54, the Canadian population in the ratio 1.65. Canada is 10 per cent higher on the NRR, the ratio of increase over a generation, but only 7 per cent higher on the ratio of increase in twenty-five years.

Table 9. *Average interval between female generations, United States and Canada, 1940–64*

Year	United States	Canada
1940[a]	27.23	28.89
1950[a]	26.35	28.08
1960[a]	25.97	27.41
1962	26.08	27.39
1963	26.16	27.37
1964	26.25	27.45

a. Three-year average around census: for the United States 1939–41, etc.; for Canada 1940–42, etc.

The Family Cycle

The facts cited above can be placed in a context of the family cycle. The Canadian family has a lower turnover than the American—the person emerges later from the family orientation period, delays his marriage, which is to say the founding of his own family, starts having children later, and has the children over a longer span of time.

Paul Glick has shown how the trends in the United States now as compared with the beginning of the century have been toward (1) younger age at marriage, (2) children sooner after marriage, (3) children leaving home at a younger age, and (4) more favorable mortality rates for the parents.[14] These all combine to produce a new element in the population—the couple still living and in good health, whose children have left home. In a high proportion of cases the wife takes a job; in middle-class occupations the husband has yet to reach his highest income. Indeed, the late possession of a good income even comes to affect the physical structure of cities over the entire continent: the high-rise, high-rent apartments which are increasingly a feature of the cities of the United States and Canada are inhabited in large part by these couples who no longer need the suburban home and back yard in which they raised their children. Canada is slightly behind, but only very slightly, in the various demographic and economic characteristics which make up the trend. However, a difference of one year in marriage age when applied in two successive generations means that parents are two years younger at the launching of their children, a magnification effect which amplifies the difference between the United States and Canada.

Convergence

The regions and social classes in both countries tend increasingly to resemble one another in family size. With the advent of birth control people can have the size family they want. It might have been thought that this would give play to individual preference; some would want many children, others would prefer to spend their incomes in other ways. In fact, people seem to use their freedom to have just two to four children.[15]

The negative association of fertility with social class in the thirties seemed to be due to the ability of the upper income and education classes to control the size of their families. Pessimists thought that children could not compete with consumer goods; as

14. *American Families* (New York, 1957).
15. Judith Blake, "Ideal Family Size Among White Americans," *Demography*, III (1966), 154–173.

soon as people had a real choice of whether to have children or not, they would not have them. Now that nearly everyone is able to control family size there are signs of a positive association of fertility and social class. These tendencies are visible in Canada as in the United States.

A Feedback Effect

The birth rates of the fifteen or so years following World War II were much higher in both Canada and the United States than in Europe. There seemed to be unlimited room for people on this continent. Only with the growing to maturity of the postwar baby crop do parents see that it is difficult to get their children into schools, difficult to place them in jobs. That these difficulties act to restrain the new generation of parents is made clear by declining birth rates throughout North America since the mid-fifties.

Mortality and Fertility in French and English Canada

One of the questions of Canadian demography has been the relation of vital rates in Ontario and Quebec. In the interest of concreteness the argument here will be confined to females. For mortality we begin with the expectation of life at age zero, shown in Table 10 from 1930 to 1963. Evidently the gap between Quebec and Ontario has steadily closed over the period, about one quarter of the 1930 gap remaining in 1963.

Table 10. *Life expectation at age zero for females, Canada, Quebec, and Ontario, 1930–64*

	Canada	Quebec	Ontario
1930–32	61.81	57.36	63.67
1940–42	66.29	63.16	68.43
1950–52	70.93	68.63	71.89
1960–62	74.30	72.87	74.48
1963	74.42	72.90	74.66
1964	74.95	73.84	75.45

If the same figures are compared with other standards (Table 11), about the same result is obtained as before, with a somewhat larger fraction of the 1930 gap still remaining in 1963. The differential, however, may well be greater at the younger ages and less at the older, if the expectations at ages 5 and 20 are extended (Table 12). It appears that the differential starts smaller than it

Table 11. *Standardized death rates for females, Canada, Quebec, and Ontario, 1930–63*

	England and Wales 1961 as standard			United States 1960 as standard		
	Canada	Quebec	Ontario	Canada	Quebec	Ontario
1930–32	16.59	18.96	16.44	13.41	15.73	12.96
1940–42	14.69	16.60	14.19	11.47	13.16	10.80
1950–52	12.24	13.78	12.04	9.27	10.55	9.00
1960–62	10.15	11.31	10.27	7.55	8.43	7.59
1963	10.10	11.31	10.13	7.50	8.42	7.48

Table 12. *Life expectation for females at ages 5 and 20, Canada, Quebec, and Ontario, 1930–63*

	Expectation at age 5			Expectation at age 20		
	Canada	Quebec	Ontario	Canada	Quebec	Ontario
1930–32	63.22	60.76	63.92	49.79	47.77	50.17
1940–42	65.71	63.64	66.67	51.78	49.89	52.43
1950–52	68.91	67.34	69.31	54.50	53.02	54.79
1960–62	71.35	70.22	71.25	56.73	55.62	56.60
1963	71.38	70.22	71.38	56.78	55.66	56.75

did with all ages and still does not entirely close. At older ages, the differential remains more or less constant through time. For example, at age 50 the excess for Ontario is about one year throughout (Table 13).

A comparison of crude birth rates (Table 14) shows Quebec to be higher throughout the period. But the earlier very high rates left Quebec with the heritage of a young population; when allow-

Table 13. *Life expectation for females at age 50, Canada, Quebec, and Ontario, 1930–63*

	Canada	Quebec	Ontario
1930–32	24.82	23.94	24.59
1940–42	25.49	24.48	25.48
1950–52	26.85	25.75	26.87
1960–62	28.41	27.38	28.24
1963	28.46	27.41	28.40

Table 14. *Crude birth rates of Canada, Quebec, and Ontario, 1930–63*

	Canada	Quebec	Ontario
1930–32	23.08	28.80	20.08
1940–42	22.16	26.49	19.05
1950–52	27.17	30.01	25.00
1960–62	25.76	25.94	25.24
1963	24.38	24.40	24.02

ance is made for this, the difference from 1960 onward is reversed (Table 15).

If ever any set of statistics agreed, it is these. On all age-adjusted measures, the figure for Quebec is about 50 per cent higher than that for Ontario in 1930, and during the succeeding generation it falls to the point where it is well below Ontario in the sixties. This remarkable fact is of course associated with the industrialization and urbanization of Quebec and with the change in outlook that has accompanied this process. Those who think in terms of a rural Quebec maintaining the traditional large families are a generation behind the times, a generation of very rapid change in all aspects of life.

Education

The trends in education in Canada and the United States are reflected in Table 16, giving median years of schooling of the male labor force. The age differentials correspond to the fact that

Table 15. *Three comparisons of fertility: Canada, Quebec, and Ontario, 1930–63*

| | Gross reproduction rates | | | Standardized birth rates | | | | | | | | |
| | | | | England and Wales 1961 as standard | | | United States 1960 as standard | | | Intrinsic birth rates | | |
	Canada	Quebec	Ontario	Canada	Quebec	Ontario	Canada	Quebec	Ontario	Canada	Quebec	Ontario
1930–32	1.551	1.928	1.288	20.38	25.52	16.83	20.81	26.03	17.21	22.25	27.41	18.29
1940–42	1.368	1.645	1.178	18.16	21.69	15.39	18.56	22.14	15.75	19.75	23.64	16.44
1950–52	1.713	1.846	1.571	22.41	24.23	20.57	22.92	24.74	21.06	25.15	26.80	23.20
1960–62	1.861	1.768	1.821	24.22	23.35	23.67	24.76	23.83	24.21	27.58	25.94	27.32
1963	1.795	1.725	1.785	23.31	22.06	23.19	23.82	22.52	23.71	26.54	25.07	26.67

Table 16. *Median years of schooling of male labor force by age groups, United States, 1962, and Canada, 1961*

Age group	United States	Canada
25–34	12.4	10.0
35–44	12.2	9.6
45–54	11.1	9.0
55–64	9.0	8.3

Source: Economic Council of Canada, *Second Annual Review*, p. 81.

schooling has been increasing in both countries by about two years per generation. But the United States increase has been greater, and the differential between the two countries in the sixties is wider for young people than for old. The story is told strikingly by the percentages who have completed four years of high school and university (Table 17).

Table 17. *Educational attainment of the male labor force by age groups, United States, 1960, and Canada, 1961*

Age group	Percentage of labor force with 4 years high school only		Percentage of labor force having completed university	
	United States	Canada	United States	Canada
Total, 25–64	24.6	8.7	11.1	5.6
25–34	30.8	8.7	14.7	6.0
35–44	29.5	9.5	11.9	6.3
45–54	20.0	8.5	8.8	5.0
55–64	12.2	7.4	7.0	4.2

Source: Economic Council of Canada, *Second Annual Review*, p. 81.

The Economic Council of Canada takes the "widening education gap" between the two countries with appropriate seriousness. Considering that within each of the countries the relation of income to education is close, can the difference between the two in schooling account for at least part of the difference in income? That it might is suggested by the fact that Canadians with university education actually have higher incomes than graduates in the United States.[16] The Council concludes that

the over-all rates of return to the economy for total investment in education would be relatively high—perhaps in the range of 10 to 15 per cent. . . . Relatively greater emphasis should be placed on facilitating expanding investment in education in relation to expanding investment in other assets . . . in general accordance with the growing concern in many parts of the Canadian economy that the shortage of skilled and trained technical, professional and managerial manpower is even more critical than the problem of enlarging the physical facilities required for increasing output.[17].

The statistical proof that education causes wealth is not without some logical difficulty. The statistical results taken by themselves are equally consistent with the supposition that it is the wealth that causes the education. Suppose one started by assuming that education was merely a consumer good, and that the more income people had the more schooling they bought for themselves or their children. On this model Canada would not become richer by increasing its spending on education any more than by buying luxury automobiles and private yachts.

In fact, education is both a consumer good and a producer good. Because it is partly a producer good, the difference in income between two individuals will be partly redressed by the one with less education going back to school, and the difference between two countries' averages will be reduced by closing the educational gap. Based on this fact, the policies of Canadian governments have dramatically affected not only the intellectual but the economic landscape. Newspapers talk of the establishment of new colleges and the expansion of existing ones as the "growth industry" of Canada in the sixties, just as automobiles and housing were the growth industries which spurred the economy in earlier decades.

Wealth

A final word might be said about Canadian wealth and poverty. In 1964, personal disposable income, the best available indicator

16. Economic Council of Canada, *Second Annual Review,* p. 89.
17. *Ibid.,* p. 91.

of welfare, was $1,643 (Canadian dollars) in Canada against $2,248 (U. S. dollars) in the United States. Prices in the two countries, each in terms of its own currency, were not very different on the whole—clothing and automobiles were cheaper in the United States, while services and food were cheaper in Canada. What is the place of demographic facts in determining that Canadian real income per head is 25 per cent less than United States real income? The following are relevant:

1. The higher birth rate of Canada means a higher proportion of children, who are an expense to their parents before they can become an asset to the economy. In 1963 the percentage of the population under fifteen years of age in Canada was 33.7, in the United States 31.1. The dependency ratio ("under 15" and "65 and over" to "15–64") was .707 against .676.

2. Differences in labor force participation favor the United States. The difference is not great for males of 15–64 years of age—91.8 per cent for Canada against 92.9 per cent for the United States in 1960; but is very large for women—32.0 per cent against 43.2 per cent.[18]

3. If education qualifies labor, then the quality of Canadian labor is lower, as measured by the average difference of years of schooling in favor of the United States.

4. The effect of the ratio of population to land would seem to favor Canada; mineral, timber, and agricultural resources are less per capita for the United States. The 1966 census will count about 20 million Canadian residents, spread over 3.9 million square miles, while the 197 million inhabitants of the United States share 3.6 million square miles—a density of 5 persons per square mile for Canada against 55 for the United States. The more temperate climate of the United States makes its land more useful for agricultural purposes (though one would have to weigh the drawbacks of Arctic snows against Southwest desert), but on the other hand in neither country is agricultural land pressed to the margin; agriculture has not only become highly efficient in returns to its human input but also in returns to its land input. Agricultural efficiency rose faster than industrial in both countries in the fifties.

18. *Ibid.,* p. 57.

5. If agricultural and other resources favor Canada, the dispersion of population, also a fact of the ecological order, handicaps her. Canada needs and has more capital per worker than the United States, partly because dispersion requires relatively more roads, railways, and airports. Climate demands more extensive structures for shelter of people and goods, and Canadians have to spend more on heating them. Partly as a result of climate, seasonal swings are wider and hence capacity is less fully utilized. Manufacturing runs are shorter, which means more make-ready time.

6. Finally, the greater differentials in wages among regions and among industries in Canada than in the United States suggest that geographical, occupational, and industrial mobility of the human factor is not as great as in the United States.[19] Mobility of capital, like the cautious attitude of Canadians to risk-taking, and charges of inefficiency and lack of imagination in higher management, are some things that Canadians are uneasy about.

What are the prospects of improvement in the Canadian position under these six headings? (1) For age distribution, projections show that the proportion of children will diminish through the drop in the birth rate currently taking place. A projection from 1963 with 1963 mortality and fertility rates shows a dependency ratio in 1973 of .669 for Canada against .661 for the United States. (2) For labor force participation, the drop in the birth rate releases women to paid work if they want it; a strong upward trend in participation is occurring. (3) Monumental efforts are being made to build up higher education in Canada. (4) and (5) Overall population density is increasing in Canada somewhat faster than in the United States, as the ratio of populations moves up toward and passes one Canadian to ten Americans, but there is no likelihood that density will ever be equal in the two countries. On the other hand, the concentration of Canadian population in fewer places will tend to reduce some of the costs of dispersal, an advantage which may offset for the nation the harm done to particular regions and localities. If such resources as oil, water, and base metals are exhausted in the United States earlier than in

19. *Ibid.*, p. 62.

Canada, the rising prices will favor the Canadian standard of living. Whether the advent of such technical improvements as numerical control of machine tools will reduce the disadvantage of smaller scale remains to be seen. (6) With further development of education and transport there may well be more mobility of labor. Such mobility will be an advantage insofar as it takes place within Canada, but it also entails the risk of increasing seepage to the United States, especially of mature and educated labor force. This is part of a worldwide movement from poor countries to richer ones, inevitable with free migration, and from which Canada is suffering less than Britain. Will localities like Nova Scotia and nations like Canada come to tax emigrants an amount equal to the state contribution to their education? Such a tax would seem eminently fair.

Two Cultures: An essay on nationalism, class, and ethnic tension

Hubert Guindon

In highly industrialized societies, the increasing scale of economic organizations goes hand in hand with a corresponding degree of concentration of political power in the central governments. Canada, however, in the last decade has in a climate of political tension experimented in another direction; namely, an increase in the political and economic relevance of the provincial governments at the expense of the federal government. One of the factors bringing this unexpected turn of events has been in no small measure, as most observers will agree, cultural dualism, within which the French-Canadian culture has been more aggressive and forceful. The question therefore becomes: What are the changes, the social forces, within French-Canadian society that brought about this development?

In this essay the social and cultural factors that seem to have been of paramount importance in producing change in French Canada—a new middle class and a resurgence of nationalism—are singled out and analyzed. There are three parts to this study. The first deals with neo-nationalism and traditional societies. In this section, an attempt is made to trace the emergence of modern nationalism in Europe and in traditional societies. Furthermore, elements of a conceptual model that could be useful in interpreting nationalist movements in a comparative fashion are described in some detail. The second section of the essay is an attempt to utilize the model in analyzing social and cultural

changes in French-Canadian society. In a final section, the impact
of the aforementioned cultural and social changes on ethnic accommodation is raised.

Neo-nationalism and Traditional Societies

In his essay on nationality, Lord Acton gives a brilliant account
of its emergence.[1] Until the French Revoluton the exercise of state
power was legitimized by dynastic rule. The rights of nationalities
were neither recognized by governments nor asserted by the
people. Wars between countries were not wars between nations
and did not capitalize on national feeling, but were wars involving dynastic rivalries and conflicting claims between monarchs.
Dynastic rule became despotic, claims Acton, with the brutal
suppression of Poland because of the nature of its monarchy. A
monarch without royal blood, a crown bestowed by the nation,
was an anomaly and an outrage in that age of dynastic absolut-
ism. "This measure awakened the theory of nationality in Europe,
converting a dormant right into an aspiration, and a sentiment
into a political claim."[2]

The legitimacy of dynastic rule was destroyed by the French
Revolution. With the overthrow of dynastic rule and feudal social
structure, a new legitimation of the power of the state had to be
created. Since tradition meant feudalism, it had to be discarded,
and "descent was put in the place of tradition and the French
people were regarded as a physical product: an ethnological, not
an historical unit."[3] In this way the idea of the sovereignty of the
people, uncontrolled by the past, gave birth to the idea of nationality independent of the political influence of history. Nationality
sprang from the rejection of the two authorities—of the state and
of the past. "Every effaceable trace and relic of national history
was carefully wiped away the system of administration, the

1. John E. E. D. Acton, *Essays on Freedom and Power* (London, 1956), pp.
141 ff.
2. *Ibid.*, p. 146.
3. *Ibid.*, p. 148.

physical divisions of the country, the claims of society, the corporations, the weights and measures—even the calendar."[4]

Nationality had been ignored by the Old Regime; the revolutionary wars and the Napoleonic Empire proceeded to outrage it. Napoleon attacked nationality in Russia, delivered it in Italy, and governed in defiance of it in Germany and Spain. Men were made conscious of the national element of the French Revolution not by its rise but by its conquests. With the demise of Napoleon and the Restoration, the governments of the Holy Alliance devoted themselves to suppressing with equal care the revolutionary spirit by which they had been threatened and the national spirit by which they had been restored. The antinational character of the Restoration, most distinct in Austria under Metternich, had the opposite effect of transforming the theory of nationality—that is, the right of national groups to statehood—into a political doctrine. "Beginning by a protest against the domination of race over race, its mildest and least-developed form, it grew into a condemnation of every state that included different races and finally became the complete and consistent theory that the state and the nation be coterminous."[5]

Lord Acton's account of the emergence of the principle of nationalities as a political doctrine can be supplemented by a consideration of De Tocqueville's brilliant analysis of the continuity between the Old Regime and the Revolution.[6] Revolutions seldom start outright with an attack on the legitimacy of the political structure as such but rather as a plea for redress of injustices within the structure itself. His analysis of the *cahiers de doléances* that preceded the Revolution abounds with the practical characteristics of such complaints, covering a wide area of social arrangements. What stunned De Tocqueville was the fact that the centralized bureaucratic structure that had largely been set up under the Ancien Régime was left untouched by the Revolution. Indeed, the kings had progressively substituted their own

4. *Ibid.*, p. 149.
5. *Ibid.*, p. 156.
6. Alexis de Tocqueville, *The Old Regime and the Revolution*, trans. Stuart Gilbert (Garden City, N. Y., 1955).

politically appointed administrators, the feudal lords, to handle
bureaucratic requirements of daily life, thereby extending ter-
ritorially the political dominance of the Crown over the feudal
lords. While the former did the work, however, the latter pocketed
the proceeds, a factor that De Tocqueville considers of great importance in focusing unrest and resentment of the people upon
feudalism. In fact, in those areas of France where the feudal lords
still performed their administrative duties as well as reaping the
rights and privileges of their office, the Revolution was resisted.
This would suggest that revolutions build up gradually from discontent over the unequal distribution of facilities to meet the
prosaic requirements of daily living, to the gradual focusing upon
agents responsible for this state of affairs, to demands for a change
of structure, and finally, to a challenge of the legitimacy of the
overall political structure.[7]

The centralization of bureaucratic power under the monarchy
was retained, however, because of its functional utility as a structure to maintain the political power and cohesion of the state
under the new symbols of legitimacy. Had this bureaucratic centralization not occurred and had it not been maintained, the
chances of France remaining a unified political state would have
been greatly reduced. In summary, the theory of nationality in
Continental Europe provided the symbols whereby the nation-
state was made legitimate after the liquidation of the feudal
political order.

The Emergence of Nationalism in Traditional Societies

From a consideration of the development of nationalism, it is
important next to consider some of the structural features of
contemporary or "current" nationalism. Paradoxical as it may
seem, at the very time that the principle of nationality was reor-
ganizing the political shape and foundations of Europe, the European powers were expanding, developing, and consolidating their

7. This model is to be found in explicit form in Neil Smelser, *A Theory of Collective Behavior* (New York, 1962), chap. iii.

imperial holdings over other parts of the globe. National groups of the imperial powers controlled the political apparatus of the colonies. These endeavors were carried on with the help of the army and the churches.[8] In order to deal with local cultures, the imperial elite within the colonies would work with indigenous political structures of a tribal or feudal character or create such native political leadership. Administrative and political boundaries were carved with little or no regard for the ethnological homogeneity or heterogeneity of the indigenous populations.

The symbol of "legitimation" for the empire-builders was the "spread of civilization." In providing this legitimation, the Christian churches were of paramount importance. The religious legitimation took the form of converting the indigenous populations to Christianity, thereby heeding the prescription of the Gospel. The "spread of civilization" involved the armies, to assure political stability; the capitalists, to spread the benefits of industrialization; and the clergy, to bring them the Kingdom of God.

Colonial rule swiftly and deeply affected the local traditional cultures as well as the traditional social structure of the various indigenous groups. Not infrequently, the nature of traditional indigenous culture before the Western presence is clouded in mystery and is the object of historical speculation and of archeological investigation. The very success of the imperial ventures gave rise to an indigenous middle class recruited from the various indigenous groups, a middle class whose status, power, and prestige were derived from its formal though subordinate participation in the expanding institutions of the imperial regimes. While the newly acquired status of the middle class was honored by its co-nationals, it was bestowed upon them by the ruling aliens. The social mobility of the middle class was accompanied by a high degree of acculturation. The local clerically staffed schools gave its children their basic education and not infrequently the more promising would have some years in the metropolitan centers overseas.

Irrespective of the occupational dissimilarities, whether they

8. Hans H. Gerth and C. Wright Mills, *Character and Social Structure: The Psychology of Social Institutions* (New York, 1964), pp. 192 ff.

were minor civil servants, teachers, industrial white-collar workers, or non-commissioned officers in the army, the members of this
newly arisen middle class had many common characteristics: they
were bureaucratically employed, they were culturally marginal to
the traditional local cultures, they had been shaped by the same
school system, they had alien ethnic superiors, and social distance
kept them from intimate social contact and integration with the
Western elite. These common characteristics made them a status
group with a distinctively characteristic style of life, with common class interests that led to class awareness, if not to the growth
of political class consciousness.

Thus the growth and extension of colonial governments and
administrations gave birth to a new indigenous middle class. It is
within the ranks of this new indigenous middle class that nationalist movements were born.

The Structural Dilemma of Nationalist Movements

Next, an analysis may be made of what may be called the
structural dilemma of nationalist movements in traditional societies.[9]

Nationalist movements in traditional societies seldom, if ever,
begin as revolutionary movements launching a full-fledged attack
on the legitimations of the political structure of the state. The first
phase is more aptly labeled a quest for social and political reform.
This quest, which more often than not takes the form of a request
from legitimate authorities, is voiced by the new indigenous middle class and very frequently in terms of its class interest. The
symbolic basis for the requested changes invariably reflects the
ideological acculturation of the native elite. For instance, in the
British Empire it was based on the extension to the colonies of
increased "home" rule, i.e., increased and extended political participation of the citizenry. This, however, only reflected the colo-
nists' acceptance of the political ideology that brought about such
changes in Britain itself.

9. This whole development is to a great extent dependent on Smelser's model on
collective behavior.

The second phase of nationalist movements begins when there is an effort to extend the social base of national claims and of the nationalist movement itself. The initial social base of nationalist movements, as has been noted, is the native bureaucratic or liberal bourgeoisie. It is a social class of recent emergence and of relatively small size. As a class it possesses very little political leverage to bring about political reforms because of its restricted social base. In its search to extend its social base it faces what might be called a structural dilemma.

Two sets of structural constraints must be overcome by the nationalist movement to expand its social base. The first set of constraints stems from the nature of colonial rule and the local groups which have a vested interest in the persistence of the status quo. The constraint is that these groups, politically established or supported by the state, control the means of violence in the country. The other set of constraints stems from the preindustrial character of the local culture and its traditional commanding institutions. While they accommodate with the status quo, they are marginal to, if not resentful of, the ongoing social changes.

In order to overcome these structural constraints, the national movements must successfully launch a twofold symbolic attack: on the alien presence and control of the state on the one hand, and on the traditional culture and the social control of traditional institutions and traditional political leaders on the other.

This leads the nationalist movements to the third phase wherein they are transformed from reform to revolutionary social movements. They are revolutionary because they attack the very legitimacy of the exercise of power of the state as presently constituted; they are equally revolutionary because they attack the legitimacy of basic values legitimizing indigenous traditional social structures. As a class, the newly emerged native elites have an economic and political stake, not in arresting but in pursuing the socioeconomic changes initiated by the colonial regimes. Thus not only their marginality and acculturation but their class interests compel them to pursue and accelerate socioeconomic changes. The attack upon the legitimation of colonial rule as well as of the traditional social structure is centered on the positive acceptance of industrialization. It then focuses on the fact that the purpose of the colonial regime's political apparatus is to protect and assist the economic interests of the investing capitalist from the imperial center, not to accelerate the economic development of the local people.[10]

The same core values of modernization and industrial development are used to challenge the traditional culture, its social institutions, and its traditional leadership. Neo-nationalist movements based on the values of modernization therefore are necessarily ambivalent toward the traditional culture which was not based on such values. However, the need for ethnological continuity in the new nation-state requires not that all the elements of traditional cultures be rejected but that some be retained, glorified, and used as a basis to form a new consensus.

The fourth and final phase of successful nationalist movements is to forge a new consensus in support of the new nation-state. This requires, to varying degrees, wresting the masses from the symbols of tradition, creating and celebrating a new kind of man, a product of the changing society, by initiating and controlling the formal and informal means of socialization—the schools, the public mass media, etc.—and finally, establishing a considerable degree of bureaucratic control and centralization over the whole territory to avoid the fractionalism of tribal or local cultures once the political dominance of the aliens has been removed.

Neo-nationalism, the Quiet Revolution, and the New Middle Class

From an assessment of the emergence of modern nationalism in Continental Europe of the nineteenth century and a consideration of the social basis of neo-nationalism in the traditional societies of the present, elements of a conceptual model that might prove useful in analyzing social changes in contemporary French-

10. These themes are to be found abundantly in the writings of C. Wright Mills, notably in his *Causes of World War II* (New York, 1958).

Canadian society have been developed. This model will now be used in assessing, in global terms, the direction of change in the ideologies and the social structure of French Canada.

The French Revolution was a social revolution designed to overthrow the feudal social order. The major social changes brought about in a violent fashion as a result of the French Revolution were an end to the dynastic exercise of power and to the political, fiscal, and economic privileges formerly held by the feudal lords and landed aristocracy, the accession to political ascendency of the liberal bourgeoisie, the abolition of the privileges of the estates, and changes in feudal ownership of land.

That no similar situation existed in French Canada is quite obvious. The feudal system of land tenure never had serious content within New France. Bush country was no major attraction for whatever feudal nobility emigrated to New France. In fact, agricultural settlement was marginal to the social organization of New France and did not keep pace with the agricultural settlements of the British colony to the south.[11] What feudal trappings there were in New France were an urban phenomenon and revolved closely around the political control of the administrative structure of the colony. The main economic drive was the development and exploitation of the fur trade industry, carried out by a metropolitan bourgeoisie, supported by the military and viewed with suspicion by the clergy. With the British conquest the traditional society collapsed. The military was recalled and what liberal bourgeoisie of any significance were left were supplanted quickly by their British counterpart from the south.[12]

The pattern of landownership, formally feudal in the political form of its distribution and allocation, was not so in social fact. It was neither politically oppressive, socially resented, nor economically burdensome. Under pressure to develop agricultural settlements in order to maintain ownership, the feudal landowners could manage to meet this requirement only by parceling out ownership as an incentive or inducement to settlers to carve out arable

11. See Léon Gérin, *Aux Sources de Notre Histoire* (Montreal, 1946), and also Hubert Guindon, "The Social Evolution of Quebec Reconsidered," *Canadian Journal of Economics and Political Science,* XXVI (Nov., 1960), 533–551.
12. Michel Brunet, *Canadians and Canadiens* (Montreal, 1954).

land in bush country. This process had one major effect: it avoided the development of a class of indentured agricultural workers. The *colon* was never an indentured servant, although some of the *corvées* of the feudal agricultural system were implemented. Léon Gérin was therefore correct in stating that the French-Canadian rural society, which was left untouched by the conquest, consisted in a "juxtaposition of [landholding] families which are very nearly all equal; nearly all engaged in farming; nearly all sufficient unto themselves."[13]

With the collapse of the political ties with France, the exodus of the entrepreneurial bourgeoisie, the absence of feudal landownership as an oppressive social structure, the withdrawal of the military and political elites, all this some thirty years before the revolution in France, it should not be a subject of amazement that the French Revolution, its ideology, its break with the past, and its new set of legitimations of the present, did not receive a sympathetic ear within its ruling elite of French-Canadian society —the clergy, the intelligentsia, or the habitants. The differences between metropolitan French and French-Canadian social structure were so great as to render meaningless in French Canada the revolutionary upheavals in France.

Nationalism did not feed therefore on a rejection of the past, of tradition, or of feudal social structure which did not exist, as it had in Continental Europe. Since Canadians were unattracted to French republicanism, because of the difference in social structure, the Crown, whether British or French, was not an object of resentment, and loyalty to the monarchy was not considered national treason. As a result, when the American Revolution or Rebellion, quite bourgeois in character and interest, occurred, the loyalty of the new British subjects of French descent, while crucial for the British Crown, could be easily pledged by the Fench-Canadian peasants and its clerical elite in exchange for political concessions assuring its cultural survival, namely, the right to stay French and Catholic. The tradition of political guarantees for

13. Léon Gérin, *Le Type economique et social des Canadiens* (Montreal, 1938), as quoted in Everett C. Hughes, *French Canada in Transition* (Chicago, 1963), p. 4.

cultural survival of the French Canadians as a community was thereby begun.

If French-Canadian national feelings were unaffected by the Continental context, the same is equally true of the British who moved into the newly acquired country. The British Canadians were not deprived of their military forces and their political elites. Rather than spurring a rejection of the British connection, the immigration of the United Empire Loyalists from the American colonies strengthened the emotional ties to the Crown and motherland. The effect of the American severance from Britain gave impetus to British-Canadian nationalism and its determination to forge a British North America. Furthermore, the political upheavals of Continental Europe had not had the same repercussions in England, where the accession of the liberal bourgeoisie to political dominance had been achieved without revolutionary upheavals.

The theory of the nation-state, of the right to statehood on the basis of national homogeneity, was a product of Continental Europe where despotic rule and feudalism were violently overthrown and where it served the political unification of feudal territories into nation-states. Neither French Canada nor English Canada, although for different reasons, was greatly affected by these ideologies. The granting of some political guarantees to French Canadians' survival as a culturally distinct community assured French-Canadian acquiescence to a common state. The absence of political repercussions to these doctrines in England, together with the multi-national character of the British Empire, also inclined the British-Canadians to consent to a multi-national state in Canada.

French-Canadian society in the nineteenth century was a rural society. It consisted in a loosely integrated collection of rural parishes geographically expanding. As a social system it required an equilibrium between land and people.[14] Since the pattern of landholding was one of diffuse ownership among small farmers with large families, the stability of the system could only be main-

14. See Horace Miner, *St. Denis: A French-Canadian Parish* (Chicago, 1939), chap. xi.

tained by handing down the family farm to one inheriting son. The equation between land and people could thus be kept intact. But this also meant that the system required an ever expanding geographical base in order to absorb the surplus population. As long as arable land remained plentiful there was no major problem. When it became scarce this social system became acutely vulnerable. It is within this context of geographically expanding parishes that a developing set of supraparochial institutions gave birth to an ethnic elite. Faced with a surplus population with no land to till, the traditional elite was in need of structural relief for its continued survival.[15]

Structural relief could only consist in industrialization, which is the one thing the traditional elite could not deliver since it was not and had not been primarily an entrepreneurial bourgeoisie and therefore lacked capital. The vulnerability of the traditional elite set the stage for an easy introduction of industrialization even if it meant dependence on foreign capitalists. The capitalists transformed the French Canadians into urban dwellers. To service the needs of the recently urbanized masses, the traditional power elite had to transform its institutions into large-scale bureaucracies, giving birth in the process to the new middle classes of French-Canadian society. Industrialization helped finance the development of urban bureaucracies, but the new middle class was formed within the context of traditional institutions headed by the traditional power elite, but undergoing fundamental changes to meet the demographic need of the urban masses.

The institutional segregation of the new middle class sets it off in one respect from the new middle class of traditional societies of colonial regimes. There, its emergence was the direct result and outgrowth of the colonial political and economic structure. The bureaucratic overlords were cultural aliens, of more or less recent arrival, and in direct political control of the bureaucratic structures. In French Canada, the new middle class was an outgrowth of traditional institutions, ethnically homogeneous in composition, in the process of urban transformation.

15. Guindon, "The Social Evolution of Quebec Reconsidered," pp. 545–546.

Modernization: Its Initial Claim to Power

The new middle class equated its social role with progress and the growth of its institutions with modernization. Its cohesion was thus first achieved under the banner of modernization, not nationalism. This value of modernization was a product of the training and education of the new middle class. In the process of developing urban social bureaucracies, the need for functional specialization and training brought the new generation in contact with the various specialized social, human, biological, and economic sciences of industrialized societies. This new training was the basis of the internal status of that class within the developing hierarchies. This new competence had been achieved through cultural borrowing, and the new theories of organization welcomed within the developing bureaucracies were foreign to the traditional culture. Not only was this new knowledge the basis of status; it also became the yardstick by which traditional institutions were evaluated.

Marginal to traditional culture by training, the new middle class became politically restive by class interest. Because it settled mainly in bureaucracies that did not produce profits, it required outside financial resources, namely state funds, to expand its scope, develop its services, and perform its social role. Functionally indispensable in bringing about the institutional changes required in the urban setting, it became politically aroused and aggressive.

Its demands were directed toward the provincial government headed by the Union Nationale. By refusing to acquiesce quickly to its demands, the Union Nationale incurred its wrath and Duplessis, its leader, became its favorite scapegoat. While Premier Sauvé was successful in tapping its support, Premier Barrette, an ex-railroad employee of working-class origin with no formal training who represented a rural riding with strong rural traditions, could not become a symbol of the new social order. He was defeated, his incompetence being adequately celebrated in political cartooning by emphasizing his "boîte à lunch." In such a

context, the slogan of the Union Nationale, "vers les Sommets,"
seemed ludicrous and no match for the structurally appropriate
slogan of the Liberals: "Y faut qui ça change." The Liberal party
thus became the political expression of the new middle class, the
champion of its interests and aspirations. It heralded a bureaucratic revolution under the banner of modernization and was
spontaneously acclaimed internally and externally. Its election in
1960 publicly consecrated the political dominance of the new
middle classes in French-Canadian society.[16]

The New Middle Class: Shifting Ideologies and the Shaping of Society

The positive acceptance of modernization has been and still is
the unifying ideology of the new middle class. The violent controversies manifest in the various segments of its intelligentsia do not
center on the desirability of this assumption, but rather on conflicting views on the methods of accelerating its historical implementation.

Social change seldom begins with attacks on the legitimacy of a
social structure. The new middle class in French Canada con-
formed to this expectation. Rather than the legitimacy of a party,
an agency, a government, the first attempts consisted in trying to
secure a bigger share of facilities, financial and administrative, to
develop modern competent bureaucracies. Failing to secure these
facilities, the new middle class identified a responsible agent—the
Union Nationale and its leader. Their challenge was reformist, not
revolutionary; the political structure was not attacked, but the
incumbents of political office were, as incompetent. Incompetence
was defined in terms of ruling arbitrarily, of retarding progress, of
allocating funds to cronies rather than to qualified people.

In the bureaucratic institutions of health, education, welfare,
and public service, the challenge to priestly rule or political ap-
pointees was not an attack on religion or on the older people, but
on incompetence. It no longer was sufficient to be a priest to run

16. Hubert Guindon, "Social Unrest, Social Class and Quebec's Bureaucratic
Revolution," *Queen's Quarterly* LXXI (Summer, 1964), 155.

an agency or a university department, a nun to run a hospital board or the nursing department, or a public official with a long record of service to head a ministry. What was necessary was that one should be professionally qualified. If he were not, he must forfeit the right to bureaucratic power. That scientific or technical competence should be the overriding concern in the selection, hiring, and promotion of bureaucratic personnel marked the claim to supremacy of bureaucratic leadership over traditional leadership.

A second characteristic of the attack on traditional leadership was that competence and training were the *only* prerequisites to claim office. A university teacher competent in his discipline and in his role as a teacher need not be Catholic even in an officially Catholic institution. In this way the Weberian idea of bureaucracy was the yardstick to measure institutions. The allocation of institutional position should be rational and open to achievement rather than ascription.

Modernization, bureaucratic rationality, and personal qualification became the tools for the new middle class to assess the worth of not only the institutions but also the ideologies of the past. Ethnically homogenous, the new middle class was not initially ethnically conscious. In fact, nationalism was suspect during the first decade after World War II. Faced with the depression, the main stream of French-Canadian nationalism withdrew its support from capitalism. It could not indorse socialism, however, because of its atheistic materialism and its cultural matrix, which was Anglo-Saxon and Protestant and therefore foreign to the traditions and philosophical world view of a Latin and Catholic people. It endorsed instead corporatism as the ideal sociopolitical structure of the state.[17] The new middle class, at least those members of it who were trained outside the ethnic universities, did not take corporatism seriously. It had no sympathy for its political elitism and was fully aware of its economic sterility.

Not only did the new middle class of the period reject the

17. Consult the works of Esdras Minville and especially those of Francois Albert Angers during the thirties and forties. See also the review *Action Nationale* during this period.

political philosophy of the nationalism of the thirties and early forties but it remained skeptical about its indictment of American culture. Rather than fearing the assimilative effect of American culture, it admired the technological and scientific basis of that culture and found in American society the model for modernization it sought to establish in French Canada. The attempts by nationalist groups in the thirties and forties to make the French Canadian an ethnically conscious consumer had failed and were looked upon by this postwar-trained middle class as an indication of naïve ignorance about the economics of the market place.

What is somewhat more surprising is that in the early postwar period the new middle class did not deeply share but rather remained skeptical of the nationalist suspicions toward the government and its encroaching jurisdiction within the network of French-Canadian institutions. While the Massey Report, one of whose authors was Father Levesque, founder of the Laval Faculté des Sciences Sociales, tended to legitimate centralization, and while it was castigated publicly and violently by the French-Canadian nationalist intelligentsia, it left the new middle class rather indifferent. Maurice Lamontagne's book on Canadian federalism[18] was an attempt to show how the modernization of French Canada could best be achieved within the context of a strong central government. It was strongly criticized by the same intelligentsia but was warmly received in academic and political circles, labor unions, and by the majority of the new middle class. Maurice Duplessis, in turning down federal aid to education, was not initially acclaimed by the new middle class for doing so but incurred its censure instead. Indeed, his action was applauded only by the Action Nationale and the nationalist wing of its intelligentsia. He made the decision politically and eventually an attitude toward federal aid to education became the cornerstone of the strategy of political parties in Quebec in their public platforms.

Finally, to illustrate the little inclination toward nationalism of

18. *Le Fédéralisme Canadien* (Quebec, 1954).

the new middle class from 1945 to 1955, one may refer to the celebrated asbestos strike,[19] which rallied the sympathy of the new intelligentsia for the workers and directed its attack on the provincial government for interfering in collective bargaining and supporting management and for its callous disregard for the workers' health. The strike was viewed as a class conflict, not an ethnic conflict; the government was attacked not for ethnic treason but for political interference with the rights of the workers. The new middle class ideology in the immediate postwar period claimed change in the name of modernization and democracy. The values of the middle class were those of modern liberalism with emphasis on progress and social change articulated partly in class interests but not in terms of ethnic conflict.

If modernization was the initial claim to power of the new middle class, if at the beginning the middle class was rather hostile and suspicious of traditional nationalism, this is so obviously not the case in the sixties as to require some explanation for the change and shifts in the ideological positions of the middle class.

The Resurgence of Neo-nationalism

In the mid-fifties neo-nationalism as a force dissenting from traditional nationalism made its appearance. The main exponents of neo-nationalism were French-Canadian historians, Michel Brunet being the main spokesman of the new wave. Brunet made a celebrated attack on three tenets of traditional nationalism that were described as myths impeding modern development that should be cast aside. These myths were called: *l'agriculturisme,* or the glorification of the rural life; *le messianisme,* or the concept that French Canadians had a spiritual mission in the North American context; and *l'anti-étatisme,* or the conservative suspicion of the propriety of state-initiated social and economic activity. This declaration for modernization under the aegis of nationalism and the attack on traditional nationalist tenets heralded the

19. P. E. Trudeau, *La Grève de L'Amiante* (Montreal, 1956).

emergence of the social power of nationalism within the new middle class. Traditional nationalism was offensive not because it opposed modernism and industrialization, which it did not, but because it subordinated them to what was felt to be a more basic, more important value, namely, religion.[20] Brunet did not disagree with the tenets of the thirties; he shared their suspicions of the central government.[21] Brunet's pessimism was based on what he perceived to be an inevitable fact—the incapacity of total social development for French Canada because it lacked statehood. He viewed the federal government as a political structure ethnically appropriated by English Canadians and as a tool of English-Canadian national interests and aspirations. This he stated as a sad yet inescapable fact which French Canadians must recognize and accept and which worked necessarily in the direction of depriving French Canada of a necessary tool to achieve modern development. Co-operation necessarily meant being short-changed, and in such a setup French Canada could only be perceived as a burden by the rest of Canada. French Canada, because of ethnic appropriation by the central state, was doomed to a condition of arrested development. The only solution lay in relying exclusively on the government of Quebec to transform its province into a national state and to use the full powers of its limited scope to achieve partial development.

For a decade the new middle class remained aloof from, if not hostile to, the tenets of nationalism since its emphasis subordinated modernization to traditional religious values. Nationalism became ideologically compatible when it became decisively modern, slaying as myths the traditional beliefs of agriculturism, messianism and antistatism. It became, in the last decade, increasingly nationalist in its effort to overcome the structural constraints to its growth. The constraints to the growth of the new middle class are a function of the specialized character and the smaller scale and size of the bureaucracies it staffs. The specialized character restricts the channels of mobility and the smaller scale and

---

20. This is the striking difference between nationalist intellectuals like Minville, on the one hand and Michel Brunet, on the other.
21. *Canadians and Canadiens.*

size restrict the level of mobility. A direct outgrowth of urbanization rather than industrialization, fathered by a clerico-political elite rather than an entrepreneurial bourgeoisie, the channels of mobility of the new middle class were located in the bureaucracies of private enterprise, secondary manufacturing, finance, and trade. Thus its channels of mobility were both restricted and specialized.

If the channels of mobility were restricted by the specialized nature of the bureaucratic tasks to be performed, the levels of mobility were equally restricted by the smaller scale of the bureaucracies themselves. The French-Canadian bureaucratic pyramids have a narrow base—geographically, socially, and organizationally—because of their small scale. This means that upward mobility is more restricted, less diversified, and less extended.

Given these two constraints, one can view the new middle class as seeking and needing space for expansion, occupationally and organizationally. This, indeed, is the most important structural clue to understanding the restive or restless character of the new middle class in French Canada and the various competing ideologies, the political attitudes, and the ideological agitation so rampant within its ranks in the last five years. To overcome the restricted social mobility of its small bureaucratic pyramids, it has adopted a twofold strategy: (1) a bureaucratic transformation of traditional institutions, and (2) a reaffirmation of linguistic identification, so that by expanding linguistic space and ethnic jurisdiction it can also increase job outlets.

The New Middle Class, Nationalism, and Ethnic Accommodation

Ever since 1760 the French and the English in Canada, for better or for worse, have had interlocking destinies and a shared fate. The pattern of ethnic interaction in the two centuries that have since elapsed can be roughly divided into three periods: (1) from conquest to Confederation, (2) from Confederation to 1950, and (3) from 1950 to present.

From Conquest to Confederation

The conquest, as it has been said, involved the take-over by the British of the political and economic institutions of New France. This was greatly facilitated by the massive exodus of the middle-class entrepreneurs and political administrators of New France. It was thus achieved swiftly, completely, and without conflict, for the French Canadians who remained were either farmers or priests. French Canada became a rural society with a clerical elite. Since French Canadians were concerned with ethnic and religious survival and were living in quasi-self-sufficient rural parishes, their interaction with the English political rulers and the economic elite was mediated by a clerically led ethnic elite. The *habitants* in the rural parishes could and did live out their lives in a French environment, with no direct contact with the ruling aliens. The parochial institutions that did exist were staffed by co-nationals. Until 1867, the history of French Canada is a history of rural expansion and consolidation. Inter-ethnic contact was thus held to a minimum, mediated by an ethnic elite.

While the French Canadians were rural dwellers, the English were urban, and the social and economic and ethnic division of labor was also to a large extent geographical. Nor did the rural French Canadian meet the English farmer, who was geographically concentrated in the Eastern Townships, so that even rural settlements were neatly divided along ethnic lines. The rural French, for the better part of a century busily involved in reproduction and parochial settlement, were not to meet the English. Contact with the English came about with industrialization, but even then its impact was cushioned by social distance—since the English were status superiors—and by informal interaction, since the linguistic environment of work, while formally English, was and still is informally French for the working class.

From Confederation to 1950: Patterns of Mutually Satisfying Institutional Self-segregation

The second era in ethnic accommodation extends from Confederation to the postwar period. During this time two major sets of events affected the pattern of ethnic interaction. The first of these concerns the extension of Canadian sovereignty to the Pacific with the settling and development of the West. The second concerns the progressive industrialization of Quebec. Both of these affected the course of ethnic interaction between French and English in Canada: the first set of events affected the patterns of accommodation of the French minorities outside Quebec; the second set the stage for ethnic interaction within Quebec.

Minorities outside Quebec. It is doubtful whether Canadian nationalism existed in any meaningful way within English Canada before Confederation. While the French Canadians were concerned with ethnic and cultural survival, the English Canadians were concerned with political supremacy and political sovereignty. Political supremacy was threatened internally by the demography of ethnicity. A potential external threat to political sovereignty was always present in the successfully secessionist neighbor to the south. Political sovereignty could only be upheld by depending on the military strength of Britain. Political supremacy could only be achieved by demographic growth and development of the political structures of the country.

In these conditions Canadian nationalism could not and did not exist. The birth of Canadian nationalism coincides with Confederation, the political structure that facilitated the geographical extension of sovereignty from the Atlantic to the Pacific. Nationalism is often closely related to geographic expansion and conquest. The conquest and settling of land co-ordinates group activity, channels energies, provides a common vision and dreams, nurtures and develops nationalist sentiments. In a process of circular reinforcement, nationalism in turn legitimates the spatial enterprise. Former Prime Minister Diefenbaker intuitively knew this when, in his attempt to revitalize Canadian nationalism, to stir the national soul, and to activate the national purpose, he proposed his vision of opening up the North. Not only was Diefenbaker's vision of the North good sociology, but it was also good history. For the birth of Canadian nationalism indeed coincided with the settling of the West. Initiated in the East, English-Canadian nationalism was realized in the West. Its dreams enacted in the

Prairies, Canadian nationalism has ever since found its most coherent and sharply defined expression in the Prairies.

Notwithstanding what might or might not have been the intentions of the founding fathers of Confederation, notwithstanding
whether Confederation was or was not a pact between two races,
in empirical fact the settling of the West set the stage for the
pattern of ethnic conflicts in Canada. The national dilemma of the
1960's reflects the same basic strains in national consensus that
arose in the 1870's. George Grant,[22] who laments the defeat of
Canadian nationalism, nonetheless recognizes in Diefenbaker a
true Canadian nationalist defeated by the concerted and co-
ordinated efforts of the antinational ruling classes whose economic interests are tied to the continental economy and who, by
the way, did not respond to Diefenbaker's vision of the North.
Grant explains Diefenbaker's unpopularity in French Canada and
the traditional ill fate of the Tory party with French-Canadian
voters quite accurately.

A product of Prairie nationalism, Diefenbaker could not appeal
to French Canadians because of his basically American conception
of federalism. His emphasis on unhyphenated Canadianism, quite
an acceptable doctrine as far as the rights of individuals were concerned, became a threat to the rights of French Canadians as a
community. While Grant's diagnosis is correct, his contention that
Prairie nationalism is a deviation from traditional nationalism is
much more open to question.

The West was settled by the action of the central government,
which financed, directly or indirectly, the system of transportation and facilitated immigrant settlement in the western enterprise. When ethnic conflict arose on the school question, Ottawa
upheld legislation that curbed the possibility of the existence of
French Canadians as communities. That this occurred not only in
the West but also in New Brunswick and later in Ontario would
indicate that unhyphenated Canadianism enjoyed a central rather
than a marginal status in traditional Canadian nationalism. The
"nuisance value" of French Canadians, to quote P. E. Trudeau's
expression, is still celebrated today, as the Dunton-Laurendeau

22. *Lament for a Nation* (Princeton, 1965).

Commission discovered, and this celebration increases as one moves farther away from Quebec, east as well as west. The consequence of the assimilationist impulse of traditional Canadian nationalism has been greater in Quebec than among the French minorities in other provinces. The latter, reduced to immigrant status as they moved out of the boundaries of Quebec, developed ethnic institutions as demographic density permitted, centered around the national parish. The greater impact, however, of these historical events took place in Quebec.

The French Canadian in Quebec. In Quebec the consequence of the assimilationist impulse was to restructure loyalty to and identification with land and institutions. Loyalty became more restricted in space and more selective in institutions. Loyalties of individuals and groups tend to take root and must find expression in space and time. They therefore are affected by proximity and daily interaction. This is why emotional ties to farm, town, and neighborhood need little conceptual elaboration and remain constant in times of stress, national fervor, or national indifference. These kinds of ties, basic to patriotism, are constant, irrespective of the direction of nationalist sentiment and feeling associated with larger social structures. A German Jew can still remember fondly his city of birth and childhood despite the nightmare of national socialism. Localized, these loyalties are not parochial and are very often more deeply embedded, more deeply internalized, than loyalties toward larger and more abstract structures, such as national governments. The French-Canadian loyalties in Quebec, as a consequence of the assimilationist impulse outside Quebec, became restricted in space and selective in institutions. The army, the central government, the federal bureaucracies, while legitimate sources of employment and appropriate institutional setups within which to eke out a living, or even a career, were thus, from their very beginning, not objects of emotional commitment and of devotion.

For the French minorities outside Quebec, the assimilationist pull from the civil and industrial society was counteracted by the norms of kinship and religion. The solution to the dilemma created by the contradictory pull of these opposing norms was and is perfect bilingualism. That way, full membership and participation in all of the institutional life of a community could be achieved. Thus could one be spared the sanctions of both imperfect citizenship and loss of ethnic membership. Without it, one's loyalties had to be twofold and camouflaged. The French-Canadian could stay French only in Quebec, in public as well as in private, in official as well as in unofficial life. His linguistic environment within the confines of his province encompassed his school, his place of work and worship, his hospital, his town hall, and the public streets, and his loyalties could be more sharply differentiated.

Quebec: Industrialization and the pattern of self-segregated institutions. From Confederation to the postwar period the pattern of ethnic accommodation between French and English in Quebec developed within the context of rapid industrialization, especially after the turn of the century. Historically ethnic accommodation has been constructed successfully in Quebec on the basis of mutually desired self-segregated institutions.[23] In the fields of education, religion, welfare, leisure, and residence, institutional self-segregation has been total. The only two areas of societal living where inter-ethnic contact has been institutionalized are those of work and politics. The pattern of ethnic contact at work was established with the introduction of industrialization. Anglo-Saxon industry moved into a society faced with an acute population surplus, a distinctive political and religious elite, and a developing set of institutions anchored in the rural parish. This society, politically stable, economically conservative, and technically unskilled, provided ideal conditions for investing Anglo-Saxon capitalists. They could invest their capital, open industries, and be supplied with an abundant source of unskilled labor seeking employment. The managerial and technical levels were filled, with no protest, by the incoming group, who also brought along their own set of institutions servicing their own nationals. This social setting provided an easy introduction to industry. The

23. Guindon, "Social Unrest, Social Class," p. 155.

French-Canadian elite was ideologically co-operative, protective
only about its continued control over its demographic substruc-
tures. This fitted in quite well with the aims of the incoming
groups who could develop their economic pursuits with a minimum involvement in the local ethnic society. Industry was relieving the economic burden of the demographic surplus of French-
Canadian rural society. The local elite's leadership was not being
challenged. This led to a mutually satisfying pattern of self-
segregated institutions. The English could live in Quebec as au-
tonomous and separate communities, with their own churches,
hospitals, schools, and ethnic neighborhoods. Very often, especially in the provincial cities, they could and did incorporate as
separate towns, where the limits of the town often coincided with
the limits of class and ethnicity. The pattern of self-segregation
conditioned the social setting of inter-ethnic contact, which was
held to a minimum. The lower classes, the working class, met the
English in the formal structure of the job, while the middle classes
met the English much less frequently, and when they did it was
almost always on ritual occasions and in a ritualized manner. This
pattern of mutually self-satisfying, self-segregated institutions
worked with no dissent up to and including World War II. This
historical pattern is now being challenged by the recently
emerged French-Canadian new middle class. The traditional
ethnic division of labor is now under attack and the present climate of uncertainty has arisen as a result.

From 1950 to the Present: Ethnic Tensions and Social Mobility

With the postwar emergence of the new middle class, a new era
in ethnic interaction has set in, and a search for a new deal in
ethnic accommodation is being sought by the French-Canadian
new middle class under the impetus of reformist nationalism. As
noted above, neo-nationalism in traditional societies is linked with
social change in the direction of modernization. Reformist in
outlook, the new middle class seeks to extend its scope, size, and
mobility. It becomes revolutionary when it successfully enrols the

support of the peasants and working classes in taking over control of the state by successfully indicting colonialist rule. This situation is not paralleled in French Canada. Despite the inroads of separatism, separatist ideology has not succeeded in enlisting the support of the working classes or the rural people, and the colonialist indictment has been rejected. Historically, the exploitative view of the English presence is inaccurate and does not reflect the way it was initiated. Rather than rally to separatist unrest, the lower classes joined the Creditiste ranks in proclaiming the possibility of the middle-class dream for all.

The new middle class in French Canada, like its counterparts in traditional societies, however, has a stake in modernization. Having achieved political dominance, the provincial state to a large extent is seeking to meet its demands. In seeking to overcome the constraints to its growth and continued mobility, it is seeking a new social convention in ethnic accommodation. The old pattern of ethnic accommodation and its institutional arrangements met the needs of incipient industrialization. At that time, the ethnic division of labor reflected the complementary needs of both ethnic groups, and ethnic competition did not take the form of occupational competition.

The new middle class, however, by training, outlook, and culture increasingly similar to its ethnically alien counterpart, is also increasingly in competition with it. In its search to expand its channels of mobility and widen its areas of development it is examining the assumptions of institutional self-segregation. Now that it is politically in control, its views may be acted upon. Thus the traditional patterns of financing education, welfare, and health—wherein the pattern of institutional segregation has often meant better services, better facilities, and better salaries for the English involved in these areas within the confines of the province—are being questioned. The differentials in resources and income are not new, but the fact that these differentials are viewed as special privileges is recent and new. That in its search for resources to expand its bases the new middle class will seek to change traditional institutional arrangements in these areas is a foregone conclusion. That such changes are upsetting to the English Quebecers is already apparent. Bred by the church, having achieved control of the provincial state, the French-Canadian new middle class is now anxious to move from social to industrial bureaucracy. Bureaucratic state capitalism as well as linguistic expansion in the management of private industry are only assorted tools in its ongoing attempt to increase its social and occupational space.

3

The Canadian Economy: An overview

William C. Hood

The Setting

Although Canada is a country of only 20 million people, it is rather highly industrialized, well endowed, and wealthy by the standards of most of the world, if not by those of the United States.

It is not of course a major power. Its recent fortunes have reflected in myriad interwoven ways the changing tension between the two gigantic powers which face each other across Canadian territory.

The world economy is important to Canada and in its way Canada is important to the world economy. Canada is an important supplier of grains to the world food markets, and as the problem of hunger in the world mounts, Canadian food may be of even greater importance in world trade than it is today. Canada is rich in a variety of resources—oil, uranium, potash, nickel, iron, copper, wood, asbestos, and many others—and benefits from supplying these to other countries. It nurtures the hope that it may supply many of them in increasingly fabricated form. In the last several years Canada has had a surplus on its international merchandise account. Its deficit on invisible items is substantial, however, and each year it imports substantial amounts of capital.

In building the Canadian nation, Canadians have always been keenly conscious of their gigantic and growing southern neighbor. To an important degree, the nation was forged to resist the threat of domination by the United States. The earlier concern with military domination has now given way to concern about cultural and economic domination. But this concern is matched by a great admiration for and wish to emulate much that characterizes the United States. The tug of war between the desire to be like the United States and the desire to be separate from it has confused Canada's sense of national purpose and thwarted the emergence of distinctly Canadian qualities in the nation's economic and cultural life. A major problem of economic policy in Canada is to try to achieve for Canadians in their economic life a balance between independence of the economic power of the United States and the deep need and grudgingly admitted wish to benefit from it.

Canadians are not of course a homogeneous group struggling to maintain a separate nation in the colder half of the continent they share with the United States. Like the United States, Canada has welcomed people of many cultures coming to join Canadian nation-building. Canada differs though in that two main groups, speaking different languages and inheriting two of the great European cultures, have linked their destinies. That great cooperative venture has both enriched and complicated national life.

The building of the Canadian nation was in many respects undertaken in defiance of natural economic forces. It was on that account costly. These costs of maintaining an independent nation have contributed to the development of a sort of national schizophrenia. They have also made it imperative that government play a rather large role in developing the Canadian economy. There is a long tradition of government participation or partnership in economic affairs in Canada. That tradition is maintained today, and a growing role for government in the economy of Canada is very likely in the future.

In sketching a picture of the contemporary Canadian economy, its performance, its focal points of change, and its major policy problems, one has to sketch against this background. Canada has a relatively small but highly endowed industrial base which is heavily integrated with the international economy. The two founding groups—French and English—are still seeking their mutual accommodation in a nation born out of fear and supported by envy of the United States.

The Recent Performance of the Canadian Economy

I shall begin this sketch with a very brief review of the recent performance of the Canadian economy. I intend this to be a matter-of-fact reference to certain of the main indicators of performance, and I shall not offer elaborate tables and charts. After noting salient facts from Canada's aggregate record I shall direct attention to some of those points in the economy where significant developments are taking place and conclude with reference to a few of the major problems of policy.

Developments of the population and the labor force as they represent basic aspects of the demand for and supply of output in the economy provide a good starting place. From 1950 to 1960 Canada's population increased by the very substantial amount of 30 per cent. The corresponding figure for the United States was 19 per cent. Canada's population is increasing less rapidly in the present decade but still more rapidly than population is increasing in the United States (1960–65: Canada, 9.7 per cent; United States, 7.7 per cent). These high rates of growth reflect the very high rates of natural increase and of net immigration in the late forties and the fifties. The natural rate of increase of the Canadian population in the decade following the war was higher than in most Western countries. An important consequence of this population growth has been the very rapid growth of the labor force. It has been growing more rapidly than the population, and of course the growth in younger age groups has been especially pronounced. Thus in the sixties as a whole, the average *annual* increase in the members of the labor force aged 20–24 will exceed the increase in labor force members in this age group for the entire previous decade. A further factor contributing to the growth of the labor force is the increasing participation of women. The participation rate for married women, though still substantially below that in the United States, is expected to increase threefold in the period 1950–70.

The real output of the Canadian economy in the years 1950 to 1965 increased at the compound annual rate of 4.5 per cent. This is not high by the standards set by many other industrial economies. It is higher than the rate of 3.7 per cent set by the United States economy during the same period, however. Allowing for the more rapid rate of population growth in Canada, the per capita rate of growth of real output in that period was the same in both countries: 2.1 per cent. By this rough measure of living standards, Canada has not been gaining on the residents of the United States over the period as a whole, although it did better in the latter part of the period. In the sixties, real GNP per head has risen 3.7 per cent per annum in Canada, compared with 3.1 per cent in the United States, and this in spite of Canada's more rapid rate of population increase. Using the very rough indicator of productivity provided by the ratio of real GNP per person employed, the United States has fared rather better than Canada: for the period as a whole the ratio in the United States rose by 2.3 per cent per annum, while Canada managed only 2.2 per cent per annum. Again both of these figures are rather low by comparison with those of many other industrial countries.

The rate of price increase in the period as a whole has been somewhat higher in Canada than in the United States. Using the GNP price deflator as the measure, Canada has had a price rise of 2.7 per cent per annum, whereas in the United States by the comparable measure prices have risen at the rate of 2.2 per cent per annum. The performance in respect to prices compares favorably with that in other industrial countries.

The unemployment of labor resources was a particularly difficult and obstinate problem in both countries in the late fifties and early sixties. Although Canada had higher rates of unemployment as the present boom began than those prevailing in the United States, unemployment rates fell more rapidly than in the United States in spite of a far more rapid labor force growth and from mid-1963 have been below those in the United States. These unemployment figures are one evidence of the greater pressures in the Canadian economy that in recent years have led to greater price increases.

At present about 45 per cent of the Canadian labor force is employed in what may roughly be described as the goods-producing industries and 55 per cent in the services industries. The proportions of real output produced in these two categories are almost exactly the reverse. As in other industrial countries, Canada has experienced a substantial increase in the proportion of the labor force employed in the services industries—about one percentage point a year over the last fifteen years. Although the statistics may underestimate the growth of output in the services industries, the figures indicate that the growth of output has been somewhat greater in the goods industries than in the services industries. In 1965 capital formation was split about equally between the goods and services industries. In the preceding fifteen years, the weight of capital formation has shifted between these categories; in the present boom it has been concentrated more in the goods-producing industries than in the services industries.

Last year manufacturing of all kinds accounted for about 30 per cent of the economy's real output, a quarter of the employed labor force, and a fifth of the capital investment. There has been a rise in the proportion of output in manufacturing and a decline in the proportion of labor employed over the last fifteen years. In agriculture, which last year accounted for 8–9 per cent of output, labor employed, and capital investment, there has been a very sharp absolute decline in employment between 1949 and 1965 amounting to about 45 per cent. Taking the activities of mines, oil wells, and power, gas, and water utilities together, their proportion of output has about doubled over the last fifteen years, now amounting to some 10 per cent, their proportion of employment has remained quite steady at about 3 per cent, and their proportion of capital investment has also remained fairly steady at 17–18 per cent of total fixed capital investment.

A high ratio of capital to output is a significant feature of the Canadian economy, and high ratios of investment to output have characterized Canadian economic performance in the postwar years. It is estimated that the ratio of capital stock per employed worker in 1961 was 23 per cent higher in Canada than in the United States, the ratio for structures was 37 per cent higher, that for machinery and equipment only 8 per cent higher. I cannot here go into the reasons for this situation. They are to be found partly in climatic differences, in the relative importance of capital-intensive resource industries, and in the high overhead costs of the transportation system relative to population. Canada has had two major investment booms since the war and throughout the period consistently had a higher ratio of capital investment to GNP than the United States and most other industrial countries. Total public and private fixed investment has been between 22 and 27 per cent of GNP in these years.

Residents of Canada have supplied a very substantial portion of the savings required to finance capital requirements. In this, they have been served by a sophisticated, well-developed capital market, with strong banking and other financial institutions. Resident saving since 1950 has averaged about 18.5 per cent of GNP in Canada, which is about three percentage points higher than in the United States. Much of this difference is accounted for by higher saving through capital cost allowances in Canada, reflecting Canada's higher capital-output ratio.

In spite of the high ratio of saving in Canada, the even higher ratio of capital investment there has implied the necessity of securing financing abroad. Over the period 1950–65 taken as a whole, the ratio of the deficit on the current account of the balance of payments to the GNP has been about 2.4 per cent. Putting the matter another way, savings supplied by non-residents have amounted to about 11.4 per cent of the savings supplied to the Canadian economy. The net import of capital is preponderantly from the United States.

The value of Canada's merchandise exports is about 17 per cent of GNP. In the first two-thirds of the period since 1950, they grew rather less rapidly than GNP, but in the last five years taken together their growth rate has exceeded that of GNP. The United States buys more than half of Canadian merchandise sold abroad, and its share of Canadian exports is growing, though not in every year. The United Kingdom share is declining, but the shares of Europe and other countries taken as a group are rising. There is a particularly noteworthy shift in the composition of exports. Although exports of wheat and flour have been enjoying a particular and welcome prosperity in the last three or four years, farm and forest products have dropped from 65 per cent in 1950 to 45 per cent in 1965. Their place has been taken by metals, minerals, and manufactured goods.

On the import side, the United States supplies about 70 per cent of Canadian requirements now as it did fifteen years ago. Continental Europe is supplying an increasing share, the United Kingdom a declining share. Fuels, lubricants, and industrial materials bulk smaller among imports now than they did at the beginning of the fifties, but investment goods and motor vehicles bulk larger.

If one looks at the population density map of Canada, he is struck with the pattern it shows. The first impression is that most of the people live in a rather narrow band within 100 to 150 miles of the United States border. The second impression is that the population is clustered within this band, with some of the clusters, notably those in the Niagara peninsula and along the Upper St. Lawrence, being much more dense than others. It is in this way too that the economic activity of the country is clustered. One-half of the manufacturing activity of the country is centered in the Province of Ontario and most of that along the shores of Lakes Ontario and Erie. Another third of the manufacturing activity is in the Province of Quebec, and most of that is along the St. Lawrence River before it broadens out below Quebec City. Construction, trade, and finance are similarly concentrated in the areas of high population density. Other activities are less concentrated. There are, as a consequence, considerable disparities of income both within provinces and between provinces.

The Economic Council of Canada argues in its Second Annual Review that the differing industrial distributions of employment among the provinces of Canada offer only a limited explanation of the manifest differences in income per head. The core of the council's argument is the following: "The central reason why interregional differences in industrial structure apparently do not have a major effect on differences in average regional income levels is that there are significant disparities in productivity per worker in any given industry among the various regions." These general differences in productivity may, however, themselves be related in part to the differing scales of activity or degrees of agglomeration of activity in different parts of the country. Understanding of these matters is far from adequate.

Whatever the explanation, one of the most striking features of the disparities among the provinces—as indicated for example by personal income per capita—is the persistence of the discrepancies. With the exception of the Prairie provinces, where the Great Depression struck with particular severity, the provinces have maintained roughly the same deviations from the national average over the last forty years at least.

The highlights of this review of Canadian performance are the following: a very rapidly growing population has contributed both to the demand for output and to the labor supply necessary to produce it. The economy has enjoyed a higher rate of growth of output than the United States and, in the last few years, also a higher rate of growth in output per head. But with declining unemployment, rapidly growing demand, and a not very satisfactory performance of productivity, the upward movement of prices has gained somewhat more momentum in Canada than in the United States. Accompanying Canadian growth has been a decline in the relative position of agriculture and an improvement in the relative importance of manufacturing output and output of minerals and petroleum. More broadly, while the labor force has grown much more rapidly in the services industries than in the goods industries, output has grown rather more rapidly in the goods industries.

A highly capital-intensive economy, Canada has added vigorously to its capital stock throughout the last fifteen years and especially in the capital booms of the period. Saving by residents, which is at a higher rate than in the United States and which is encouraged by generally higher interest rates and a well-developed and efficient capital market, has fallen short of requirements by more than 10 per cent, and Canada has accordingly relied upon foreign sources, mainly the United States, for the additional financing it has needed. The United States is the principal supplier of imports and the main market for exports, and Canada continues to run a substantial deficit on merchandise and current accounts with the United States.

Although the Canadian economy has been prosperous and growing at a rate that is high by recent North American standards, regional differences in economic performance persist. They reflect regional differences in productivity that are not confined to particular industries.

Canadian economists are not unhappy with the overall performance of the economy in the last few years. Indeed, some of the developments now taking place augur very well indeed. Others pose major problems for policy.

Focal Points of Change

Energy Sources

One series of developments of recent years which provides a basis for optimism is that associated with the supply of energy by and for the Canadian economy. Traditionally Canada has been rich in many, though not all, sources of energy, and changing technology has called into prominence new sources with which it is liberally supplied.

The exception to the rule has been coal, which is now of course declining as a source of energy. While Canada has large deposits of bituminous coal, these are located in Alberta and the Maritime provinces, far from the central markets. Production and marketing of coal from these sites have been subsidized, but domestic production has met rather less than half of the nation's needs during the last thirty-five years. Although declining in importance for transportation and heating, coal continues to have importance in the production of electric power and in metallurgical industries. It is a moot question, depending on technology, how much the demand for coal in these uses will grow.

Canadian climate and terrain have combined to provide handsomely for the generation of hydroelectricity. The abundance of hydro power has been an enormous boon to Canadian industrial development. Nor have all the resources in this field been fully tapped yet. But it must be reported that the development of the last of the major sites for the production of hydroelectricity is now being contemplated or is underway. These sites are Hamilton Falls in Labrador, the Outardes and Manicouagan rivers in Quebec, the Nelson in Manitoba, the South Saskatchewan in Saskatchewan, and the Peace and Columbia rivers in British Columbia. Development of some of these sites has only recently become technically feasible with improvements in the capacity to transmit power economically over long distances. There are of course many smaller sites to be developed, and with the co-operation of the United States, potential power in the Bay of Fundy tides may eventually be harnessed. Anticipating the future, active experimentation with the production of nuclear power has been conducted. There is already one nuclear power plant tied in with the power grid in southern Ontario, a second plant with five times the capacity (1 million kw.) is under construction in that province, and a third is being planned in Quebec. There are important deposits of uranium in Canada with which to fuel these and future nuclear power plants.

Finally, in the postwar years, Canada has enjoyed an enormous surge in the discovery and production of oil and natural gas, especially in the West. The needs for crude petroleum in all parts of the country west of the Ottawa River are now supplied entirely from domestic sources. The eastern part of the country is supplied by imported crude; but a large volume of crude is exported from western Canada. The production of natural gas has increased about tenfold in the last decade. Virtually all the domestic requirements, which have grown enormously, are now supplied from Canadian fields; something on the order of 30 per cent of total production is exported. Associated with the development of production of oil and gas has of course been the creation of a pipeline network to collect and distribute the product and an important petrochemical industry.

All of these developments in the field of energy sources in recent years have given a more secure foundation to the prospects for Canada's economic growth. There may remain some doubt whether there will be a substantial increase in the use of coal in power production; if there is such an increase it will be only to the extent that coal from the United States is cheaper to use than domestic uranium.

Potash and Other Fertilizers

Associated with the development of the petrochemical industry in Canada has been a considerable growth in the production of nitrogen and phosphate fertilizers. Domestic sales increased about 180 per cent between 1957 and 1965, and in that latter year roughly one-half of production of nitrogen fertilizers and one-quarter of production of phosphate fertilizers were exported.

Much more important than this development, however, has been the emergence of potash as a major output of Saskatchewan and Manitoba. Indications of potash deposits were found in western Canada in 1943, and since then a vast, rich potash belt has been revealed. These deposits are among the richest in the world, and their quantity is adequate to meet total world demands at present rates of consumption for a thousand years. Exploitation of these deposits began in earnest in the sixties. By the end of the sixties, a capital investment well in excess of $500 million dollars will have been made and Canada will be the largest world supplier, the annual value of potash exports amounting perhaps to $250 million. At that, potash would not be the largest single export item (wheat exports in the last four years averaged $850 million), but the scale of the operation is nevertheless such as to warrant particular mention. Along with the production of oil and gas, the petrochemical industry, and the spread of more mixed farming in the Prairies, potash is contributing substantially to a notable diversification of the Prairie economy.

Agriculture

I have already referred to the changes taking place in employment and output in Canadian agriculture, but these changes are dramatic enough to warrant further mention in any review of the focal points of change in the Canadian economy. Although output per worker in agriculture remains substantially below the comparable figure for manufacturing, the gains in productivity are phenomenal. These result from many causes, among which must be mentioned the increased use of machinery on farms of increased size and better farming methods, including use of fertilizers, insecticides, and weed killers. But whatever the causes, the fact is that on Canadian farms today upward of 25 per cent more output is produced by more than 40 per cent fewer farm workers than was the case fifteen years ago. Canada is not unique in her experience with changes of this character in agriculture (though they have been more extreme than in the United States), but these changes are transforming the economy into a much more urbanized and industrialized system.

Manufacturing

Some of the changes in manufacturing to which passing reference has already been made have been signs of strength. There are other developments that are more worrisome. On the positive side is the growth of the manufacturing industry itself, the increased diversity of its output, the growing share of manufactures in exports, and the increased capability of domestic products to serve domestic needs. On the other hand, while the devaluation of 1962 gave a substantial boost to the international competitiveness of manufactures, this advantage has been eroded somewhat since then by the rise in wage costs per unit of output which has been accelerating in the last couple of years. In the United States, labor costs per unit of output have had a downward drift throughout the sixties until mid-1965, when a reversal may have set in. The trend of labor costs per unit of manufacturing output in

Canada is symptomatic of a more general problem in the Canadian economy.

Low Rates of Productivity Growth

The growth of productivity in the Canadian economy has been somewhat less than in the United States economy and less than is required to give assurance of improvement in its competitive position. The Canadian standard of living is substantially below that of the United States. Productivity and living standards are difficult to measure on any objective basis, but the best statistical evidence which can be mustered supports the generalization. Canadian residents want and increasingly demand a living standard equivalent to that of their neighbors in the United States. Unless productivity gains exceed those in the United States, Canadians will be frustrated in this ambition. Moreover, attempts to secure income increases which on the average exceed the growth of productivity will exacerbate the difficulty by impairing Canada's competitive position. While this problem is a long-term one for Canada, it appears in a particularly acute form when the economy is operating close to the limits of its growing capacity, as it is at present.

The Current Account Deficit with the United States

Another important current development that is intimately connected in a complicated way with the problems just discussed is the growth in the current account deficit with the United States. Let me briefly recount some of the facts concerning the deficit. In the four quinquennial periods beginning with the year 1946, successive deficits on current account with the United States have run as follows in billions of Canadian dollars: 3.75, 5.30, 7.75, 8.01. There is a cyclical variation in this deficit. It tends to be low in periods of slack activity and high when the economy is running in high gear. The deficit in 1965, at just over $2 billion, was the highest on record and represented a jump of 62 per cent over 1962, which was a year of exchange crisis and of import restrictions. The deficit on merchandise account was $1.2 billion, and of course a substantial portion of the deficit on non-merchandise account is accounted for by interest and dividend payments on the capital imported from the United States in financing the deficits of 1965 and previous years.

Canada is able to finance a considerable portion of its current account deficit out of the proceeds of transactions with other countries, but this portion varies. In the four successive quinquennial periods since 1946, it has run 61, 42, 22, and 35 per cent. Within quinquennia, the variation has been even greater. The large and variable remainder of national financing has to be obtained on the average by imports of capital from the United States.

The Growing Role of the Provinces in the Economy

There is one other very significant development in the Canadian economy: the change in the character of the demand for public services, which is bringing the provinces into a much more prominent role in the economy. With the prosperity and peace of the postwar period there has come a decline in the weight of defense expenditures by the federal government and a rise in the demands for expenditures on highways, education, municipal services, and a variety of social services that under the Canadian constitution are the primary responsibility of the provincial governments. Expenditures on capital formation by the federal government—which in 1950 were 29 per cent of all government capital expenditures, and 27 per cent in 1957—were by 1964 only 17 per cent. Total expenditures on goods and services by the federal government were 42 per cent of such expenditures by all governments in 1950, but by 1965 were only 34 per cent. This change has necessitated a continuing reappraisal of the division of revenues between the federal government and the provinces. A net result of the financial arrangements between the two levels of government to date has been that the amount of outstanding bonds of the provincial and municipal governments has increased by roughly twice as much as that of the federal government in the last decade and is now within 17 per cent of the federal government total of approximately $21 billion.

The added burdens on the provincial governments and the need to redistribute revenues among levels of government have made for some tension between the provinces and the federal government. Constitutional issues concerning the respective rights of provinces and the central government have been raised. These developments have emerged from circumstances that are quite independent of the new sense of purpose in the Province of Quebec. But the "quiet revolution" in that province has added an additional dimension to the adjustments among governments in the Canadian federation.

Summary

I have not been able to refer directly to all focal points of change in the Canadian economy. Those I have mentioned would, I think, be included in any observer's list. Canada is becoming a more industrialized economy. New discoveries of energy sources encourage the belief that economic growth will be securely based on adequate economical supplies of energy. Some new products are achieving prominence in the list of outputs and exports. I have selected three for special mention—oil, natural gas, and potash. It happens that all of them are produced in the Prairie provinces and are contributing greatly to the growing diversity of that region's activity. There are changes taking place which bring in their train difficult problems of policy. Among these I have mentioned particularly the relatively slow growth of productivity, the rise in the current account deficit with the United States, and the growing weight of the provincial governments in the economic life of the nation.

Major Problem Areas of Policy

The Problem of Slow Productivity Growth

Slow productivity growth presents one of the most perplexing general policy problems. This is partly because productivity has so many dimensions and partly because there are severe limits on what government can do to promote growth in output per man-hour. In fact, of course, responsibility for efficient production is widely shared throughout the community. Though perplexing, the problem is important, for high productivity is essential for the realization of national aspirations to a high standard of living and a sense of independence. There are several government programs in Canada designed to improve productivity performance.

Very great importance is now attached to the provision of educational facilities for the stream of youths through the schools and universities and for workers on the job or between jobs. The educational programs, in which both federal and provincial governments are participating, include increasingly generous income allowances for university students and for persons who have already entered the labor force. The co-operation of employers in various aspects of these programs is being sought and obtained. The general objective is to raise the average educational attainment of the members of the labor force and to insure that the training of individual members continues to be adequate throughout their working lives for the tasks they have to do.

A major reorganization of the federal government's administrative machinery for dealing with manpower problems has just been put into effect. A new Department of Manpower, separate from the older Department of Labour but including responsibility for immigration, has been established. It will administer and improve the National Employment Service and will also administer a recently inaugurated manpower mobility program. Under this latter program loans or grants may be made to workers and their families to help defray costs of moving and resettling when it is clear that such a move is in the worker's and the public interest.

Special taxation measures have been enacted to encourage research and development. Corporations are allowed to deduct from income for tax purposes all expenditures on research of a current or capital nature other than for the acquisition of land in the year in which they are made, and in addition are eligible for a grant or tax credit equal to one-fourth of capital expenditures other than for the acquisition of land and increases in current expenditures on research. In addition, the government of Canada announced in June, 1965, a program to permit government underwriting of up to 50 per cent of the costs of developmental projects undertaken in Canada, including the cost of special equipment and prototypes. Industry decides on the projects and applies for government approval under the program. If the results of a project are put to commercial use, the company involved will be required to repay the government's contribution with interest. The federal government and some of the provincial governments operate research bodies which conduct and support both pure and applied research relating to agriculture as well as industry. There are also capital financing programs of several types.

I should also mention the existence of several programs to assist in establishing viable economic activities in areas that have hitherto been distressed. These include special tax incentives for the location of industries in such areas and rural development schemes.

These are some of the major undertakings by federal and provincial governments in Canada that are specifically designed to improve the productivity of the economy.

Fiscal Problems of Federalism

Another group of major policy problems facing the authorities in Canada may conveniently be referred to as the fiscal problems of federalism. There are two main classes of problems in this area. One is that of achieving and maintaining an appropriate matching of revenues at the two principal levels of government with the responsibilities carried by government at each of those levels. The other is that of achieving the degree of co-ordination of government policies necessary to insure that fiscal policy may be effectively employed as an instrument of economic stabilization policy.

In respect to the first of these main problems, the overriding aim of federal-provincial financial relations must be: (1) to see that the rates of growth of tax revenue from all sources accruing to the federal government and to the provinces adequately reflect the growth in the total costs of their respective functions; (2) to see that the division of revenues among the provinces permits and induces each province to provide services to a minimum national standard without necessitating punitive disparities in taxation; and (3) to divide functions and revenues so as to achieve the most effective administration of functions, the most efficient tax collection procedures, and the least violation of the principle that responsibility for financing expenditure should devolve upon the spender.

The problem of achieving the appropriate matching of revenues and responsibilities at each level of government is a continuing one requiring new responses from time to time to meet changing circumstances. In Canada since the war the practice has developed of undertaking major revisions of the fiscal agreements between the provinces and the federal government every five years. Another major revision will be required for the period 1967/68–1971/72. In addition, a federal royal commission with a wide mandate to review the federal tax system and to make recommendations is expected to report early in 1967. In the next year, then, Canadian governments will be facing up to this aspect of the fiscal problems of federalism in earnest.

The problem of co-ordinating the fiscal policies of the two levels of government to enable fiscal policy to contribute effectively to stability of prices and employment is one on which only modest progress has been made to date, partly because not much deliberate use in peacetime of the federal fiscal authority as a stabilization instrument has been made until recently. Measures in each of the last two federal budgets, however, were introduced primarily as stabilization measures. Of course, the federal government must take the lead in using fiscal means of stabilizing the economy. On the expenditure side, the power of the federal government to make significant variations is more limited than that of the provinces taken as a group. I have already referred to the much greater weight of the provinces' capital expenditures. On the revenue side, if one deducts from the federal government the revenue transferred to the provinces and adds this to the revenue collected directly by the provinces, then at the present time one finds that the revenues of junior governments taken together are running roughly one-third above those of the federal government. An important consideration to be taken into account in dividing revenue fields between the provinces and the central government must be the efficacy of changes in revenues from different sources in influencing the level of economic activity. Although the technical aspects of this matter cannot be pursued here, certain it is that no matter how the fields of taxation are shared between the federal and provincial governments, effective fiscal policy will require concerted action by the two levels of government with respect both to revenues and expenditures. Machinery for such co-ordination has begun to be developed, but it would only be fair to say just begun.

Problems Arising From the Current Account Deficit and Capital Account Surplus with the United States

Three policy problems arise from the current account deficit and capital account surplus with the United States. The first of these is the problem of reducing the deficit. The current account deficit is by no means an unmitigated evil. In periods of high activity a net import of goods adds to the domestic supplies in Canada and mitigates price pressures which damage Canada's competitive position. Beyond this, a large proportion of imports into Canada is capital equipment which enhances the productivity of the Canadian economy. Even so, Canada is anxious to cut down the deficit to the extent that full exploitation of its competitive advantages will permit.

Measures outlined above to improve productivity will, to the extent that they succeed, contribute to the reduction of the deficit. And other more specific measures have been taken. For example, the policy in recent years on the export of energy or energy sources has been liberalized.

Undoubtedly the most dramatic and most discussed measures taken in recent years to restrain the growth of the deficit are those which Canada and the United States together have taken in respect of automobiles and parts for new automobiles. From mid-

January, 1965, Canada has permitted the manufacturers of automobiles to import motor vehicles and parts duty free from all
countries provided that such manufacturers maintain a ratio of
production to sales and a ratio of Canadian content in their
domestically produced vehicles at least as high as prevailed in the
1964 model year. The United States government for its part
permits duty-free entry of automobiles and original equipment for
automobiles from Canada, subject to certain provisions limiting
content from sources other than Canada or the United States. It
is the expectation that fewer models of cars will be produced in
Canada, but that such models as are produced will serve a much
larger portion of the North American market for these models than
heretofore. It is also expected that the most efficient of the Canadian parts producers will enjoy an increased volume of sales both
in Canada and the United States. It is hoped too that the prices of
cars to Canadians will eventually be lower in relation to the prices
to Americans than they traditionally have been. It is important
to add that it is not the Canadian expectation that the deficit on
trade in automobiles and parts with the United States will be
turned into a surplus, but rather that it will grow less rapidly than
it would have otherwise. I should also note that in connection with
this automobile program a further measure was taken that establishes an important precedent. It was recognized that the automobile program would create serious problems of adjustment for
some parts producers and for some workers. Accordingly, an assistance program was introduced under which loans have been
made to qualifying parts manufacturers, and transitional assistance
benefits have been paid to affected workers.

While it is not likely that improvements in the balance of
payments could be induced by identical measures applied in
other industries, it may be assumed that the Canadian government is actively investigating all suitable and acceptable means of
encouraging Canadian industry to service domestic and foreign
markets with their products.

One of the problems connected with the capital account surplus with the United States derives from the American balance of
payments difficulties and the controls that have been placed on
the export of capital from the United States. I do not wish to enter

upon the technical details of the American interest equalization tax and guidelines and the effects that the latter are having on the Canadian capital market. I do wish to refer to the fact that, in negotiating an exemption from the application of the interest equalization tax to new issues of Canadian securities and later from the guideline on the purchase of foreign securities by non-bank financial institutions, Canada agreed that it would not be its desire or intention to use the proceeds of borrowing in the United States to add to the official reserves of Canada. Indeed, a target ceiling on the total official reserves and net creditor position in the International Monetary Fund is now being established. The target was reduced in negotiations in the fall of 1965 by $100 million below the figure agreed upon at the time of exemption from the interest equalization tax. While this agreement in respect to the ceiling on reserves has not to date prevented the monetary authorities from achieving the credit conditions they have regarded as appropriate to the domestic situation in Canada, it is a factor which must always be taken into account and which conceivably in some circumstances could complicate the achievement of a public policy appropriate for domestic stabilization.

Canadians are concerned directly with the magnitude of their capital imports. This concern stems partly from a sense of exposure to the risk that for any of several reasons a significant part of this capital flow might be interrupted and thus necessitate concentrated and painful adjustments in the Canadian economy. It stems partly also from apprehension concerning the growing ownership and control of Canadian enterprise by United States residents which has been an accompaniment of the inflow of capital. An important long-term policy problem facing Canada then is to find suitable ways and means of reducing reliance on foreign capital. In part the solution is to be found in measures to reduce the current account deficit. But in important degree the solution must also be found in measures to increase the amount of domestic saving and, perhaps even more significant, the concentration of Canadian saving in channels that lead to the financing of the types of large and risky enterprises which now so often rely upon equity capital from the United States.

4

The Canadian Industrial Structure:
An essay on its nature and efficiency

H. E. English

Structure is a residual concept in the minds of many economists. To some, structural considerations are those which cannot
be explained by the grand aggregates or by the quantifiable part
of the disaggregation process. But to Canadian economic historians it has been the key to the kingdom—the kingdom, that is, of
original ideas in social science. More recently it has also been the
favored theme of some Canadian politicians, but in their hands its
use has been less fortunate, for they have tended to confuse
structural and general disequilibrium. There are indications that
the Economic Council of Canada may yet identify the structural
concepts that have real significance for Canada's present problems and future prospects.

There are two principal kinds of structural questions: one concerns the pattern of industries, the other the internal organization
of particular industries. Both are important in understanding
Canada's economic development and present problems. The pattern of Canadian development has received much attention because the conventional wisdom in Canadian economic history is
the staple theory, which is structural in nature.[1] Questions of
internal industrial structure have been less thoroughly studied, but
with the rising importance of manufacturing and the controversy

---

1. The list of Canadian economic historians who have developed the staple theory is an honor roll of Canadian economists, headed by Harold Innis and W. A.
Mackintosh.

over Canada's ability to compete internationally and over the role
of foreign ownership in Canadian industrial development, questions of structure have been catapulted into the foreground of
debate on economic policy in Canada. A subtitle encompassing
both aspects of the following essay on structure might well be
"From Codfish to Car Parts."

The Staple Theory and its Application to Canada

As M. H. Watkins has stressed, "The fundamental assumption
of the staple theory is that staple exports are the leading sector of
the economy and set the pace for economic growth."[2] He notes
that the theory has its greatest explanatory value in rather special
circumstances—where the domestic market is limited and natural
resources are abundant relative to labor and capital. Economic
development then consists in diversification around the export
base. The form of development will be governed by the nature of
the staple and of the "spread effects" it generates. At heart it is a
technological theory of economic development, under which the
initial impetus may come from the demand side in world markets—a change in the size of demand (increased population or
higher incomes) or in the pattern of tastes; or—in the supply
side—the development of new processes of exploration, processing, or transportation. Any or all of these aid the development of
new resources in a new land. But the nature of the development is
governed by the character of the staple. Several spread effects can
be identified. It may or it may not call for production of inputs in
the new country (backward linkage); it may or it may not afford
opportunities for further processing near the resource (forward
linkage); it may or may not generate a demand for consumer
goods which can be satisfied by new production facilities in the
new land (final demand linkage). The realization of these spread
effects will depend both on the demand generated for domestic
investment and on the availability of savings and other factors of

2. "A Staple Theory of Economic Growth," *Canadian Journal of Economics and
Political Science*, XXIX (May, 1963), 144.

production, perhaps most of all on the presence of entrepreneurial talents. If these factors are available locally or can be imported, an export boom can readily develop. It will be more intensive and longer sustained if the spread effects are large, and further assisted if other staples appear.

But while staple theory explains success when it occurs, it does not guarantee it. There are the dangers that concentration on particular staples may accentuate fluctuations in the developing economy when world demand for the staple slumps, and that factors and institutions may be so specialized that they are not readily adaptable to other industries. The plantation economy of the tropics is often cited as an example of the latter. Then too, population growth may outstrip the growth of production.

Application to the Canadian case has revealed much of the variety which is associated with the nature of the staple. Until the nineteenth century the Canadian staples, codfish and fur, were of the type that generated almost no spread effects, and the otherwise inhospitable land encouraged little settlement except for imperial reasons. New England, for superior locational reasons, developed agriculture, lumbering, and shipbuilding, and nurtured shipping routes to the West Indies from its ice-free ports. In the nineteenth century came settlement in Upper Canada and lumbering, followed by expansion to the West and the founding of the wheat economy. These activities brought about the building of sawmills and flour mills and later, the construction of railways and the production of agricultural implements. In the East, processing of food became more diversified with construction of cheese factories. All these activities were tied to export, the only purely domestic requirement being for construction materials for modest housing.

Such figures as are available suggest that even in the latter part of the nineteenth century export income declined as a percentage of national income. But domestic activity was not sufficient to prevent considerable emigration to the United States during this period.

In the twentieth century the wheat boom of the first decade

was followed by the artificial stimulus of war. Then came the rise of the pulp and paper industry in the twenties and much fuller development of non-ferrous metals mining and smelting from the late twenties onward. Canadian economic development and the changing industrial pattern, especially in the period since 1910, are illustrated in Tables 1 and 2:

Table 1. *Estimates of gross national product for goods-producing sectors in Canada, 1870 and 1910, and average gross domestic product, 1926–29 and 1953–56 (in millions of dollars)*

	1870	1910	1926–29	1953–56
Primary industries				
Agriculture	153	509	850	1,818
Fisheries	5	21	71	419
Forestry	44	86	40	88
Mining	4	59	183	984
Total primary	206	675	1,144	3,309
Manufactures	87	508	1,202	6,782
Percentage of primary	42	75	105	205

Source: M. C. Urquhart and K. A. H. Buckley, *Historical Statistics of Canada* (Toronto, 1965), pp. 133, 141.

Until 1910 the primary industries were clearly of dominant importance. Agriculture, especially wheat, and forestry, especially lumbering, dominated both primary and manufacturing sectors, except for the traditional manufacturing activities producing simple textile and iron and steel products required in the frontier communities. Among the so-called newer secondary industries only that producing transportation equipment for the railways was of any importance.

By the late twenties manufacturing was for the first time more important than the primary industries taken together, even though mining was beginning its spectacular rise. Among the manufactures there was greater diversification in the processing industries, including the first boom in pulp and paper manufacture and new kinds of mineral processing.

But the major step toward a more diversified economy has

come about in the last generation between the boom years of the late twenties and the comparable boom years of the mid-fifties. In this period mining has become much more important, now comprising about 30 per cent of primary production. The great new iron and oil resources have been mainly responsible for this in-

Table 2. *Value added in selected Canadian manufacturing industries, 1870 to 1957 (Percentage of total)*

	1870	1910	1926–29	1957
I. *Resource-based manufactures*	25.9	28.9	25.6	23.9
Food and beverages	8.7	9.2	7.8	6.2
Wood products				
(mainly lumber)	16.5	13.2	5.4	3.9
Pulp and paper	0.6	2.3	7.6	6.9
Non-ferrous metals	n.a.	3.1	2.8	4.6
Primary chemicals	n.a.	0.1	1.1	1.4
Non-metallic minerals	0.1	1.0	0.9	0.9
II. *Traditional secondary industries*	63.2	56.0	53.5	46.5
Textiles	10.6	12.7	11.3	7.9
Clothing	6.9	8.6	5.2	3.6
Other	3.7	4.1	6.1	4.3
Iron and steel products	16.8	14.0	12.9	15.1
Other[a]	35.8	29.3	29.3	23.5
III. *Newer secondary industries*	10.9	14.3	19.5	27.7
Electrical apparatus	n.a.	1.6	3.3	5.8
Transportation equipment	6.8	7.4	7.7	9.8
Petroleum and coal products	1.8	1.8	2.3	5.5
Chemical products	2.1	2.9	3.4	4.8
Rubber	0.2	0.6	2.8	1.8

a. Includes such industries as tobacco, food processing (other than that under I), furniture, paper products, publishing, leather products, non-metallic minerals, and non-ferrous products.

Source: Gordon W. Bertram, "Historical Statistics on Growth and Structure of Manufacturing in Canada, 1870–1957," in J. Henripin and A. Asimakopulos, eds., *C.P.S.A. Conferences on Statistics, 1962–1963 Papers* (Toronto, 1964), pp. 103–113.

crease. However, at the same time as these new natural resource developments have occurred, manufacturing has grown so rapidly that it is now twice as important as the combined primary industries. Furthermore, within manufacturing, in spite of the great spur to processing given by Canada's resource production, those manufactures which are not directly related to resource industries have outstripped the processing industries. Newer secondary industries producing automotive products, electrical apparatus, and chemicals now contribute a quarter of Canada's manufacturing output. Even in the more traditional sectors of manufacturing new developments have changed the pattern of production. Whereas the iron and steel products category was previously dominated by a range of small-scale production activities (hardware), it now represents a vigorous primary industry and a growing range of machinery manufactures.

This postwar phenomenon is still only partly comprehended by Canadians, though I am convinced that the business community is better aware of the change than are many political leaders and publicists. Some of the latter fail to understand that the only plausible explanation is the growth of the domestic market to a size that enables the establishment of a range of manufacturing industries which could never in the past have been supported by the Canadian market, segregated as it is from world markets. Some years ago a symposium of economists met under the auspices of the International Economics Association to consider "The Economic Consequences of the Size of Nations."[3] They agreed that there appeared to be a threshold market of about ten million people and that beyond that size a nation could support, primarily on the basis of domestic demand, a substantial range of manufacturing activity. The Canadian population reached the ten million mark by the end of the thirties, but more important, the population of central Canada, Quebec, and Ontario grew from about six million in the late twenties to about twelve million in the early sixties. There is ample evidence that the industrialization afforded by this market between Windsor, Ontario, and some point east of Montreal on the St. Lawrence has transformed industrial attitudes toward the long-term advantages of investment in this region. Perhaps from the twenties, certainly since World War II, the staple theory no longer deserves pride of place in the explanation of Canadian economic growth.

3. E. A. G. Robinson, *Economic Consequences of the Size of Nations* (London, 1960).

The Problem of Realizing Industrial Potentials, 1946–62

Unfortunately, the story cannot yet be told as dramatically as it will be in the future because special short-term circumstances have adversely affected the course of development in the postwar period, and certain basic inhibiting conditions have persisted. Between 1946 and 1953 an extended period of artificial stimuli related both to postwar reconstruction needs and the Korean conflict supported a pattern of industry in Canada which was not entirely appropriate to normal peacetime competitive conditions. When import competition from the United States again reappeared in 1953, many firms and industries discovered that they were too diversified and that their tariff protection was not sufficient to enable them to meet it. Many concluded that their disabilities under peacetime conditions must be fundamental. Rates of return in secondary manufacturing could not match those in the resource industries, which were engaged in a massive investment boom under the impetus of the Paley Report that had predicted substantial world shortages of the sort of raw materials Canada could produce. As the boom reached its peak, huge imports of capital goods, paralleled by massive inflows of foreign capital, caused some observers to conclude that Canada was indeed a very dependent and vulnerable economy. They had forgotten that Canadian imports had previously enjoyed the happy tendency to react sensitively to business fluctuations.

The mid-fifties boom was neither long enough nor balanced enough to inspire confidence in Canadian industry. The circumstances of the late fifties left it shaken. The drop in investment in the resource industries after excessive expansion of new capacity was accompanied by weakness of policy in both Canada and the United States. So closely is Canada tied to fluctuations in the United States that part of its problem was probably unavoidable. Furthermore, the restoration of the competitive position of European industry was likely to affect both countries in similar ways. But Canadians have only themselves to thank for an employment record that was inferior to the American record in the late fifties. The perverse tight money policy adopted in Canada maintained a higher capital inflow than was warranted and, under the flexible exchange rate, produced an artificial premium on the Canadian dollar. The immediate effect of this was to handicap Canadian exporters and to wipe out protection of domestic industries. However inappropriate the policy, it had one unintended salutary effect. It forced a tightening up of management and the abandonment of some inefficient lines of manufacture and prepared Canadian industry for the days when a more appropriate exchange rate would be restored. When this occurred in 1962, it heralded better export opportunities—though the method of bringing it about left much to be desired, involving as it did a totally unnecessary exchange crisis and the abandonment of the flexible exchange rate system.

Evidence of Economic Maturity: The Export of Specialized Manufactures

Since 1963, a reasonably normal international exchange relationship has been achieved, and there is thus an opportunity to observe the competitive effectiveness of Canadian industry. Unfortunately, there is a long lag in production statistics so that a comparison between 1953–55 and 1963–65 cannot be made for some time. But the export figures are available and give further dramatic indication of the long-term improvement in Canada's industrial potential.

Manufactured exports have been the only major category to grow steadily in relative importance during the period, and almost all subcategories have shown similar increases, with those in the automobile group being exceptionally large. Although the effect of the 1965 automobile pact between Canada and the United States is only beginning to be felt, there can be no doubt that export figures reflect the start of a dramatic response to the incentives and opportunities provided. In dollar terms, the amount of automotive and parts exports almost exactly doubled between 1964 and 1965. Of the $304 million of exports in 1965, nearly $150 million comprised passenger cars (up from about $68 million in 1964); parts other than engines comprised $128 mil-

Table 3. *Pattern of Canadian exports, 1963–65 (Percentage of total)*

	1963	1964	1965
Agricultural products	17.6	18.7	16.2
Fisheries products	2.4	2.3	2.3
Forest products	27.0	29.9	29.9
Newsprint and pulp	17.3	16.1	16.1
Minerals and metals, raw	17.1	16.4	16.7
Iron ores and concentrates	4.0	4.4	4.3
Non-ferrous metal ores and concentrates	6.0	5.2	5.7
Petroleum and natural gas	4.6	4.5	4.6
Asbestos	2.1	1.9	1.9
Minerals and metals, processed	14.2	13.8	14.3
Iron and steel	2.7	2.8	2.7
Non-ferrous metals	10.9	10.2	10.8
Manufactures	13.9	15.7	17.9
Chemicals	4.0	3.8	4.0
Textiles	0.9	0.9	1.0
Machinery			
Agricultural	1.7	1.8	1.9
Other	2.0	2.1	2.8
Electrical equipment	2.0	1.8	2.0
Automobiles	1.3	2.2	4.2
Aircraft	1.6	3.1	2.5
Percentage of total trade accounted for above	92.2	92.8	97.3

Source: Dominion Bureau of Statistics, *Trade of Canada*, Dec., 1965.

lion (up from $63 million in 1964). Trucks and motor vehicle engines made up the rest. It should be added that Canadian imports of similar products have grown relatively less but by larger absolute amounts, resulting in a greater deficit for Canada in her trade with the United States. This was expected, as it will take a while for Canadian production facilities to adapt fully to the plan. It is considered probable that the deficit would have grown more rapidly in the absence of the scheme.

The Remaining Structural Problem

These trade figures confirm the impression one gains from the longer-term trends, namely, that Canadian industry is meeting the test of international competition more effectively. Some observers have been so impressed with the change that they have overlooked the unrealized potential that remains. It is possible to come to grips with the problem only by examining the internal structure of industry, and by applying the theory of pricing, especially under various degrees and forms of oligopoly. Adopting the analytical framework of Professor J. S. Bain of California, let me briefly pose the structure and behavior questions to which attention should be directed:

1. With respect to structure, what is the incidence of competition, monopoly, and "pure" and "impure" oligopoly? What particular forms of each are found in Canada? What are the relative sizes of firms? How significant are the competitive fringes? What are the particular institutional considerations which affect Canadian industrial structure?

2. With respect to behavior, both the static or short run and the long run should be considered. In the short term, what pricing behavior is observed? How important is collusion? How significant are selling policies? What structural factors govern behavior? With regard to the longer term, the same questions may be asked and two additional ones added: What investment policies are adopted? What governs the choice between new product development and more conservative pricing and selling practices?

3. Finally, with respect to performance, how well do Canadian industries approximate the competitive norm? Are departures from that norm in any way warranted by the inappropriateness of the competitive norm for Canada? What are the principal obstacles to realizing economic efficiency in Canadian industry? What policies for changing structure and behavior might be appropriate?

Distinctive Internal Structural Characteristics of Canadian Industry

As in most modern industrial economies, the incidence of pure competition in Canada is low (being relevant only for agriculture and fishing), and monopolistic competition is approximated only in retailing and perhaps in a few types of food processing industries and the needle trades. One of the most interesting consequences of pure competition in certain primary industries has been its effect on regional political attitudes. The concentration of fishing and agriculture in the outlying provinces and the heavy dependence of these provinces on industries which have this structure has meant that Prairie and Maritime voters have often leveled the charge of monopoly against the manufacturers of Ontario and Quebec and have also complained of the harmful consequences of tariffs and other forms of protection western and eastern primary producers were forced to bear.

The rise of the pulp and paper and non-ferrous mineral industries in the interwar period has altered the picture in this respect. The pulp and paper firms, especially with their stress on pulp and newsprint, comprise a pure oligopoly, while the leading non-ferrous metal firms—International Nickel, Alcan, and Consolidated Mining and Smelting—are by far the dominant producers of their commodity lines. But the fact that they all rely on the export market for the major share of their sales means that there is less inclination to worry about the consequences of near-monopoly in Canada. Since the newsprint producers have to sell to large and influential buyers and non-ferrous metal producers have had to face the United States government as a principal buyer in times of national emergency, monopsony or oligopsony pressure has often been present as well.

Among manufacturing industries, oligopoly is general, as is primary dependence on the domestic market. The two principal categories which are distinguishable in market structure characteristics are producer goods and consumer goods, because the producer goods are subject to oligopsony influences while consumer goods are not. Each of these categories can be subdivided to take account of product heterogeneity in some industries, though this phenomenon is more common in consumer goods sectors. The principal Canadian industries can be divided as follows:

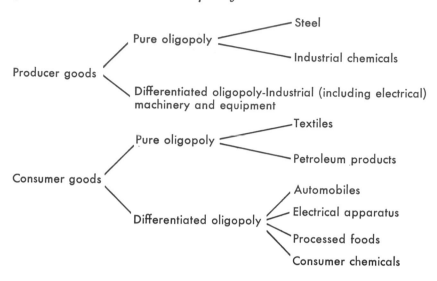

Of course, the classification breaks down when it is noted that textiles and petroleum products are in part producer goods and only in part consumer goods.

This classification is valid alike for Canada and the United States. Overall studies of Canadian industrial structure suggest a great similarity in industrial organization of Canada and the United States. Gideon Rosenbluth found greater concentration in most Canadian industries, largely because of the smaller size of the market.[4] There are a few relatively large companies in all those instances where economies of scale are of some importance, but unlike American industry, there are very few producers on the fringe of most Canadian industries. Regional markets help to support such firms in the United States; and there is some evidence of the development of smaller, more specialized firms in Canada as regional markets grow in the East and West. But to a much greater degree than in the United States, Canadian industries concentrate on the main product types in each category and are dominated by a few large firms.

The Canadian situation is made distinctive by two institutional

4. *Concentration in Canadian Manufacturing Industries* (New York, 1957), pp. 75–93.

factors—the importance of tariff and other forms of protection and the prevalence of foreign ownership in many Canadian manufacturing industries. The tariff as a price-modifying mechanism will be discussed under industry behavior. It is important here only to point out that its influence is uneven. In general, tariff levels are higher for goods at advanced stages of manufacture and lower for industrial materials. The rate levels of the Canadian tariff are as follows: steel, under 10 per cent; primary textiles, mostly 10–15 per cent; industrial chemicals, some 15–20 per cent, some under 10 per cent, zero for many end uses; industrial machinery, 20 per cent, but under 10 per cent and often zero for export industries, or if not made in Canada; consumer textiles, often 25 per cent or more; consumer chemicals, 15–20 per cent; consumer durables, 17.5 per cent for automobiles, 22.5 per cent typically for electrical.

United States tariffs are slightly lower for many categories and only half the Canadian levels for many durables, but are much higher for important types of industrial chemicals (because of a historical anachronism) and are accentuated by the "American selling price" system of valuation. The United States tariff probably represents effective protection to a lesser extent than the Canadian, both because Canadian rates are consistently higher for advanced manufactures (thus insuring enhanced protection for the value added at those stages) and because pricing and other aspects of market behavior are more directly related to international trade in Canada.

The incidence of foreign ownership is also uneven, being greater in industries based on elaborate and expensive exploration and research activities (petroleum, electronics, chemicals) and in those in which it is also helpful to be able to spread costs of product differentiation. In the mining industries, as of 1962, corporations of which more than 50 per cent was owned by non-residents held 65 per cent of the assets, though the figure varied from 52.4 per cent for metal mines to 83.9 per cent for mineral fuels. For the processing and manufacturing industries the 1962 percentages of foreign ownership were as follows:

Petroleum and coal products	99.3
Rubber products	92.0
Tobacco products	85.3
Transportation equipment	84.2
Chemical products	76.4
Electrical products	66.6
Machinery	63.7
Primary metal	60.2
Metal fabricating	51.3
Non-metallic mineral products	51.1
Paper products	40.9
Food manufacturing	31.2
Textiles and clothing	30.7
Wood production	28.0
Leather products	27.1
Furniture and fixtures	21.5
Beverages	13.3
Printing and publishing	10.9

Some of these figures seem out of line with the general observation that tariff rates are higher for goods at advanced stages of manufacture. Thus the low figure for beverages, which are dominated by alcoholic beverages, contrasts with the high figure for tobacco. Here the selling costs seem to have been spread southward rather than the other way. Apparently superior Canadian product development is the explanation.

The Effect of Structure on Industry Behavior and Performance

Turning to industry behavior, not only the normal effects of oligopoly structure, but also the influence of the special considerations cited must be identified. Basic differences are probable between pure and differentiated oligopoly in respect to their pricing and their policies. For example, pure oligopolies must take more care to insure price stability. This has generated a tendency toward price leadership, zone or basing-point pricing, or various forms of more explicitly collusive activity. In Canada there is evidence that such industries behave as one would expect. Price leadership has existed in the petroleum industry, zone pricing in steel, and certain other industries have attracted the attention of the Combines Investigation Act, paper, wire, and cable being well-known examples. Price sensitivity is, as expected, less evident in the differentiated oligopolies.

More important than these considerations, however, is the practice of pricing on the tariff. It is one of the familiar though embarrassing features of oligopoly theory that there is no easy or general explanation of price determination. The consequences of instability are serious, and the motives for finding means for insuring stability are consequently strong. Oligopolists search for a rule of thumb, but—given the usual profit—it is unlikely that the level of price which suits one firm will suit all, unless the firms are in a similar cost position and recognize this to be true. Pricing on the basis of the price of imports plus the Canadian tariff is a heaven-sent "rule of thumb." It is widely and easily recognized, especially since the relevant import prices are almost always American, a fact which is uniquely important for Canada. The price ceiling so determined introduces a kink in the demand curve which insures that the maximum profit price is almost certain to be at the level set by the tariff. (Incidentally, the extent to which the Canadian price is able to remain above or below the price of duty-paid imports probably reflects the degree of positive or negative preferences for the domestic product.)

The sharing of the market still presents a problem. It will be affected by the importance of economies of scale relative to the size of the market and the height of the tariff protection, which will in turn determine how well undersized firms can survive. In those industries or product lines for which the Canadian market is adequate to support plants of minimum efficient scale, all firms can earn an excess profit the size of which is governed by the height of the tariff. In industries or product lines for which the Canadian market is not adequate to support a plant with which to achieve the minimum efficient scale, the market may support one or more high-cost production units, though—if plant economies increase continuously with scale—one would expect that a single producing unit would be most profitable in these circumstances.

In fact, there are apparently numerous situations in which there are in Canada more producers of a given manufactured good than would be warranted by the economies of scale. The motive for each firm to drive rivals out of the market so that further economies can be enjoyed is not sufficiently strong to generate a rational organization of production. Instead, firms vie with one another for increased shares by the usual means of advertising and other selling activity, style changes, and real product improvement. For consumer goods, the former are more important, for producer goods, the latter. But essentially the maintenance of an inefficient structure in such oligopoly situations must depend on the presence of a positive incentive to preserve the status quo, or of a negative incentive, that is, the penalty that will be experienced by anyone who tries to change it. If profits are adequate, and in particular if a dominant firm has a strong profit position, this will act as a strong stabilizing force in maintaining market shares. There are indications that this was the case in the automobile industry before the automobile pact was negotiated. The leading firm had nothing to gain from an industry rationalization which would improve the relative profitability of the other two firms. Hence an extra inducement was needed to assure acceptance of the scheme. But in general, the negative incentive is probably the more important for Canadian oligopolists. First, there is the risk each rival faces that he may be the one to fail in the battle for market shares. But secondly, in the Canadian context, there is the fact that branch plants have great resources to back them up in any struggle. Hence the temptation to struggle is modified. Foreign ownership thus probably insures that, given the tariff and other elements of Canadian protection, the branch plants will avoid disruption of market structure for fear of repercussions involving costly rivalry among the parent firms.

A number of interesting cases can be cited to demonstrate the effects of differences in degree of protection, number of firms, scale of output required for efficiency, and extent of foreign ownership in particular industry situations. Four will be outlined briefly—the electrical appliance industry, the industrial chemicals industry, the machinery industries, and the primary steel industry.

1. The electrical appliance industry is dominated by six firms

(though for each main product line, production is more concentrated). As the products are consumer durables, the demand is large and mass production techniques are applicable. It is pretty clear that Canadian plants have not been of efficient scale, that the maintenance of the inefficient structure of production has depended upon the tariff, and that the prevalence of foreign ownership has discouraged individual firms from striving for increased shares except by the kind of selling activity which tends to be counteracting so far as established firms are concerned, though it also provides a barrier to the entry of new competitors.

2. In the industrial chemicals industry, low Canadian tariffs in many important lines have meant that only very few producers (often three or less) supply each line, though about six foreign-controlled firms having overlapping product patterns lead the industry. In those product lines on which foreign tariffs are low or absent, firms have sought to export to achieve efficient scale of output. Where foreign tariffs have been high, the Canadian producer has had to be satisfied with short runs and high cost.

One of the most vigorous forms of competition in this dynamic industry has been the competition to see who could first establish production facilities to supply a new product. Short-term gains have sometimes been possible for the winner, but the advantage has not normally lasted long, and the outcome has often been excess capacity. The recent experience with nylon producers makes an interesting case study. For many years, nylon was patented and under comfortable protection; the patent-holding firm was the sole producer, hence able to get all economies available given the size of Canadian and occasional export demand. Then the patent expired and several other firms subsequently announced plans to produce in Canada. Their entry has almost certainly affected the ability of all to achieve low-cost production of at least some types of nylon; yet all apparently have sufficient incentive to produce, given the protection available. Tariff protection apparently provides no guarantee of the continuation of profitable or efficient production.

Finally, the industrial chemicals sector illustrates the effect of the historic conflict of interest between primary export industries and manufacturing industries supplying producer goods. The pressure exerted by Canadian export industries has resulted in the inclusion of numerous end-use items in the chemical tariff schedule. These permitted those industries to obtain their chemical inputs at import prices. The effect has been to reduce the market available to Canadian producers of those chemicals. So long as there was no hope that they could become efficient producers on the basis of the small Canadian market and whatever export markets they could expect to supply on a continuing basis, the Canadian tariff may have been essential to their survival. But now that Canadian producers could be efficient suppliers of many industrial chemicals in world or continental markets (a fact which has been demonstrated in certain lines where foreign tariffs were not prohibitive), the chief value of the Canadian tariff, which has only inadequately protected them, is as a negotiating instrument.

3. In the industrial machinery industries, another type of experience has been evident. Tariff levels are substantial, though types of machinery which are not made in Canada are imported at low duties or none at all. Foreign ownership is quite general, though not universal. There has been less tendency for too many producers to appear on the Canadian market, both because of the limited demand and because fewer leading producers were available in the United States and elsewhere to set up rival branches. The lack of a large mass market for specialized lines of producer goods has meant that mass-production techniques cannot be applied. However, the high cost of product research and development facilities often favors the large United States firm.

In some categories—electronic office equipment and communication equipment, for example—Canadian operations have been fully integrated into the international production organization of the companies involved. These are product lines for which tariffs are of little importance, because price is secondary to quality. There are also cases where expensive product development activity requires large-scale operations to enable spreading of fixed costs. In other instances, there would be opportunities for development of specialized Canadian exports, but the Canadian market alone is insufficient to achieve competitive cost levels. Numerous opportunities for integration of Canadian and American production appear to exist, but are not exploited primarily because of the commercial policies of the two countries.

In this connection, the farm machinery industry is of special interest. Since 1944, there has been free trade in most lines. Canadian production has become more specialized as a result of this development, and both exports and imports have grown proportionately, though the flows of trade have become more north and south than they were in the interwar years. Canada's biggest production and export opportunities have been in self-propelled combines. The agricultural machinery industry's experience has been cited as an example of what would happen if free trade were applied more generally. This is only partly valid. Most Canadian manufacturers are better located to supply the North American market than are the Canadian producers of farm machinery, because the market for other manufacturers is centered farther east in the area between Boston, Chicago, and Washington.

But this is a digression from the main theme. The case cited suggests that the Canadian machinery industries are much better suited to integrated operation and that the protection which may have made possible the establishment of firms in the first place now merely postpones the realization of Canadian manufacturing potential.

For both the chemicals and industrial machinery groups, research and development are important, and it has sometimes been stated that Canadian, like European, firms cannot compete with the great United States giants in the development of new products. There can be no doubt that the subsidiary relationship gives Canadian firms with United States parents substantial advantages—access to technology and a basis for readily integrating production facilities. The distribution network already available in international companies could also be more fully exploited by Canadian subsidiaries if trade barriers were reduced. Those firms that are Canadian owned or have operated exclusively in the domestic market, often on the basis of technology obtained by licensing arrangements, would be at some disadvantage in adapting to the closer integration of Canada into the world economy.

But more fundamentally, the possibility of spreading the costs of research and development, and of selling distinctive Canadian products, can much better be borne if the market available is expanded.

4. The primary steel industry is dominated by four firms, three of which are Canadian owned while the other is controlled by British interests. As noted earlier, tariffs on steel are low. The experience of the industry in recent years is unique in several respects: it succeeded in extensive import replacement in the late fifties, at the time of the overvalued Canadian dollar, and prices for the main types of primary steel and many rolled products remain at roughly United States levels. The Canadian tariff is not incorporated in pricing steel sold in Canada, and the modest United States tariff has been absorbed in exports. This record is an important demonstration of the improved potential for efficient manufacturing in Canada and probably also of the value of low tariffs in discouraging inefficient production structure. The absence of foreign control may have left the firms more willing to compete for shares of the market, though oligopsony power and the temptation to squeeze the Dominion Steel and Coal Company, which is less well located to supply the Canadian market than are other steel producers, are probably more important.

Thus it can be seen that the performance of Canadian industry is affected by its oligopoly characteristics, but that the specific effects of protectionist policies and, to a lesser extent, of foreign control of Canadian firms operating under these policies, are of considerable importance in explaining the behavior of particular oligopolies and the economic efficiency of the results achieved.

Rationalization Policies for Canadian Industry

The foregoing discussion indicates that a central feature of Canadian policy for improving the productivity of Canadian industry is the reduction and probably the removal of obsolete trade barriers. The Economic Council of Canada implied this in its Second Annual Review, and further attention will be paid to this subject in the council's future research studies. Just as it feels that improved labor market policies are required to insure that Canadian labor inputs are fully competitive at all levels of skills with those of other countries, so the council is pointing out that efficient use of Canadian real capital will depend on the ability to use capital facilities in more specialized ways made possible in the context of access to international markets and exposure to international competition. But in designing the policy environment it is important that the kind of commercial policy arrangement adopted should be appropriate and that transitional policies should be chosen so as to avoid unnecessary burdens of adjustment and unequal sharing of those that must be borne.

There has been much confusion in Canada and elsewhere over the position adopted by the Canadian government in the course of the recent round of GATT negotiations. Many have implied that Canada's offer was limited for a country which has considered itself a champion of multilateral tariff reductions. The government has argued that Canadian industry would find the sort of linear and partial tariff reductions contemplated in the Kennedy Round a rather inadequate basis for restructuring its manufacturing industry. For great free-trade areas like the United States or the EEC, the reduction of tariffs by 25 per cent or even 50 per cent makes some contribution to better choice of product specialties and is as well an act of economic and political partnership. For Canada it would require a move toward heavier dependence on export markets in order to achieve the scale of production required to meet increased international competition. As long as the other trading partners of the United States and Canada have residual tariffs, Canadian producers would have to absorb duties on a larger share of their output than would rival producers elsewhere. For these reasons those that could adapt to international trading opportunities would much prefer a scheme involving the elimination of tariffs rather than their further gradual reduction. At the same time, because of the greater adjustment required of Canadian industries, a transition period and appropriate adjustment policies would be desirable to insure that those who must make the greatest adjustments need not bear the lion's share of the costs. A clear commitment to a comprehensive program of adjustment policies could play an important part in gaining support for the required commercial policy changes.[5]

Among adjustment policies the kind of direct assistance of labor and capital covered by the Trade Expansion Act of 1962 would be important for Canada's trade, but there is also considerable demand for amendment of the Combines Investigation Act to permit firms to get together in agreements to specialize, to merge, or to set up joint sales and research agencies to put themselves in a stronger position to compete internationally. When (and only when) a commitment to tariff reduction has been undertaken, there might be a case for amendment or more flexible application of the combines laws. Some businessmen and financial writers call for co-operative action prior to the commercial policy commitment. This would not seem to be in the public interest. As already hinted, most foreign-owned firms should be able to adapt quite readily, given their international affiliations, so that the main purpose of any approved or tolerated collusion would be to enable those firms with a traditional orientation to the domestic market to adapt to the new circumstances. One should be skeptical of any general or long-lasting departure from the application of laws for insuring competition because no convincing evidence has yet been advanced that the European-type argument for the creation of giant enterprises to meet the United States giants is based on sound appraisal of the economies of scale in either production or research in Canada.

In conclusion it might be noted that the Canadian economy

---

5. It is not the purpose of this paper to explain various commercial policy choices. A recent Canadian-American Committee Statement, *A New Trade Strategy for Canada and the United States*, details what might be an appropriate policy for Canada. Canadians would prefer, for political reasons, a broad free-trade arrangement rather than one which included only Canada and the United States. If such an arrangement is not possible, some Canadians, including some politicians and government officials, have proposed further industry-by-industry deals like that covering automobiles and parts. There is a danger that further such arrangements between Canada and the United States might be used as a precedent for special deals by other GATT members, and for the undermining of the principle of non-discrimination. Furthermore, the choice of individual industries in removal of trade barriers tends to leave aside the hard-core protectionist sectors in any economy, which can only be effectively included in a broad free-trade deal.

has now developed to the point that the old conflict of interests between primary resource industries and secondary manufacturing industries is no longer relevant, and internal structural problems can only be solved by appropriate and substantial changes in commercial policy and complementary adjustment policies.

5

Le Syndicalisme au Canada

Gérard Dion

Dans son organisation, sa structure et son action, le mouvement syndical canadien reflète assez parfaitement toutes les ambiguités géographiques, constitutionnelles, sociales, et économiques de l'état canadien. Le Canada est un pays vaste, peu populeux pour son territoire. La population est irrégulièrement dispersée selon les régions avec une très grande concentration dans l'Ontario et le Québec. Des vingt millions d'habitants, 90 pour cent vivent à l'intérieur de cinquante milles de la frontière américaine qui s'étend de l'Atlantique au Pacifique. Près de 30 pour cent de la population totale du pays est de langue française et habite pour une bonne part dans la province de Québec. Les Canadiens français ont une culture et des traditions différentes des Canadiens d'expression anglaise et, en raison de la constitution fédérative du pays, dans le Québec, ils peuvent conduire leurs affaires avec beaucoup d'autonomie.

Le Canada est composé de dix provinces et la juridiction du travail relève de ces entités politiques, alors que le Gouvernement d'Ottawa n'a juridiction que sur environ 10 pour cent de la main-d'oeuvre. La concentration des ressources naturelles et de l'industrie dans certaines régions de même que les coûts du transport et des communications accroissent la tendance de chacune des régions à se développer indépendamment l'une de l'autre. La Colombie britannique est séparée du reste du pays par les montagnes rocheuses et est voisine des marches américains. Elle est riche en ressources naturelles (mines, bois), ses industries ont une haute productivité, et les salaires sont élevés. Les Prairies, constituées des provinces du Manitoba, Saskatchewan, et Alberta tirent leur richesse de la production du blé. En Alberta, cependant, il y a des puits d'huile. Cette région est dépendante totalement du marché international. Le Québec et l'Ontario forment la partie la plus populeuse et la plus riche du Canada. En plus de ressources naturelles abondantes, c'est le centre de l'industrie manufacturière canadienne. La région de l'Atlantique, composée de quatre provinces, est peu populeuse et possède le plus bas niveau économique du pays. Elle est peu industrialisée et les mines de charbon s'en vont déclinant.

Comme force sociale vraiment importance, le syndicalisme est assez récent. Il est vrai que nous avons eu des unités syndicales au Canada depuis plus d'un siècle. Mais parce que le syndicalisme est nécessairement lié au développement de l'industrialisation, qu'il la suit de pas à pas, on peut dire que c'est surtout depuis la second grande guerre mondiale qu'il a pris un essor considérable. Pensons seulement qu'en 1939, les effectifs syndicaux canadiens étaient même quelque peu inférieurs à ceux de l'année 1919 (1919: 378,000—1939: 359,000).

La Situation syndicale

Les Groupements syndicaux

Le mouvement syndical canadien est constitué d'unités locales qui, pour la plupart, sont rattachées à deux grandes centrales: le Congrès du travail du Canada (CTC) et la Confédération des syndicats nationaux (CSN). En effet, ces deux centrales, en 1965, groupaient ensemble 83.8 pour cent des effectifs syndicaux alors que 12.1 pour cent des travailleurs syndiqués appartenaient à d'autres unions non-affiliées et seulement 3 pour cent à des unités locales indépendantes.

Le Congrès du travail du Canada (CTC). Le Congrès du travail du Canada, issu, en 1956, de la fusion du Congrès des métiers et du travail du Canada et du Congrès canadien du travail, est de beaucoup le groupement le plus important. A lui seul, en 1966, il englobait près de 74 pour cent de tous les travailleurs syndiqués canadiens. Il est formé d'unités locales rattachées soit à des unions internationales ou à des unions nationales, mais ces dernières sont beaucoup moins nombreuses (18 unions nationales et 92 unions internationales). Toutes ces unions internationales, sauf trois, sont aux Etats-Unis affiliées à l'AFL-CIO. En 1965, les unions internationales englobaient 84 pour cent du total des effectifs du CTC et les unions nationales y compris les syndicats locaux à chartre directe, 16 pour cent.

Dans chacune des dix provinces du Canada, il existe une fédération affiliée au CTC qui s'occupe des intérêts des travailleurs à ce niveau. Cependant, l'affiliation aux fédérations provinciales pour les unités locales appartenant à des unions internationales, bien que fortement encouragée, reste facultative. Il en est de même aussi pour l'affiliation aux Conseils du travail que l'on rencontre dans chaque ville. Comme plusieurs unités locales se prévalent de ce privilège, ceci n'est pas sans causer des problèmes de représentation syndicale au niveau provincial. La plupart des grandes unions internationales, enfin, possèdent au Canada un ou plusieurs districts pour s'occuper des affaires canadiennes.

La Confédération des syndicats nationaux (**CSN**). La Confédération des syndicats nationaux, bien qu'elle soit considérée comme une centrale syndicale canadienne, recrute ses adhérents surtout dans la province de Québec et presque la totalité de ses membres sont d'expression française. Fondée en 1921, elle s'appelait jusqu'en 1960, la Confédération des travailleurs catholiques du Canada. Depuis bien longtemps avant cette date, elle avait perdu dans les faits son caractère confessionnel; mais il reste que l'on retrouve chez elle une homogénéité culturelle qui, s'ajoutant à une organisation structurelle plus centralisée, lui donne un pouvoir de représentation beaucoup plus considérable que ne lui permettrait le nombre de ses adhérents. Aussi, bien qu'officiellement la CSN se proclame une centrale nationale par opposition aux unions internationales et qu'elle soit ouverte à tous les travailleurs, lorsqu'elle se présente devant le gouvernement d'Ottawa pour y faire des représentations, elle peut prétendre être le porte-parole des travailleurs canadiens-français.

L'organisation de la CSN est beaucoup plus centralisée que celle du CTC: elle possède un fond de grève commun pour tous ses adhérents. Selon les données du Ministère du travail du Canada, elle est formée, au début de 1966, de 800 unités syndicales dont la plupart sont affiiliées à ses 16 fédérations. Ses effectifs se chiffraient alors à 188,000 membres, mais depuis ceux-ci se sont accrus considérablement. A son dernier congrès en septembre 1966, le secrétaire rapportait 204,000 membres.

Autres groupements. Quelques unions internationales indépendantes possèdent au Canada un certain nombre de membres, comme l'International Brotherhood of Teamsters, les United Electrical Workers, l'International Union of Mine, Mill and Smelter Workers, etc. Ensemble ces unions groupent plus de 100,000 membres. Dans le Québec, les professeurs de l'enseignement public sont groupés en une organisation particulière, la Corporation des enseignants du Québec, qui possède 50,000 membres. Enfin, on rencontre certaines unions affiliées à l'AFL-CIO aux Etats-Unis qui ne sont pas affiliées au CTC. Mais c'est quantité négligeable.

Les Effectifs syndicaux

En janvier 1966, les effectifs syndicaux canadiens s'élevaient à 1,736,000 membres. Et ceci constituait 30.7 pour cent des travailleurs salariés non-agricoles et 24.5 pour cent de tous les travailleurs salariés. Depuis dix ans, le pourcentage des travailleurs syndiqués par rapport aux travailleurs salariés non-agricoles a quelque peu diminué, car en 1956, il était de 33 pour cent (voir Tableau 1). C'est donc dire que dans l'ensemble l'un des objectifs poursuivis lors de la fusion des deux centrales, l'expansion du mouvement syndical n'a pas été atteint, car l'on n'a pas réussi à syndiquer les nouveaux venus sur le marché du travail.

Le Tableau 3 indique le mouvement de la main-d'oeuvre et le taux de syndicalisation dans différentes industries depuis dix ans.

Les secteurs où les accroissements dans l'emploi ont fait le plus de progrès sont les services, la finance et l'assurance, le commerce, et la fabrication. Si l'on considère le taux de syndicalisation dans chacun de ces secteurs, il est remarquable de constater que c'est dans les secteurs où la main-d'oeuvre décroit que des gains sont faits (mines, industrie forestière), alors que la pourcentage de

Tableau 1. *Variation dans les effectifs syndicaux en Canada 1956–66*

Année	Effectifs	Variation sur l'année précédente		Pourcentage des travailleurs non-agricoles en emploi rémunéré
		Nombre	Pourcentage	
1956	1,342,000	84,000	6.2	33.0
1957	1,376,000	34,000	2.5	31.9
1958	1,444,000	68,000	4.8	34.0
1959	1,449,000	5,000	0.3	33.1
1960	1,449,000	0	0.0	32.0
1961	1,437,000	−12,000	−0.8	31.1
1962	1,413,000	−24,000	−1.6	30.0
1963	1,439,000	26,000	1.8	29.7
1964	1,483,000	44,000	3.0	29.4
1965	1,589,000	96,000	6.4	29.7
1966	1,736,000	147,000	9.3	30.7

Source: Ministère du Travail, *Organisations de travailleurs au Canada*, Rapports annuels (Ottawa, 1956–66).

syndiqués diminue dans les autres où l'emploi global a connu une hausse sensible: construction, fabrication, services, avec une seule exception, les utilités publiques.

Quand on examine le taux de croissance des effectifs des deux centrales syndicales, on constate qu'il est à peu près le même à chaque année depuis dix ans et que chacune des deux centrales, sauf pour la CSN depuis les deux dernières années, maintient à peu près le même pourcentage de membres par rapport à l'ensemble des travailleurs syndiqués canadiens (voir Tableau 2).

Tableau 2. *Effectifs du CTC et de la CSN 1956–66*

Année	CTC			CSN		
	Effectifs	Changement sur l'année précédente	Pourcentage des travailleurs syndiqués canadiens	Effectifs	Changement sur l'année précédente	Pourcentage des travailleurs syndiqués canadiens
1956	1,030,000	—	76.8	101,000	—	7.5
1957	1,070,129	40,129	77.8	99,372	−1,628	7.2
1958	1,444,120	73,991	79.9	104,225	4,883	7.3
1959	1,153,756	9,636	77.9	97,092	−7,163	6.9
1960	1,122,831	−30,925[a]	77.5	101,942	4,850	7.0
1961	1,070,837	−51,994[a]	74.5	98,457	−3,485	6.8
1962	1,049,145	−21,692[a]	74.2	102,186	3,729	7.2
1963	1,079,909	30,764	75.0	110,577	8,391	7.6
1964	1,106,000	26,111	74.6	121,540	10,963	8.2
1965	1,181,000	75,000	74.3	150,040	28,500	9.4
1966	1,282,000	101,000	74.0	188,000	37,960	11.0

a. Cette diminution est attribuable à l'expulsion de certaines unions commes les Teamsters, les Marins, etc.
Source: Ministère du Travail, *Organisations de travailleurs au Canada*, Rapports annuels (Ottawa, 1956–66).

Syndicats canadiens et Syndicats américains

Le mouvement syndical canadien possède cette caractéristique tout à fait spéciale dans l'univers, à savoir que sept travailleurs syndiqués sur dix sont membres d'une union internationale dont la direction est en dehors du pays, et, en l'espèce, aux Etats-Unis. Quatre-vingt-douze unions internationales ont des membres au Canada. Idéalement, on ne peut pas dire que ce soit là une situation normale. Dans un pays libre, une institution aussi importante que le syndicalisme devrait être entièrement autonome: c'est ce que soutiennent ceux qui connaissent mal le genre de liens institutionnels qui rattachent les groupements canadiens aux unions américaines et qui ignorent le degré d'autonomie dont l'action syndicale canadienne jouit dans la pratique. Aussi, dans l'opinion publique, on voit rebondir de temps à autre des pressions pour que les syndicats canadiens soient uniquement canadiens. De plus, dans le Québec où existe une centrale concurrente purement canadienne, il arrive que la concurrence syndicale se fasse autour de cette question.

Les travailleurs canadiens, membres des unions internationales, ont dans leur ensemble toujours apporté la même réponse: ils sont restés fidèles aux unions internationales. Mais la question n'est pas pour cela résolue. Au niveau des centrales, le CTC est complètement autonome de l'AFL-CIO quoiqu'en certains cas ses possibilités d'action soient diminuées. En bien des circonstances, les deux groupements ont affiché des orientations et des politiques différentes, principalement en matière de politique nationale et internationale.

Les unités locales canadiennes affiliées à des unions internationales ont aussi, en général, au sein de leur constitution une autonomie assez grande dans la détermination de leurs politiques de négociation collective. Les grandes unions ont des districts canadiens qui s'occupent de l'élaborer. Malgré l'absence de règle constitutionnelle et malgré la faible proportion des effectifs canadiens dans la plupart des grandes unions, elles ont des représentants canadiens au sein du Conseil exécutif; et leur influence dépend de leur personnalité. Le choix des représentants se fait selon une grande diversité de méthode. Mais s'il n'est pas rare que ceux-ci soient choisis sur le plan régional ou local avec l'assentiment du Conseil exécutif, c'est plutôt celui-ci qui en a l'initiative. Aujourd'hui, la plupart sont des résidents canadiens. En ce qui concerne la fonction de recherche, en dehors des grandes unions qui peuvent se permettre la mise-sur-pied d'un département canadien, on a recours à ce qui se fait aux Etats-Unis. Lorsqu'il est question de déclaration de grève, comme le fonds de grève est administré par le Conseil exécutif des unions internationales, les unités canadiennes doivent se soumettre à son approbation.

En dehors des questions de sentiments et de prestige, l'existence des unions internationales au Canada pose des problèmes quasi-insolubles dans les cas de conflits de juridiction entre deux unions en territoire canadien. Parfois ces conflits ont lieu entre deux unions internationales, parfois aussi entre une union internationale et une union nationale canadienne. On sait que c'est un des rôles principaux de l'AFL-CIO, comme du CTC, de protéger la juridiction des unions et de régler les conflits juridictionnels, et que l'autorité des centrales est purement morale. En ces dernières années se sont présentés des cas qui ont mis en opposition le CTC à l'AFL, au sujet de problèmes purement canadiens.

On connaît bien l'affaire des marins. La Seafarers' International Union of North America, affiliée au CTC et à l'AFL-CIO a été l'objet d'une enquête gouvernementale et ses dirigeants ont été condamnés pour violence et racketeerisme. Elle a été expulsée du CTC et une union canadienne a été fondée par le CTC. L'AFL-CIO a refusé de collaborer avec le CTC pour cette opération de nettoyage et a soutenu les éléments indésirables de l'Union internationale. L'Union internationale des marins est encore sous tutelle gouvernementale au Canada.

Enfin, la présence et l'action au Canada de deux départments de l'AFL-CIO, le Building and Construction Trade Department et le Maritime Trade Department, n'est pas sans créer au CTC des problèmes qu'il faudra un jour résoudre. Comme l'explique John Crispo,

In practice both the BCTD and the MTD and their local councils in Canada have been used as bases of defiance for some of their affiliates when they were at loggerheads with the CLC. As a result, the existence of such bodies has further diminished the already reduced efficacy of suspending or expelling unions from the CLC for failing to abide by its policies. By way of illustration it is only necessary to point out that when the Teamsters' Union and the International Union of Operating Engineers were expelled from the Congress they remained in good standing with most local building and construction trades councils. Even more significant is the fact that these local building and construction trades councils sometimes ally themselves with their parent trade department in the AFL—CIO in a none too subtle attempt to force the CLC to adopt policies in keeping with the interest of the building and construction trades unions individually or collectively.[1]

L'Action syndicale

Les syndicats canadiens, comme les syndicats américains, ont fait de la négociation collective leur principal champ d'action. Au Canada, la négociation collective est fortement marquée par une grande décentralisation. C'est le régime de conventions collectives particulières à chaque établissement qui prévaut et la législation du travail qui existe présentement, avec l'accréditation pour chaque unité de négociation, encourage cette tendance. Parfois, on verra aussi des négociations groupant plusieurs établissements d'une même compagnie, mais elles sont généralement limitées à une ville ou à une région géographique. C'est ce genre de négociation que l'on retrouve dans quelques industries: chemins de fer, automobile, salaisons, pouvoirs électriques, téléphone, et radiodiffusion. Quant aux négociations intéressant plusieurs employeurs, elles sont limitées géographiquement à une localité ou à une région et se rencontrent dans des industries très compétitives comme l'imprimerie, le vêtement, la chaussure, le commerce de détail, le meuble, et le transport.

1. *Dominance or Independence? The Problem of Canadian Autonomy in Labour-Management Relations,* Sixteenth Annual Conference, Industrial Relations Centre, McGill University (Montréal, 1965), p. 84.

Bien que les négociations avec les associations patronales soient restreintes, le même résultat peut-être obtenu grâce au phénomène des réseaux d'imitation. Peu d'études ont été faites, mais il semble évident que ces réseaux existent dans l'industrie manufacturière, les mines, et l'industrie forestière. Ces réseaux sont cependant régionaux, à cause de la concentration régionale des industries. Les seules exceptions sont dans les salaisons et dans l'industrie de boîtes métalliques où l'on essaie d'imiter ce qui se fait aux Etats-Unis. Malgré l'autonomie locale dans la négociation collective, les politiques, les stratégies d'action sont grandement influencées par ce qui se fait aux Etats-Unis. En bien des cas, dans l'industrie manufacturière—acier, automobile, boîtes de conserve—les unités locales canadiennes des unions internationales adoptent avec peu de changements les programmes de négociation établis aux Etats-Unis. Cela ne provient pas d'une imposition de la part des dirigeants américains, mais simplement parce qu'il est normal qu'au Canada on recherche les mêmes avantages et les mêmes standards de conditions de travail. La similitude entre ces mêmes industries, quand ce n'est pas la même compagnie, encourage le développement de ce type de négociation. Et cela est vrai, non seulement chez les unités locales canadiennes affiliées aux unions internationales, mais encore chez les unions purement canadiennes.

Le poids de l'économie américaine sur celle du Canada, la proximité des deux pays, s'ajoutant aux désirs des travailleurs canadiens de bénéficier du même standard de vie que les travailleurs américains, ne peuvent empêcher cette tendance d'être de plus en plus grande. A la suite de l'accord canado-américain dans l'industrie de l'automobile, Walter Reuther a fermement averti les fabricants d'automobiles qu'ils auraient à uniformiser les salaires et les conditions de travail des deux côtés de la frontière.

Comme l'action syndicale dans le domaine de la négociation collective se fait par les unions elles-mêmes qui agissent indépendamment les unes des autres, que les diverses régions du Canada forment plus ou moins des marchés isolés, et, enfin, que le Gouvernement du Canada ne possède peu juridiction dans le domaine du travail, il est impossible, au Canada, de rencontrer une politique à travers tout le pays, en ce qui regarde les salaires et les conditions de travail. Il n'y a pas de doute que cette forte décentralisation devra être atténuée, mais comment y parvenir avec deux centrales syndicales en concurrence, avec la grande autonomie des unions au sein du CTC, et avec la constitution fédérative du Canada?

Les Centrales syndicales et la Politique

Les positions politiques des deux centrales syndicales sont sensiblement les mêmes sur les problèmes généraux du rôle de l'etat dans la vie économique, sur la sécurité sociale, et sur la politique internationale. Il reste cependant que face à une question aussi importante que celle de l'équilibre des pouvoirs entre le gouvernement du Canada et ceux des provinces, la CSN prend partie en faveur de l'autonomie provinciale alors que le CTC supporte des thèses visant à la consolidation et à la concentration des pouvoirs entre les mains du gouvernement fédéral. Cela se comprend quand on considère que la grande centrale canadienne recrute ses membres dans tout le pays alors que la CSN est une centrale surtout québécoise. D'ailleurs, il faut dire ici que la Fédération des travailleurs du Québec affiliée au CTC adopte les mêmes positions que la CSN avec qui elle a présenté un mémoire conjoint au gouvernement du Québec en avril 1966.[2] Mais elle ne peut les faire prévaloir au sein de sa centrale.

L'action politique elle-même est un sujet de divergence entre le CTC et la CSN. Avant la fusion des deux groupements qui ont donné naissance au CTC, le Congrès des Métiers et du travail du Canada (AFL) suivait la tradition américaine et se refusait à faire de l'action politique directe partisane, alors que le Congrès canadien du travail appuyait le parti CCF. Pour éviter des heurts, à la réunion de fusion en 1956, il ne fut pas question d'action politique. Mais au Congrès suivant, en 1958, le CTC a décidé d'encourager fortement ses groupements affiliés à appuyer le NPD. Parce qu'il comprend des unions qui doivent rester à

2. *Mémoire de la Confédération des syndicats nationaux, de la Fédération des travailleurs du Québec et de l'Union catholique des cultivateurs soumis au Comité de la Constitution de l'Assemblée législative du Québec*, texte français et anglais (Avril, 1966), 22 pp.

l'écart de toute action politique, le CTC lui-même se borne à coopérer dans diverses commissions du NPD et à faire de l'éducation politique sans affiliation formelle. Au 30 décembre 1965, 596 syndicats locaux représentant 20,057 membres étaient ainsi affiliés au NDP et la plupart venaient d'Ontario.[3]

Quant à la CSN, si elle laisse à ses corps affiliés la liberté de soutenir un parti politique, jusqu'ici elle s'est toujours refusée à s'engager dans l'action politique directe. La raison principale de cette attitude est que d'après des sondages effectués auprès de ses membres, ceux-ci ne veulent pas que leur centrale s'engage dans cette voie. Ce qui n'empêche pas la CSN d'apporter une attention très grande à l'éducation politique. Au cours de la dernière campagne électorale du Québec, la CSN et la FTQ n'ont pas donné de directives à leurs membres et même se sont dissociées de tous les partis politiques, y compris les candidats portant la banière de l'aile québécoise du NPD.

Dans l'ensemble, il faut dire que jusqu'ici l'action politique du CTC en faveur du NPD n'a pas donné de résultats extraordinaires, mais on espère qu'avec le temps elle portera des fruits plus tangibles.

Les Facteurs de Changements

Parmi les facteurs qui sont de nature à amener des changements dans le syndicalisme et l'action syndicale au Canada, on peut mentionner la nouvelle configuration de la main-d'oeuvre et l'émergence d'une conscience salariale, l'accélération des changements technologiques, l'inévitabilité de la planification, et la montée du nationalisme canadien-français.

Nouvelle Configuration de la Main-d'oeuvre et Émergence d'une Conscience salariale

Les industries qui ont connu un accroissement de main-d'oeuvre supérieur à la moyenne durant les dix dernières annés

3. *Le Travailleur Canadien*, Mai, 1966, p. 57.

Tableau 3. *Evolution de l'emploi et des effectifs syndicaux dans les industries canadiennes, 1956–65*

	Pourcentage des travailleurs syndiqués				Pourcentage des changements dans l'emploi
	Tous les travailleurs		Travailleurs dans l'industrie		
Industrie	1956	1965	1956	1965	1955–64
Industrie forestière	4.0	2.8	42.5	55.0	−28.1
Mines	4.0	3.6	51.0	65.4	−20.9
Industrie manufacturière	42.0	42.5	40.5	33.2	+23.5
Construction	10.0	10.7	46.0	38.0	+20.7
Transport et communication	21.0	18.6	64.0	65.8	+11.4
Services publics	2.0	2.6	41.0	53.7	+24.2
Services personnels	13.0	14.1	19.0	12.7	+64.6
Commerce	2.1	3.0	4.0	5.1	+26.3
Finance-assurance	—ᵃ	—	—	—	+48.3
Total	98.1	97.9	33.0	29.7	22.6

a. Moins de 1 pour cent.
Sources: Ministère du Travail, Division de l'économique et de la recherche, *Les conditions de vie et de travail au Canada;* Ministère du Travail du Canada, *Organisations de travailleurs au Canada,* Rapports annuels, 1956–65.

sont surtout celles qui donnent de l'emploi aux collets-blancs (voir Tableau 3). La syndicalisation parmi cette catégorie de travailleurs a été lente à démarrer. Cependant elle commence à faire des progrès. Au dernier congrès du CTC, le comité d'organisation mentionnait dans son rapport:

Pendant la période de 1964–65, environ 20,000 nouveaux employés de bureau se sont affiliés au Congrès, soit en obtenant une charte directe soit par l'intermédiaire de syndicats affiliés au CTC, ce qui représente une augmentation marquée sur les années précédentes. En 1963, par exemple, les syndicats affiliés au Congrès n'ont recruté que 3,915 nouveaux employés de bureau.

Il en est de même en ce qui regarde la CSN.

De plus, dans le Québec, depuis deux ans, on commence à faire l'expérience de syndicalisation chez les professionnels. Il y a même à la CSN une fédération d'ingénieurs. Ceux-ci sont organisés dans la ville de Montréal, à l'Hydro-Québec et chez les fonctionnaires de l'Etat québécois. Les 22 syndicats de professionnels à l'emploi du Québec groupent plus de 2,000 fonctionnaires. Le gouvernement vient de signer une convention collective avec le syndicat des médecins omnipracticiens. Au début, les associations de professionnels ont vu d'un mauvais oeil la syndicalisation de leurs membres salariés. Cela s'est manifesté surtout chez les ingénieurs. Mais en ce moment, elles n'y font plus d'objection. Une des difficultés communément rencontrée est la détermination de l'unité de négociation. Au cours de 1966, les ingénieurs de l'Hydro-Québec ont fait une grève de trois mois pour cette question.

Depuis longtemps les collets-blancs constataient qu'ils étaient dans une situation défavorisée vis-à-vis des ouvriers, mais ils conservaient un complexe anti-syndical: ils avaient peur d'appartenir à un syndicat. Avec la syndicalisation des professionnels—professeurs, ingénieurs, médecins, réalisateurs de télévision, etc.—le syndicalisme leur apparaît moins une forme dégradante d'action collective. Il est en train de se développer chez eux non une conscience de classe, mais une conscience salariale. Ils sentent qu'ils ont des intérêts communs qui ne sont pas ceux de l'entreprise pour laquelle ils travaillent. En ce moment, ils se syndiquent avec les centrales ouvrières existantes. Mais l'avenir nous dira si, comme les professeurs, ils ne se créeront pas leur propre centrale.

Jusqu'à récemment, les fonctionnaires avaient le droit de se grouper en association, mais la loi ne leur permettait pas de négocier collectivement avec le gouvernement. L'an dernier, le gouvernement du Québec a modifié sa loi de la fonction publique et accordé aux fonctionnaires le droit de s'affilier à une centrale syndicale ainsi que celui de négocier collectivement et même de faire la grève. Le gouvernement du Canada a présenté à la Chambre des communes un projet de loi dans le même sens.

Après huit mois de négociation, le gouvernement du Québec a signé ses deux premières conventions collectives, l'une avec les employés manuels et l'autre avec les fonctionnaires. En plus des clauses économiques, le gouvernement a accordé à chacun des syndicats une forme de sécurité syndicale que l'on appelle au Canada la Formule Rand, et qui consiste en ceci: le maintien d'affiliation et la retenue des cotisations syndicales pour les travailleurs déjà membres du syndicat et si d'ici six mois, le syndicat reussit a grouper 70 pour cent des travailleurs, le gouvernement effectuera la perception d'un montant equivalent a la cotisation syndicale chez tous les travailleurs compris dans l'unité de négociation. Le gouvernement a aussi négocié avec les fonctionnaires qui ont un statut professionnel: après une grève de plus de deux mois on est arrivé à signer une convention collective. La syndicalisation des fonctionnaires semble donc un fait acquis qui ira se généralisant et tous les organismes gouvernementaux seront soumis à la négociation collective avec le droit de grève.

Les Changements technologiques et les Syndicats

Depuis longtemps le problème des changements technologiques est une cause de conflits entre syndicats et direction d'entreprises. Avec l'évolution grandissante des techniques de production, le nombre de ces conflits ne peut que s'accroître et prendre une importance plus considérable tant pour la paix industrielle que pour le progrès de l'économie. Certaines normes de solutions semblent se dessiner à la suite d'évènements récents dans lesquels le gouvernement du Canada a été obligé d'intervenir. Nous voulons parler du Rapport Freedman et du règlement de la grève des débardeurs qui a paralysé les ports de Montréal, Québec, et Trois-Rivières durant trente-huit jours.

La Commission Freedman avait été instituée par le gouvernement fédéral pour régler un litige entre le CNR et ses employés itinérants à la suite de changements technologiques. Pour accélérer ses services et réduire ses coûts d'opération la compagnie a décidé de supprimer les terminus intermédiaires et de prolonger la distance que doivent parcourir les équipes. La décision du Juge Freedman dégage le principe général à l'effet que, nonobstant l'état actuel du droit et de la pratique en relations industrielles chez nous, l'employeur ne peut décider seul en une telle matière, laquelle devrait être l'objet de négociation entre les parties intéressées et donner ouverture aux mécanismes et aux recours prévus par les lois du travail pour la solution des conflits d'intérêts, en case de mésentente. Si la mésentente survient pendant la durée d'une convention collective, le Rapport Freedman suggère qu'une distinction soit faite entre les changements technologiques mineurs, ne touchant pas de façon substantielle le régime du travail, et les changements majeurs de nature à altérer considérablement le régime. Afin d'établir cette distinction, il suggère la procédure de l'arbitrage obligatoire. Si la décision est à l'effet qu'il s'agit d'un changement mineur, l'employeur pourrait y procéder immédiatement; si, au contraire, il est décidé que le changement en est un majeur, l'employeur ne pourrait le mettre à exécution durant le cours de la convention collective existante et le problème deviendrait matière à négociation lors des pourparlers en vue du renouvellement de cette dernière, comme toute autre matière faisant l'objet de ces pourparlers.[4]

La grève des débardeurs de Montréal, Québec, et Trois-Rivières s'est terminée par l'intervention personnelle du premier ministre du Canada. La fédération des arrimeurs se refusait à accorder l'augmentation de salaire réclamée par les syndicats sans avoir le droit de modifier graduellement ses installations et de réduire le nombre de travailleurs. Selon le règlement auquel on est arrivé, l'augmentation de salaire a été accordée et aucun changement sera fait avant l'expiration de la convention dans deux ans. D'ici là, une commission d'enquête réglera le cas des changements technologiques projetés.

Nous ne serions pas surpris si dans un avenir rapproché, le gouvernement du Canada et les gouvernements des provinces en viennent à fixer des normes touchant les conflits subséquents aux changements technologiques: obligeant les compagnies à donner un avis préalable et rendant la matière sujette à négociation et même à arbitrage, ainsi que le demandent les syndicats.

L'Inévitabilité de la Planification

Il n'y a pas de doute que le Canada est engagé dans un processus irréversible de développement qui entraîne une certaine plan-

4. The Freedman Report, "Technological Changes and Collective Bargaining," *Relations industrielles*, XXI (Avril, 1966), 274–300.

ification. Même si on ne s'entend pas sur les formes qui pourra prendre cette planification, tous sont d'accord pour la prévoir, les employeurs marchant à reculons, les syndicats ouvriers la préconisant. Le gouvernement du Canada et certains gouvernements provinciaux ont déjà établi des Conseils économiques qui font des recherches et se préparent à présenter des plans indicatifs.

En dehors de toute question de doctrine et de politique, la planification économique va rencontrer des difficultés très particulières en raison: (1) de la constitution qui divise les pouvoirs entre le gouvernement fédéral et les gouvernements provinciaux; (2) des caractéristiques de notre économie, de sa dépendance envers les pays étrangers et spécialement des Etats-Unis; (3) des besoins d'un pays qui avec sa géographie comprend plusieurs marchés du travail; et enfin (4) de la structure et de l'organisation des groupes productifs: les associations d'employeurs et les syndicats ouvriers.

Jusqu'ici le CTC, qui préconise la planification ne semble pas avoir porté une attention très grande aux obstacles internes qu'il aura à surmonter s'il veut une participation efficace du mouvement syndical à la planification. Car c'est non seulement tout le régime actuel des conventions collectives avec la prédominance des négociations au niveau de l'établissement qu'il faudra modifier, mais encore une restructuration de la centrale qu'il faudra faire pour lui donner une possibilité d'action sur le plan économique. On voit facilement dans quelles complications on s'engage, car il faudra l'assentiment d'une centaine d'unions internationales jalouses de leurs prérogatives sur lesquelles le CTC a bien peu d'influence. Il est à espérer que le Comité de structure formé au dernier congrès va envisager cette question.

La Montée du Nationalisme canadien-français

Les Canadiens de langue française forment près du tiers de la population globale du pays et 85 pour cent de la population du Québec. Le Canada est officiellement bilingue. Certains malaises qui existent depuis longtemps ont amené le gouvernement fédéral à créer la Commission royale d'enquête sur le bilinguisme et le biculturalisme. Le sentiment national qui a toujours existé chez les Canadiens français a pris, depuis 1960, une tournure particulière à la fois positive et négative.

D'une part, à la tête de la province de Québec de qui relèvent constitutionnellement l'éducation, les ressources naturelles, le travail, la santé et le bien-être, etc., un gouvernement dynamique, progressif a entrepris ce qui a été appelé une "révolution tranquille." Après une stagnation de plus de quinze ans, il a voulu être à la pointe du progrès dans tous les domaines: éducation, sécurité sociale, économie, et législation du travail. D'autre part, la proximité du centenaire de la Confédération que l'on veut célébrer en 1967 a fait renaître, et cette fois avec plus de force, un mouvement visant à séparer le Québec du reste du Canada. Aux dernières élections provinciales du 5 juin, deux partis politiques ont présenté des candidats avec cet objectif et ils ont obtenu 8.8 pour cent des votes. Les indépendentistes ne se recrutent pas surtout chez les travailleurs ni dans les milieux syndicaux. Cependant, l'ambiance créée par cette montée de volonté d'affirmation chez les Canadiens de langue française, bien que localisée au Québec, n'est pas sans avoir des répercussions sur le mouvement syndical tout entier.

En effet, la centrale québécoise formée de syndicats purement canadiens et presqu'exclusivement québécois a profité du climat de la "révolution tranquille." Elle a toujours été contre les unions internationales et même si officiellement elle se réclame uniquement d'un nationalisme canadien sans distinction culturelle, ses organisateurs locaux, à ce que soutiennent ses adversaires, ne se gênent point pour faire vibrer la corde nationaliste canadienne-française et pour mettre de l'avant qu'elle est la seule à pouvoir exprimer parfaitement les aspirations des travailleurs du Québec. Elle mène donc, avec assez de succès, une campagne de maraudage auprès des syndicats affiliés au CTC au point que celui-ci, à son dernier congrès d'avril a été obligé de songer à prendre des mesures pour se protéger et contre-attaquer.

La non-flexibilité de la constitution du CTC qui maintient la juridiction exclusive des unions et rend difficile les changements d'adhésion des travailleurs pour joindre une union plus dynamique, a grandement facilité le maraudage de la CSN et a fait passer dans ses rangs beaucoup d'unités de négociation. Le congrès du CTC de 1966 a établi une commission d'enquête sur la structure qui doit faire des recommandations au prochain congrès de 1968. Il n'y a pas de doute qu'en raison du peu de pouvoirs que possède le CTC sur ses affiliés, la Commission va rencontrer beaucoup de difficultés et que ses recommandations dépendront pour une bonne part de la coopération que voudront fournir les dirigeants américains des unions internationales.

L'action organisatrice de la CSN l'a conduite à recruter efficacement des membres représentés jusqu'ici par des groupements affiliés au CTC et faisant partie d'unités de négociation couvrant tout le pays, comme à Radio-Canada et dans le chemin de fer. La CSN est en instance de demande de certification devant le Conseil canadien des relations ouvrières. Les deux centrales s'affrontent ainsi dans une lutte qui pour chacune d'elle a raison de principe. Alors que la CSN se retranche derrière le respect de la volonté des travailleurs et la liberté d'association, le CTC met l'accent sur des raisons d'ordre économique et syndical pour le bien des travailleurs. Jusqu'ici le CCRO a donné raison au CTC et n'a pas voulu briser les unités traditionnelles de négociation, mais le Cabinet fédéral a été saisi de la question et le Gouvernement canadien devra établir une politique qui sera sûrement lourde de conséquences dans le domaine de l'organisation syndicale. Il est à prévoir qu'à la fin ce ne seront pas des raisons proprement économiques et syndicales qui l'emporteront, mais plutôt des raisons de politique générale de manière à ne pas accentuer une frustration parmi les Canadiens français. Le problème ne se serait pas posé de cette façon au sein du CTC, les unions avaient davantage tenu compte de cette réalité canadienne-française. En ce moment, une tentative de regroupement dans le Syndicat canadien de la fonction publique (CTC) de tous les travailleurs affiliés à différentes unités appartenant à des unions internationales essaie de parer à la situation. Mais c'est une entreprise qui vient trop tard et qui, de toute manière ne pourra pas régler la question dans le cas des employés de chemins de fer.

L'existence de deux groupes ethniques au Canada, qui jusqu'ici avait causé des problèmes syndicaux surtout au niveau provincial, est en train d'obliger le CTC lui-même à s'ajuster dans toute sa structure au niveau du Canada tout entier.

Conclusion

Malgré son morcellement et ses divisions, le mouvement syndical canadien est une force sociale avec laquelle il faut compter. Il est un élément indispensable au maintien et au développement de la démocratie au Canada. Même si les dirigeants syndicaux se plaignent—et parfois avec raison—de n'être pas suffisamment écoutés, le mouvement syndical possède des voies d'accès multiples aux pouvoirs économique et politique. Son efficacité a été incontestable pour l'amélioration des conditions économico-professionnelles des travailleurs. Au plan politique, aucune décision importante n'est prise sans que les syndicats n'aient fait faloir aux yeux des gouvernements et de l'opinion publique leur point de vue. Et l'on peut affirmer que, grâce à leur dynamisme et à leur vigilance, ils ont été à l'origine ou ont joué un rôle déterminant dans toutes les grandes politiques sociales que les gouvernements ont mises en oeuvre.

Le mouvement syndical canadien est en pleine ébullition et il a encore à chercher sa voie. Les pourparlers entrepris, il y a dix ans, pour effectuer l'unité entre les deux grandes centrales ont graduellement abouti à un échec et il est de moins en moins prévisible qu'ils soient repris dans un futur prochain. Loin de là, un fossé s'agrandit, puisque la CSN, en ces derniers temps s'est laissée aller à des pratiques de maraudage qui se sont faites surtout aux dépens d'une union nationale, la CBRT, qui autrefois était le groupement médiateur dans cette entreprise. Tous les facteurs sont de nature à amener des changements convergent vers une révision des structures syndicales, surtout au sein du CTC.

6

Canadian Parties and Politics

John Meisel

A consideration of parties and politics must be a part of any attempt to survey and analyze Canada as it enters its second century. Such a consideration must be concerned in general with the political system and more specifically with Canadian political parties in relation to four aspects of Canadian society: (1) geography and physical resources, (2) human resources, (3) value systems, and (4) social and political institutions.

Current problems of Canadian parties arise in part not only from changes within each of these four factors but also from tensions which have emerged as the result of the need for new relations *among* them. No attempt is made here to present a systematic and complete statement about the place of parties in the Canadian polity and society. Rather what follows is primarily a series of almost (but not quite) discrete commentaries on some of the more noteworthy aspects of the country's politics and parties. Frequently these commentaries are of a speculative kind, suggesting areas where students of Canada might with profit seek new knowledge and insight.

The Milieu and the Parties

Geography and Physical Resources

The dominant features of Canada's geography are the immense size and variety of the country and its North American site.

Canadians have had to accommodate themselves to a country of continental proportions exhibiting an almost inexhaustible variety of resources and typographical features. At the same time they have had to find a satisfactory relationship with their colossal, powerful, and dynamic neighbor. The consequences of both of these aspects of the country's geographical base have been subjected to repeated scrutiny by successive generations of scholars and need not be surveyed in detail here. The student of politics and parties, looking at current problems against the geographical background, will nevertheless find rewarding the re-examination of at least four suggestive points.

1. The country's history, values, and political institutions have injected a fairly strong and consistent demand for a centralist approach to its problems in a setting whose heterogeneity has unfailingly generated implacably centrifugal forces. The lush profusion of regional and subregional differences has called on the one hand for a strong force at the center which would impose some coherence on the infinitely varied interests and pressures, while on the other hand making it extremely difficult for such a central force to function effectively. The need for unity and coordination has therefore often been frustrated by the basic diversity of the country and the resulting variety in its institutions.

Political parties have responded to these conditions by being loosely organized national federations, each trying to reconcile a multiplicity of oddly assorted interests. The centripetal influence of the parliamentary system has failed to make the parties highly centralized national instruments embodying coherent and consistent political values. Even so, the major parties have with increasing frequency and intensity been challenged by smaller parties expressing regional or other factional interests.

The effective functioning of the parliamentary system (heretofore assumed to have been predicated on one party's having a majority of seats) has been impaired by the consequences of the tension between Canada's centripetal and centrifugal forces. On the one hand the so-called national parties have ceased being genuinely national and have failed in attaining stable parliamentary majorities. On the other hand regional voices have recently found it more expedient to press their claims through provincial parties or through provincial wings of national parties. Their requirements have increasingly been met through action resulting from dominion-provincial negotiations. Here they have tried to attain their ends through the intercession of the provincial governments. National parties have therefore declined as the spokesmen for certain interests in the country, and their place has to some extent been assumed by other political institutions, a point to which later discussion will be devoted.

2. Canada is not only a very large country, it is also immensely rich in natural resorces. Its economic history could, until recently, be told almost entirely in terms of the exploitation of certain minerals and certain staples which have dominated the economy and which have made it dependent in part on foreign markets and world prices and in part on the massive investment of capital required by such extractive enterprises as mining and the production of pulp and paper. The exploitation of natural resources invariably depends heavily on the good will of governments who have it in their power to issue the necessary permits, create favorable conditions, and protect the investors over long periods of time. This dependence on governments has made for a continued close relationship in Canada between large-scale exploiters and developers of natural resources (more often than not, of course, from across the country's borders) and of political parties.

A good deal is known about the relations between parties, governments, and railway builders in Canada, but even after Beauharnois we still have insufficient evidence about the equally important relationship between parties and some of the interests mentioned above. The close ties between parties, governments, and developers of natural resources have no doubt led to the adoption of particular federal and provincial policies in Canada; they have also created a certain political ethos with respect to party finance. More important, they have influenced the values applied by Canadians in judging their governments and in deciding which are the proper spheres for private and public activities. Nowadays both the federal and provincial governments are concerned with the exploitation of natural resources, and the difficult decisions to be made (with respect to the use of water, parklands, etc.) become the subject of negotiations not only between individuals and governments but also between two levels of government and/or between two or more governments at the same level. The position of parties becomes more ambiguous than heretofore under these conditions and to some extent provincial and federal wings of the same parties may take different positions on an issue and may be the subjects of different kinds of pressure. Some relatively minor conflicts of this sort have occurred recently; it is to be expected that as the supply of various resources becomes increasingly scarce and as the power of provincial governments continues to increase, these conflicts will become more pronounced. It is likely that interests seeking concessions in the field of resource development will turn more and more directly to provincial officials and governments for help than to national parties. As a consequence, vital decisions in this field will increasingly be made through dominion-provincial negotiations rather than at the level of any one government. Under these conditions parochial claims may outweigh the broader national interest.

3. Canada's geographical setting has produced still another kind of tension. The conditions under which earlier generations of Canadians had to establish themselves and to earn a living led to the development of a rugged individualism often associated with pioneer life. The values of a high proportion of Canadians were essentially toughness, endurance, and self-reliance, and they undoubtedly contributed an important element to the ethos of Canadian society. On the other hand, many of the things which had to be done in Canada could only be attempted by co-operative effort and some of them only with the vigorous assistance of the state. Governmental initiative and participation in such enterprises as railways, airways, power development, and broadcasting have become commonplace. Public attitudes to the proper sphere of activity for the state have therefore become ambiguous.

The proximity of the United States and the thoroughness with which its values permeate Canadian society, at least outside Quebec, have enhanced the already strong appeal of those singing the praises of private enterprise. On the other hand, the nearby example of United States growth and prosperity (not to mention actions of the United States government) has put Canadian governments under pressure to initiate policies designed to raise the Canadian standard of living to the level attained in the United States.

There have thus been in evidence strong and persistent demands for both state action and for the entrenchment of private enterprise. Canadian parties have responded to these demands in a pragmatic way: on the whole, the Liberals—particularly after they felt themselves threatened by the Co-operative Commonwealth Federation (CCF) and later the New Democratic Party (NDP)—have been more "statist" than the Conservatives. They have advocated more loudly and assiduously measures extending the power and role of government, but the Conservatives have probably initiated as many programs of government control and/or ownership as their allegedly less conservative rivals. It is probably not unfair to sum up the matter by saying that the Liberals have found themselves more inclined to expand the activities of the state than the Conservatives, but that the latter have, when they were in power, found themselves unable and probably unwilling to resist resorting to state intervention for the sake of promoting a Canadian national policy. The presence, since the thirties, of a small but capably led CCF/NDP has, of course, been an important factor in drawing attention to welfare needs and in bringing about the extension of governmental activities.

4. The influence of the United States on Canadian attitudes toward the role of the state is an enormously important consequence of Canada's being a North American country. For while it has *geographically* been placed unmistakably in North America, emotionally and culturally it has been reluctant to accept all the implications of being in this geographic milieu. The most critical question Canadians must answer as they enter their second century is that of self-definition: what sort of country is Canada? Is it a partnership of two societies, a pluralist state, a British-dominated (in the cultural sense) country? Is it part of a West European community in which the British Isles and France play a

vital role, or is it essentially a North American state now making its own way, inevitably in close contact with its mammoth southern neighbor? The reasons for Canada's curious neglect of the nature of its own identity and the problems its definition entails need not be examined here. One aspect of this question cannot, however, be ignored completely when discussing Canadian parties. For the job of identifying the country's nature, which is invariably undertaken in part at least with reference to what happens outside Canada, has affected party competition. The Conservatives have been more alert than the Liberals to the dangers implicit in the proximity of the United States and have, on the whole, been much more wary of forging too strong a set of ties with the United States. One of the appeals of the party at the present time is its greater reluctance than the Liberals' to bring the country closer into the American orbit. The CCF/NDP has been particularly sensitive to the consequences of Canada's heavy importation of United States capital.

The nature of Canada, and particularly the degree to which it tries to remain distinguishable from, and independent of, the United States, has become an important issue separating Canadian parties and will continue to constitute a point of distinction between them. It is tempting to assume that the difference is one largely of party and election rhetoric, reflecting a desire among politicians to engage in a superficial product differentiation, but this temptation must be resisted. While there is inadequate evidence of the degree to which the general public is concerned with the issue, there is no doubt that the politicians and intellectuals consider it a real and central problem of Canadian life. The controversies aroused by the recent books of George Grant and Walter Gordon[1] bear eloquent witness to the liveliness and heat of this issue.

Human Resources

Unlike the United States, Canada has never officially accepted the melting pot concept with respect to the various ethnic groups

1. George Grant, *Lament for a Nation* (Princeton, 1965); Walter L. Gordon, *A Choice for Canada* (Toronto, 1966).

composing the population. The country's chief demographic distinction is without question the presence of two major ethnic groups: those whose mother tongue is English and the French population concentrated to a great extent in the province of Quebec. There are other important ethnic minorities, but it is the relations between the English- and French-speaking populations which have recently absorbed much of the attention not only of Canadian scholars but also of politicians. If there is any question about the survival of Canada as a viable state, it is because of the growing complexity of the relations between the two largest ethnic groups in the country.

Each of them has developed a political style of its own, or to put it more accurately, there are several political styles in Canada, of which one is associated with Quebec. This has had significant consequences on the way in which political parties have been able to fashion national coalitions encompassing the country's most significant interests. All the national parties, for example, have experienced some sort of split in Quebec. Politicians no less than others are beginning to realize that the linguistic aspect of French-English relations is only one element in a vastly complex and stubborn thicket of parallel, conflicting, and overlapping interests.

Political parties, insofar as they have been able to cope with this situation, have relied on decentralized structures providing for considerable provincial autonomy, on the avoidance of strong doctrinaire positions, and on an emphasis on personalities rather than ideas as the chief focuses of party unity. Wherever possible, they have tried to find national leaders capable of collaborating closely with an associate of the other ethnic group so as to duplicate what in the United States would be thought of as an ethnically balanced ticket. In the modern era only the Liberals have succeeded in fashioning at least a semblance of close ethnic collaboration at the highest party levels and even they have largely failed: for a long time the leading Quebec Liberals represented the old Quebec elites rather than the new forces which have sparked the Quiet Revolution. The federal Liberal party for far too long failed to perceive that the changes in Quebec have brought influence to new men and new elites who were, in the main, strongly critical of the attitudes and actions of their elders and predecessors. This older generation enjoyed until quite recently, and may still do so today, a special position of influence in the highest councils of the party. Its members were mistakenly assumed to reflect the dominant views of Quebec. Despite the foregoing, it is still one of the facts most vital to the understanding of Canadian politics that up to the present the Liberals have been infinitely more adept than the other parties at accommodating themselves successfully to the bi-ethnic nature of the country and to the differences in the political cultures of Quebecers and other Canadians.

Emphasis on Anglo-French differences or, more precisely, on differences between French-speaking Canadians and the others, should not be interpreted as a belief that that part of the country which is not French is homogeneous. There are important differences in the political styles of the various regions to which parties must adjust, but none has recently been as pronounced nor as difficult to contain as the difference between French Canada and the rest.

Value Systems

Ethnic diversity has made for contrasts in the attitudes of Canadians to the game of politics and has been responsible for some important groups expecting from politics quite different satisfactions and benefits than other groups. It is nevertheless possible to make some broad generalizations about the system of values which, on the whole, seems to underlie Canadian political attitudes and which is an important determinant of the manner in which parties perform their functions within the political system. Like all such broad generalizations, they will often be vague and altogether too sweeping, but they will serve to focus attention on some of the more significant aspects of the values underlying Canadian politics. Furthermore, they will identify a few of the areas in which detailed studies are required to substantiate or disprove the hypotheses which appear to explain some features of present-day politics and parties in Canada.

Canada is a liberal democracy, and to the extent that its citizens have political values, they can be assumed to be those usually associated with this form of political organization. As members of a pluralist society, dedicated on the whole to what C. B. Macpherson has aptly called "possessive individualism," they subscribe to a political order permitting a reasonably free competition of both ideas and interest groups. In this respect Canada differs little from Britain, the United States, or any other of the Western-type industrialized states whose political institutions assumed their present form sometime in the nineteenth century.

It is well known that the policy of laissez faire, favored by the early proponents of liberalism, has never actually existed in pure form anywhere and that the predominant philosophy in all countries which have espoused nineteenth-century liberal values has gradually accepted an increasing degree of state activity and interference. It has already been noted that the physical setting of Canada gave the country a special reason for intrusting the state with a variety of tasks and that the impetus for rugged individualism therefore became blunted by persistent demands for governmental assistance of one kind or another.

Since it is almost a universal North American reflex to denounce state action on behalf of everyone else but to seek it for one's own benefit, it would be a rewarding study to examine in some detail the patterns in which the "rugged individualism–statism" conflict occurs in various sections of the population. This research has, alas, never been attempted in Canada. The conclusion is probably valid, however, that the ambivalence in Canadian values has created an almost ideal environment for the flourishing of non-doctrinaire political parties susceptible to business and other influence. When conditions have required it, they have facilitated an easy pragmatic interaction between the private and public sectors of the economy.

On the whole, Canadian parties have been more hospitable than their American counterparts to schemes involving the state in various aspects of community life. The reasons therefor are numerous and complex. The very presence of the powerful American neighbor has to some extent encouraged the expansion of governmental activities in Canada, but a number of purely domestic factors have also been important. One of the most important has been the presence and influence of the so-called third parties, and notably of the CCF/NDP. While the explanation (based on the Hartzian model) of the better fortune of socialism in Canada than in the United States in terms of the greater strength of Toryism, offered by Gad Horowitz,[2] is highly suggestive, it is not sufficient to account for the continued survival and influence of a left-wing, reform-oriented party. The effects of a parliamentary system, the nature of the electoral law, and the particular form of Canada's federal system all have contributed to the survival of the CCF/NDP.[3] Nor should the complex sociological factors which have conspired to bring to the left-wing parties the kind of leaders who have enabled them to survive and to exercise much influence on Canadian life be overlooked. The relentless pressure of these men for social reform and for the participation by government in the economic life of the community and the very presence of an alternative, more welfare-statist party have combined to weaken the appeals of a highly individualistic philosophy without, however, by any means destroying it entirely.

Any reference to the values of a society or to a political philosophy is in danger of being misinterpreted. It is not suggested that Canadians are a deeply philosophical people who have articulated for themselves a logically consistent rationale for what they do in their capacity as citizens. All that is being implied here is that certain "inarticulate major premises" do underlie a society's public acts and that these premises form a reasonably consistent pattern which can be detected. The legitimacy of any political

2. See his "Conservatism, Liberalism, and Socialism in Canada: An Interpretation," *Canadian Journal of Economics and Political Science*, XXXII (May, 1966), 143–171, and "Tories, Socialists and the Demise of Canada," *Canadian Dimension*, II (May–June, 1965), 12–15.
3. See S. M. Lipset's interesting review articles on C. B. Macpherson's *Democracy in Alberta* in *Canadian Forum*, XXXIV (Dec., 1954), 175–177, 196–198.

system presupposes that the politically effective citizens accept the dominant premises, or their consequences, whether they are aware of them or not.

Some similarities and some differences between Canadian and United States attitudes to politics have been noted, as has the fact that Canadian parties have had to operate in a setting which is broadly similar to that of their neighbor but that the values their "clients" bring to politics have been somewhat different. Similar distinctions and similarities exist in relation to other aspects of the value system underlying party life, and they too must be noted.

Like the United States, Canada has become an opulent society. This does not, of course, mean that there are not serious problems of poverty and deprivation, but simply that the ethos and habits of behavior of the tone-setting middle classes have come to reflect the general affluence of North American middle-class life. One of the consequences of this development has been the relatively increased preoccupation of many citizens with private possessions and pursuits and the consequent decline of interest in public issues. Politics has come to absorb less attention by the public simply because there are now so many other activities and events with which it competes. Reliable comparative data about Canada and the United States are lacking, but it is reasonable to assume that the latter's central role in world politics has to some extent offset the "depoliticizing" consequences of opulence in the United States. No comparable anxiety over, or commitment to, Canada's role in world affairs has induced Canadians to consider politics a vital concern. A larger proportion of Canadians than Americans vote in elections, particularly at the national level, but it is doubtful whether mere voter turnout is a satisfactory measure of concern over politics. There are many indications (such as, for example, the generosity with which politicians are rewarded in the two countries) suggesting that Canadians take politics less seriously than Americans.

The most significant feature of Canada's value system, and the one with the most far-reaching consequences for the political process and the operation of the party system, concerns the almost total absence of a national fervor. Canada must, in many respects, be the least nationalistic country in the world. The French-speaking population has a highly developed sense of national cohesion when "national" refers to its own cultural group, but the country as a whole is almost totally lacking in a genuinely shared set of symbols, heroes, historical incidents, enemies, or even ambitions. Canada, in short, lacks a fully developed secular political culture, and the many divisions which are inevitable in a country of its extent and variety cannot be mediated within the context of a shared and similar complex of national values and emotions. It is not only that the French-speaking population has a nationalism of its own which is not shared by the other citizens; the rest of the country does not have a pronounced identity which acts as a cohesive force when regional and other differences have to be resolved. The dearth of a potent, genuinely national ideology and of many national institutions fostering a sense of Canadian identity has made the job of the national parties particularly difficult.

Social and Political Institutions

Political parties operate in Canada in a framework set by an opulent society which has given certain groups easier access to positions of privilege and power than other groups. This is, of course, by no means a unique phenomenon, since genuine equality is probably an ideal incapable of full realization. Canada exhibits the ubiquitous inequalities associated with such related criteria as income, occupation, and class, but in addition it has developed in a way which has enhanced the opportunities of certain ethnic groups, presumably at the expense of others. Canadians of Anglo-Saxon origin have established for themselves positions of prestige and power in proportions far greater than their numerical strength would justify if there were anything like ethnic equality of access in Canadian society.[4] This is not the place to explore the reasons for this nor to examine the consequences. It is obvious, however, that Canadian political parties have operated in a world in which the attitudes, values, and practices of the

4. See John Porter, *The Vertical Mosaic* (Toronto, 1965).

Anglo-Saxon groups have been dominant. It is not known whether Canadian parties have played a significant part in providing means of upward mobility for members of some of the less favored ethnic groups, as has been the case in the United States, but they have recently unmistakably become more hospitable to personalities coming from what are quaintly called in Canada, the "other" groups. It should be noted here that by and large the French-speaking population has traditionally been represented adequately, *in the numerical sense,* in the political process. The position accorded French Canadians at this level was, in fact, often used to conceal, or make palatable, their exclusion from some of the other command posts of Canadian society.

The egalitarianism which has distinguished so much of the North American industrial society and which has manifested itself particularly in social relations among individuals is evident in Canada but to a lesser extent than in the United States. Canadian society appears to be somewhat more deferential, but it cannot escape the influence of its American neighbor. This affects political parties not only in the general manner in which they operate and organize themselves, but more importantly perhaps, in the way in which they recruit their activists and particularly their candidates. Traditionally, only the CCF/NDP has recruited significant numbers of standard-bearers whose occupational background was *not* in business or the professions, and even this—Canada's most working-class party—has followed the practice of electing an unusually large percentage of lawyers to the legislature. The only exception to this consists of the adequate representation of farmers in those provinces where agriculture constitutes the basic industry, but even here it is the so-called third parties which have shown themselves more hospitable to the non-professional candidates.

An interesting development has occurred in this context during the recent era in Canadian politics: both Diefenbaker and Pearson have had considerable influence in attracting to their respective parties candidates new to the federal scene. They have, therefore, altered the physiognomy of their parties quite aside from whatever they may have done *directly* as party leaders. Their influence as a magnet for certain types of candidates has been reflected in the greater representation, among Liberals, of the urban and urbane, establishment-minded, eastern-type politicians, and the greater Conservative receptivity to a more rural outlook and personnel. It is a good question whether the location of the electoral strength of the two parties has been a cause or an effect of differences in candidates and Members of Parliament. It is probably both, but the influence of the leaders must be considered a prime cause of this particular difference between the parties. The important point that the *federal* party in a province may appeal to quite different a group of activists and even supporters than the *provincial* organization of the same party, however, must not be overlooked.

Canada's history, the traditionalism of its people, and the influence of the country's Anglo-Saxon elite have been among the chief reasons for the entrenchment of the parliamentary system and of its cornerstone, cabinet government. Although this system may have been more rigid than was desirable in a country like Canada, there are few who will assert that Canada has been served badly by its system of government. It would be idle to speculate about what Canada might have been like under another type of political system. It should, however, be noted how Canadians have adapted the system they have inherited to suit better the particular conditions under which it has had to operate.

Virtually all the important changes were introduced to make for greater flexibility so that regional and other diversity could find expression in governmental decisions. The main mechanisms are the federal structure of the country and the modifications brought about by the party system, which differs from the British model in many important particulars. Canadian federalism need not be of concern here. With respect to the party system the adaptation falls into two distinct categories: (1) a series of conventions concerning such things as strong localism in the selection of candidates, rigid regional and religious representation in the cabinet, and the selection of national leaders by American-type conventions; and (2) the presence of third, fourth, and fifth parties. These modifications have enabled the British parliamentary institutions to function effectively in the North American setting during most of Canada's first hundred years.[5] Successful governments, that is governments capable of winning and sustaining majorities in the House of Commons, have normally been able to do so by fashioning regional alliances assuring a sufficient number of seats. Usually, the common and dominant economic interests of the central provinces have provided the cornerstone for these majorities. These common interests (and W. L. M. King's adroitness) have even permitted the Liberals to survive the near-disastrous conscription crisis of the early 1940's. Since the end of World War II, however, and particularly in the most recent decade, it has proven increasingly difficult to create any kind of viable national alliance incorporating major interests in all regions. The national party system has as a consequence failed to operate in the usual British parliamentary manner relying on stable majorities. Instead, minority governments have become commonplace, and furthermore, two, three, or even four provincial governments have been in the hands of parties other than the Liberals or Conservatives. And not only are federal parties in a state of flux and uncertainty. Every provincial election held in 1966, except that in Newfoundland, resulted in an upset and in Quebec and Prince Edward Island threatened the satisfactory operation of the provincial legislature affected by it. Both Quebec and Prince Edward Island produced startling defeats of governments and so close a balance of forces in the chamber as seriously to threaten the life expectancy of the newly elected government. The Canadian public seems to be reacting in a most unexpected fashion when going to the polls, and the parties are increasingly the target of editorial opprobrium and public scorn. Canadian politics and parties are in a state of malaise. Why?

5. For an excellent related discussion see Leon D. Epstein, "A Comparative Study of Canadian Parties," *American Political Science Review*, LVIII (March, 1964), 46–59, and Leslie Lipson, "Party Systems in the United Kingdom and the Older Commonwealth: Causes, Resemblances, and Variations," *Political Studies*, VII (Feb., 1959), 12–31.

The Parties Themselves

Problems of Political Parties

There is a tendency in Canada at the present time to blame the universally recognized shortcomings of the operation of the political system on the parties and politicians, although in some quarters the Royal Commission on Bilingualism and Biculturalism is held to be the source of all evil. It must be admitted that the performance of the politicians, particularly at the federal level, has left something to be desired and has given rise to exasperation with the parties and to some extent with Parliament. But it is obviously too simple to explain the causes of the present discontent solely in terms of the inadequacy of political parties and/or of their leading personalities.

The underlying reason is the greatly intensified problem of maintaining an effective political system under the new and ever-changing circumstances, without making some fairly substantial changes in the nature and *modus operandi* of the political institutions.

Without wishing to open a discussion of the difficulties raised by equilibrium analysis in political studies, it can be said that developments in the four areas discussed in the first part of this essay have created a state of acute imbalance in the country. The needs arising from the geographical setting clash with the demands posed by the human resources and most notably those arising from the diverse value systems adhered to by different sections of Canadian society. The tensions resulting from this disequilibrium have made extremely taxing demands on the politicians at a time when they are evidently not well equipped to satisfy them. Canada is, in short, witnessing the convergence of two factors at the close of its first century: an awkward and difficult set of problems needs to be resolved at the very moment when the political institutions and those who man them are in a particularly ineffective condition.

In the remainder of this paper, therefore, the reasons for the current weakness of political parties will be discussed. This can best be done by adopting two distinct perspectives: first, to examine some secular causes of the present inadequacy of Canadian federal parties and politicians and then to turn to some more short-run considerations.

Long-run Factors

1. The low level of professionalism in Canadian politics is one of the reasons for the lack of esteem in which its practitioners are held in Canada. Unlike the United Kingdom, Canada has never had any kind of leisure class which considered a career of public service, possibly within a political party, as a legitimate and appropriate occupation for its gifted members. Politics has therefore generally been a vocation pursued by individuals who had earlier had to accumulate both experience and resources in some other career. The interests, habits of thought, and skill of most Canadian politicians were, therefore, developed in fields which did not necessarily provide a useful training for politics. In the United States, which also lacks a traditional political elite, less hypocrisy has been displayed than in Canada: a large variety of means for making a livelihood and training has been provided for would-be Solons at the municipal, state, and federal levels of government. Many seeking a political career have therefore been able to live off politics while, so to speak, serving a political apprenticeship. Canadians have both rejected overt party participation at the municipal level and excluded a large proportion of jobs from politics. There has therefore been a pronounced tendency for active politicians to be recruited from other professions such as law or business, where their habits of thought developed and set according to the logic of some activity other than the political.

This tendency has become even more pronounced in the recent era when the role of government has expanded drastically and when the skill required of governmental leaders has had to be applied to the enormously complex and technical problems faced by the modern state. Canadian cabinets have been consistently "enriched" by members brought in because of their prestige or skill acquired in business, the legal profession, or even the public service. This "depoliticization" of party leadership, particularly among the Liberals, has removed from the most vital area of political decision-making the necessary political skill required for a creative functioning of the political system.

2. One of the consequences (and later another of the causes) of the "depoliticization" of Canadian politics has been the influence assumed by public relations and advertising firms in the conduct of electoral campaigns and to some extent in influencing the general strategy of political parties. Again the Liberals have been more subject to this kind of influence than the other parties but none has entirely escaped it. Here, as in so many other spheres, Canadians have adopted some United States practices without having available the same kinds of safeguards as exist south of the Canadian border. The Liberals were much impressed with the Kennedy style in campaigning, and they adapted some of the Kennedy tactics, but they had neither a Kennedy nor a Kennedy team to keep the image-makers and admen in line. The partial adoption of American techniques suffered the fate of many practices undergoing cross-cultural diffusion: they misfired and weakened what might otherwise have been adequate Canadian methods of dealing with a Canadian set of problems.

3. Attempts by parties to attract popular candidates from non-political circles, the influence of publicity counselors, and the North American practice of seeking bland candidates appealing to the mass of "average" voters have brought into politics many recruits possessed of a very low level of political partisanship. There is much to be said for the view that a successful politician must have a strong and abiding attachment to party and that no matter how appealing fair-mindedness and non-partisanship may be to the dispassionate observer of politics, the participant is often much more effective in the long run if he is motivated by a zealous (and sometimes even unreasoning) attachment to his cause and party.

4. As in the United States, the personal influence and prestige of the represented member has suffered in Canada as the result of

the diminution of patronage spending and the growth of bureaucratic methods of helping needy individuals.

5. Reference has already been made to the links between parties and their contributors—mostly business enterprises—who,
despite protestations to the contrary, do not finance party activities out of a purely disinterested spirit of public duty. Even when
no direct influence may result from such contributions (and a
good deal more evidence than is now available is needed to assess
whether it does or not) the personal contacts and friendly relations which prevail among the leading members of the political
and corporate elites influence the climate in which important
decisions are made and the way in which certain general ideas are
considered when they are first proposed. The intellectual climate
in which party leaders operate may develop in a sealed universe
composed of their business friends and former associates going
back to their earlier careers at the bar, in the civil service, or in
business. The always difficult task of keeping up with the so-
called grass roots and with the groups newly gaining political
influence in society is thus made considerably more formidable.
This general tendency has serious consequences at the best of
times, but particularly when the winds of change are blowing
with unusual intensity and when new segments of society, notably
the younger age groups and the heretofore inactive members of
ethnic minorities, are determined to influence events. The insensi-
tivity of all national parties to developments in French Canada in
the late fifties and early sixties can, in part, be ascribed to the
phenomenon just discussed.

6. Canada's federal structure has been undergoing considerable strains and consequently change. While little has been done
so far to bring about formal amendments to the constitution
which would redefine the respective powers of the federal and
provincial governments, important alterations have taken place
through new kinds of fiscal arrangements between the dominion
and the provinces. The practice of opting out of general agreements is becoming commonplace and is certain to spread. The net
result of these changes is going to be the increasing difficulty of
maintaining the ideal of a common Canadian standard of well-

being, etc., and the greater tendency of the provinces, particularly the wealthier ones, to make their own decisions in matters of welfare, largely unrelated to what can be achieved elsewhere. The centralist trend imposed by industrialization and enhanced by the depression and World War II is, in other words, being reversed. It will, at least temporarily, be replaced by an era of flourishing provincial autonomy and in some areas even of something approaching autarchy. These changes cannot but be accompanied by the downgrading of the importance of the federal government relative to the provincial authorities. Federal politics and federal parties will, of course, share the reweighting in importance of the two spheres of government. A somewhat lower prestige of the federal parties is likely to reduce their bargaining power, the degree to which they attract able activists, and the effectiveness with which they can impose pan-Canadian considerations on the necessarily somewhat parochial outlook of the provincial parties. This may be a particularly important factor with respect to provinces like Quebec, Alberta, and British Columbia, where the party in power tends to be entirely province-centered.

7. A related development concerns the locus of major decision-making in the Canadian political system. There has been a tendency for a larger number of far-reaching decisions to be made by dominion-provincial consultation either at the level of premiers or cabinet ministers or at that of various mixed committees and officials. Since the parties cannot very well participate in these dominion-provincial joint decisions, a variety of important steps is being taken in the country without the active participation of parties as such. It is of course true that ministers are ultimately accountable to their caucus and so to their party, but it is also true that it is exceedingly difficult for a party group to reverse or check a decision made by its own ministers.

8. Party influence has declined in yet another way. Canadian society has, like its United States counterpart, become more pluralistic as its wealth and specialization have increased. This has led to the emergence of ever increasing numbers of associations of one kind or another, many of which try to influence governmental decisions. Governments not infrequently invite some of these

groups to present their views on legislation and administration of concern to them; their spokesmen are sometimes asked to sit on advisory bodies set up to participate in governmental decision-making. A growing number of decisions is therefore being made nowadays by bodies over whose actions control by Parliament (politicians) is at best remote. Parties therefore find themselves in this sense also deprived of influence—their role is being taken over to some measure by groups who have no fixed partisan attachment but whose specific interests they pursue with whatever government happens to be in power.

9. We cannot abandon our discussion of the long-run factors making for the reduced efficacy of Canadian parties without touching on a well-known and ubiquitous development which has taken its own particular form in Canada. One of the costs of massive governmental activities is the need for highly specialized knowledge in administering and even formulating the decisions of politicians. The tendency for considerable power to become concentrated in the hands of officials at the expense of the elected representatives has until now been more pronounced in Canada at the federal than the provincial level. But more recently, some at least of the provincial governments have become more professionalized. They have succeeded in attracting even some extremely able federal civil servants. The growing professionalism of the provincial governments is, of course, related to their increasing power relative to that of the federal authority, and it is another factor explaining the reduced effectiveness of federal political institutions, including the national political parties.

Short-run Factors

While the nine factors discussed above have been operating in Canada for some time and have therefore been placed under the "long-run" heading, some have also been subject to short-run fluctuations. The last-mentioned, the growing professionalization of provincial governments and the resultant improvement in the quality of provincial civil servants, is subject to change depending on the character of the provincial governments. The advent of the Thatcher regime in Saskatchewan has reversed, and the defeat of

Lesage in Quebec may reverse, the general trend for a short period of time. But the long-run direction of events is not likely to be altered; at the most the changes discussed may be slowed down or accelerated.

1. There are some factors, on the other hand, which have had a profound influence on current Canadian politics and on the prospects for the future but which are not going to last forever. The two main party leaders have each in their own way contributed a great deal to the present state of party life. Much need not be said about the recent roles of Pearson and Diefenbaker; enough is known about the political style of each and about the way in which they have acted one on the other. It is sufficient to recall that the particular relationship that has developed between them has contributed much to the bitterness, asperity, and plain churlishness of the atmosphere prevailing in recent Parliaments. Both the major parties, but particularly the Conservatives, have become somewhat demoralized by the seemingly endless and futile parliamentary battles between the parties. The struggle for the succession in each constitutes another distraction preventing them from giving their undivided attention to the numerous vital questions which should demand their full attention. To the long-run causes of Canada's present political malaise must therefore be added the current crisis in leadership being experienced by both the Liberals and Conservatives. Some observers have ascribed virtually all of the blame to the nature of the leadership, but to do so is to ignore some of the developments noted earlier.

2. Another short-run cause of the low estate now enjoyed by federal parties in Canada is the persistent survival in Ottawa of the House of Minorities. In the last five elections only once did one of the parties obtain a majority of parliamentary seats. This, too, is a development often ascribed to the quality of the present leadership of the Liberals and Conservatives. It has been shown elsewhere that this is too simple an explanation.[6] In a sense virtu-

6. John Meisel, "The June 1962 Election: Break-up of Our Party System?" *Queen's Quarterly*, LXIX (Autumn, 1962), 329–346; "The Stalled Omnibus: Canadian Parties in the 1960's," *Social Research*, XXX (Autumn, 1963), 367–390; *Les Transformations des parties politiques Canadiens*, Cahier de la Societé Canadienne de Science politique, No. 2, 1966, to be published in English as "Recent Changes in Canadian Parties," in H. G. Thorburn, ed., *Party Politics in Canada* (2nd ed.; Toronto, 1967).

ally all the comments on the current state of Canadian politics made herein indicate, *in part,* why it has been difficult to fashion the much-desired (by the major parties) parliamentary majorities. The state of public opinion which has led to no party being certain of a stable majority in the House is both the result of the general political conditions posing particularly difficult problems for the parties and one of its causes. When one party does achieve a majority the difficulty of the politicians will be reduced somewhat but it will not, as some believe, disappear. The tensions in Canadian society will continue and will require an inspired political performance from many hands if they are to be contained and subdued.

It has been seen that a number of developments have compelled Canada to close its first century in an atmosphere of uncertainty or even crisis which has led some observers to question the likelihood of the country's ever surviving its birthday party, let alone its second century. This state of affairs has posed some acute problems for Canada's parties, which are anything but in the best of condition to cope with them. The old parties are in slight disarray, and none of the third parties has so far been able to gain a sufficiently broad base of support to find itself within striking distance of political power. The current lack of capability of the parties individually, and of the party system as a whole, with respect to providing an effective unifying force within the Canadian policy is particularly to be regretted since the country obviously needs precisely this kind of leadership toward cohesion. Parties can provide it essentially in one of two ways: if one party should emerge with strong support in the major sections and regions of Canada and with a competent group of leaders, it might provide the sense of purpose and élan needed for Canada to overcome its present national confusion. Or alternatively a multiple-party system might emerge which, *as a system,* could reconcile the most pressing differences and which could inject the needed sense of direction. Whether either of these two alternatives is likely to occur, and if so, which one, is well beyond the power to forecast. But it is evident that in a society lacking large numbers of national institutions potentially capable of reconciling the various divisive forces, national political parties occupy a special position. They are among the few institutions which must, if they are to survive, focus on national goals while forever maintaining close links with smaller communities. They are, therefore, ideally suited to promote national unity and to become the agency par excellence for the aggregation of local and sectional interests in a manner compatible with some cohesive national interest. Canadian parties at the present time are undergoing the most critical test of their history: to pass this test they must not only perfect their own structures and performance but also do much to create the general conditions in which they can in fact function.

7

Canadian Federalism in Ferment

J. Murray Beck

Since 1963 Canadian federalism has been in such a state of ferment that whatever is written on the subject may be out-of-date before it appears in print. What is involved is nothing less than whether Canada should remain an orthodox federal state, or even whether it should exist at all. Economic and cultural cleavages produced by the new directions of social thought and public policy in Quebec have combined to present the Canadian federal system with the most serious challenge it has ever faced. Does it possess "the flexibility needed to evolve a new equilibrium to satisfy these conflicting demands within the framework of our traditional federal institutions?"[1] Can the country's leaders "find the unmarked channel of [a new brand of] co-operative federalism between the Scylla of national needs and the Charybdis of provincial [and, more particularly, Quebec] rights?"[2]

Canadian federalism, no less than other brands of the species, has never been static. J. R. Mallory has distinguished five forms of federalism in Canada, each owing its existence to the dominant forces of the period in which it was operative.[3] During the first few decades of the federation the vogue was quasi-federalism, stemming from John A. Macdonald's centralizing views of the constitution he had done so much to frame. The Laurier and interwar years were characterized by something more nearly approaching classical federalism, which recognized the co-ordinate and autono-

---

1. Donald V. Smiley, "The Two Themes of Canadian Federalism," *Canadian Journal of Economics and Political Science*, XXXI (Feb., 1965), 96.
2. *Canadian Annual Review for 1963* (Toronto, 1964), p. 65.
3. "The Five Faces of Federalism," in P. A. Crépeau and C. B. Macpherson, eds., *The Future of Canadian Federalism* (Toronto, 1965), pp. 3–15.

mous relationship of the federal and provincial governments. This was no more than might be expected, for the Liberals, traditionally the party of provincial rights, were in power most of the time and they were naturally disinclined to tread upon provincial toes. Mallory's third form, emergency federalism, has operated during two world wars and the period needed to wind up wartime controls once the wars were over. Its constitutional basis was the emergency doctrine of Viscount Haldane, but its acceptability depended upon the recognition by most Canadians that the federal government required almost unlimited power to prosecute the wars fully and effectively.

The fourth and fifth forms, co-operative federalism (of at least two varieties) and double-image federalism, have emerged since 1945 and are the outcome of the significant forces which have operated in Canadian government over the past two decades. After World War II the two levels of government no longer worked in the same isolation as before, but engaged more and more in co-operative ventures. They co-ordinated their activities through such devices as the continuous consultation of officials on joint programs, the delegation by Parliament of regulatory functions to provincial agencies,[4] and federal spending on matters which fall within provincial and municipal jurisdiction.[5] The outcome, according to J. A. Corry, was that the provinces could no longer "think of themselves as independent principalities, bowing only to federal dictates on foreign policy and foreign trade and a few other matters." It could not be otherwise, he wrote in 1961, once they had allowed themselves to be drawn into an interdependent economy which undermined any secure economic base of their own. Even the strongest among them "compromised their positions when they brought within their walls the Trojan horse of big enterprise with nation-wide interests and outlook, which, by its very nature, cannot be loyal to any self-centered provincialism."[6]

4. This device, which got around the impediment against the delegation of legislative authority from the Dominion Parliament to a provincial legislature, was judicially upheld in *P.E.I. Potato Marketing Board* v. *H. B. Willis Inc.*, [1952] 2S.C.R.392.
5. Mallory, "Five Faces of Federalism," p. 10.
6. J. A. Corry, "Constitutional Trends and Federalism," in Robert M. Clark, ed., *Canadian Issues: Essays in Honour of Henry F. Angus* (Toronto, 1961), p. 11.

But the so-called co-operative federalism was marked as well by the assumption of new initiatives by the federal authority. The growing public collectivism and the provision of a host of additional services by governments in the post-depression years naturally led to the imposition of a much heavier weight of taxation. To make it as unburdensome as possible upon the economy, the national government almost inevitably assumed leadership in forming taxation policy. Also, since economic concentration and the tinkering of governments had substantially reduced the self-adjusting capacity of the economy, it was just as natural that Ottawa would take over the primary responsibility for overall economic guidance.[7] As a result, in Corry's words, a province could hardly expect more than "freedom for minor adventure, for embroidering its own particular patterns in harmony with the national design, for playing variant melodies within the general theme."[8]

Indeed, in 1945, the politicians at Ottawa, basking in the unqualified success of their management of the country's finances and economy during the war, had no doubts that they alone were capable of taking the positive, aggressive steps which were needed to insure a large national income, a high standard of living, and stability of employment. According to them, this required regulation of the economy through fiscal controls and timed public investment, and such devices would work only if the provinces relinquished to the national government the exclusive right to use the income tax. So certain was Ottawa of the great good which would continue to flow from enhanced federal power that, not only did federal leaders expect the provinces to withdraw from their major flexible sources of revenue, but they even refused to commit themselves to getting out of the nuisance tax fields which they had entered for the first time during World War II.

Quebec and Ontario protested that the provinces would, in effect, become annuitants of Ottawa if they were to do as Ottawa wished and thereby lose the fiscal independence that the co-

7. *Ibid.*, p. 6.
8. *Ibid.*, p. 12.

ordinate members of a federal system ought to possess. But in the climate of that day the federal government could adopt a take-it-or-leave-it attitude and get away with it. Under the conditions which it imposed, only Ontario and Quebec could afford not to enter the agreements of 1947 by which the other provinces rented their rights in the income tax and succession duty fields to the Dominion.

After five years Ottawa was as insistent as ever on keeping the fiscal power in its own hands. This time it devised an option which was so attractive to a province with a high tax potential that even Ontario felt compelled to accept it. Only Quebec adhered to principle and stayed out of the tax-rental system. Yet the federal government soon showed signs of relaxing its adamant position. In 1953 it allowed Quebec corporations to deduct from the federal levy the full provincial tax of 7 per cent on their incomes instead of the 5 per cent which had heretofore been permitted. A little later, after Quebec resorted to a provincial personal income tax, it decided to raise the rate of deductibility for Quebec taxpayers from 5 to 10 per cent of the federal levy, thus removing or largely mitigating the burden of double taxation. Michel Brunet considers this concession so important that he calls it the first French-Canadian victory since the Battle of the Plains of Abraham. On this basis he even dates Quebec's Quiet Revolution from the mid-fifties rather than the early sixties.

Undoubtedly the desire to mollify Quebec was the determining factor in the Dominion's less stringent attitude toward renascent provincial power over finances. But there is more to it than that. During the fifties the idea of Dominion fiscal control of the economy was beginning to lose some of its old charm.[9] Certainly the feeling was growing that it could be achieved without the excessive uniformity in income tax rates deemed to be necessary in 1945. Under the prevailing circumstances monetary policy seemed to be a more appropriate tool for regulating the business cycle. Not only that, but economics and economists had discovered a new idol to worship, and along with the eleven Canadian

9. See the speech of Marcel Bélanger in Canadian Tax Foundation, *Report of Proceedings of the Fifteenth Annual Tax Conference* (Toronto, 1961), p. 310.

governments became avid devotees of economic growth. Such growth requires the development of educational facilities and natural resources, both of which are provincial responsibilities. About the same time the ordinary Canadian had adopted a new god of his own; he wanted to be assured of security against the rigors of old age, illness, disability, and the like, which too are largely matters of provincial responsibility. Finally, the rapid increase in population and its concentration in metropolitan areas were imposing vastly increased expenditures on provincial and municipal governments for city and intercity transportation, city planning, education, housing, and the like.

The cumulative effect of all this was to produce nothing short of a revolution in the relative balance of Canadian governments. Where the federal government had been spending more than three times as much as the provincial and municipal governments in 1945 and about twice as much in 1953, by 1963 the latter governments had a current income which was 15 per cent above that of the Dominion (if federal transfer payments are included). At the same time, the combined debts of the junior governments, which had been only one-fifth that of the national government at the close of the war, had so mounted that if present tendencies continue they will exceed the latter in the not-too-distant future.[10] Big provincial governments could not be expected to acquiesce as readily as heretofore in the subordinate status to which they had been tacitly relegated since 1945. And so the pendulum had begun to shift perceptibly in Canadian federalism even before Quebec's Quiet Revolution had made an impact upon it.

Ottawa had apparently recognized these new facts of life when the third in the series of five-year tax arrangements was concluded in 1957. Undoubtedly Prime Minister St. Laurent was anxious to remedy a state of affairs which had cost his native province something on the order of $300 million since 1947 because of its failure to enter the tax-rental system. But it was also possible to regard the new arrangements as the beginning of a trend toward permitting the provinces to use the chief direct taxes

10. Jacques Parizeau, "Prospects for Economic Policy in a Federal Canada," in Crépeau and Macpherson, eds., *Future of Canadian Federalism*, p. 46.

more freely even if it meant some impairment of federal fiscal control and of the maintenance of a reasonably uniform tax structure.[11] Basically these arrangements recognized a part of the income tax and succession duty fields—known as "standard taxes" —as unqualifiedly provincial. A province might rent any or all of these standard taxes to the Dominion; it might itself levy and collect any or all of them; or it might levy them and use the Dominion as its collecting agency. Furthermore, whether or not a province entered into an agreement, it was entitled to receive unconditional equalization grants sufficient to bring the combined per capita yield of the standard taxes up to the level of the average per capita yield of these taxes in the two provinces where the combined per capita yields were highest. To say the least, it was a far cry from the inflexible, take-it-or-leave-it attitude of 1945/46.

The drums of retreat were still beating in 1962. Confronted by provincial demands which it estimated would cost two billion dollars, the Diefenbaker government vacated a further portion of the personal income tax field, but insisted that the provinces levy their own income taxes and succession duties in the future. It even encouraged the imposition of such taxes by offering to collect them without charge at whatever level a province desired, provided their base did not differ materially from that of the federal tax.[12] In a sense Diefenbaker had called the provinces' bluff, for only Ontario appeared to welcome a return to the idea that "maximum prudence and economy in spending are best achieved when the government that spends the money is made responsible for the raising of it."[13]

Thus Ottawa had already backtracked significantly when, on April 5, 1963, Quebec presented its first strident demands upon the federal government. Only three days before the Canadian people were to give their first, halting approval to Lester Pearson, Premier Lesage presented his "50–50–100 ultimatum," an asser-

11. J. M. Beck, "New Look in Finance," *Queen's Quarterly,* LXIII (Summer, 1956), 222–223.
12. Among other things these arrangements provided for equalization grants based on the yields of the standard taxes at the national average rather than in the two provinces where their yields were highest.
13. See speech of George Gathercole in *Report of Proceedings of the Fifteenth Annual Tax Conference,* p. 317.

tion of the right to use half the income tax fields and all the succession duty field within twelve months. So J. R. Mallory's double-image federalism, which includes "both the straightforward central-regional relationship between the central and provincial organs and a special relationship between French and English which to some extent transcends the other,"[14] was superimposed upon the existing co-operative federalism with a vengeance. Soon it was to constitute a serious challenge to the leadership of the national government.

J. A. Corry had shown that the factors which led to strong central initiative in Canada after 1945 were equally applicable to the United States and Australia. In all three countries, however, he had observed that material factors alone were not a sufficient explanation. At least widespread acquiescence in, if not active support for, such initiative was also required. "If the people of the several states and provinces [had] remained stubbornly determined to find their principal collective expression as tarheels or bluenoses, we should not have arrived where we are."[15] On that account, he added "some nationalizing of sentiment" to the factors which made strong leadership by the national government acceptable. Yet he admitted that the evidence supporting the existence of such sentiment, particularly in Canada, was equivocal, and the course of events since he wrote indicates that the French Canadian of Quebec may yet choose to bestow his primary loyalty on the *Canadien* rather than on the *Canadian* nation.

In any case Corry found a better explanation for the acceptability of strong central initiative in the nationalizing of elites. In many occupations and interests the active persons are drawn into national associations where they come to believe that their common problems can be most readily attacked on the broadest possible front, that is, the national front. This is especially true of the business elites, whose wants directly touch the national government in many ways, and who have thus come more and more to accept the leadership of the national government, and who concentrate on exercising influence in the national political arena.

14. "Five Faces of Federalism," p. 3.
15. Corry, "Constitutional Trends and Federalism," p. 7.

"In the main," concluded Corry, "they are the active leaders of opinion, and they are likely, in the long run, to carry electoral opinion in most states and provinces."[16] This may be an accurate description of the situation as it exists in the United States, Australia, and the English-speaking provinces of Canada. But the French-Canadian elites have tended to play a minimal role in many national associations and within recent years have withdrawn from some in which they used to participate. Also, the business elites of Quebec, who are largely English-speaking, have been prime targets in the Quebec Revolution and are in no sense active leaders of opinion. Hence some major factors which are tending toward national integration and the obsolescence of federalism in the United States and Australia are either of lesser significance or work with opposite effect in Canada. The French-Canadian fact insures that a peculiarly Canadian relationship will be worked out between the central and provincial governments there.[17]

Any discussion of the status of French Canada leads almost inevitably to the nature of the bargain arrived at in 1867. Donald V. Smiley seems to go too far when he argues that the Confederation entente rested on the understanding that the Dominion would have all the authority needed for military defense and economic development, while the provinces would have jurisdiction over those matters which have a direct cultural incidence.[18] What can be stated with assurance is that the leading Fathers of Confederation had no doubt that the federal Parliament could deal with any matter of national concern, and that the Quebec Legislature alone could touch those institutions which were peculiarly distinctive to French Canadians. Today, however, the Quebecer of the Quiet Revolution does not expect merely that the basic understandings of the Confederation agreement should be honored. While he wants his province to retain unimpaired all its existing rights under the constitution—rights which have been widely expanded through judicial interpretation—he also wants it

16. *Ibid.*, p. 16.
17. Mallory, "Five Faces of Federalism," p. 11.
18. Smiley, "Two Themes of Canadian Federalism," p. 83.

to have additional ones to conform with new needs and aspirations.

Yet even if Smiley's premises need to be qualified, his conclusions are sound. It is true, as he says, that up to 1919 the federal government was preoccupied with policies of national economic development and integration, and that it did not intervene directly in matters with a cultural incidence. It is equally true that the establishment of federal grants in aid to highways, provincial employment offices, and vocational training in 1919 presaged a new development in Canadian federalism which, although it may have "challenged one of the understandings of the Confederation settlement in a most fundamental way,"[19] at least meant active intervention by the national government for the first time in matters within provincial legislative competence. It is true, above all, that this intervention eventually extended to every major provincial function, including cultural activities of every description except elementary and secondary education. The wonder of it all is that it took place with a minimum of formal constitutional change.[20] Of greater practical significance were the attitudes of the major racial groups toward it. In English Canada the increasing federal intervention "reflected a consensus . . . that Ottawa has the moral obligation to involve itself in any matter deemed to be of great importance, and to require public action, including matters within the legislative jurisdiction of the provinces."[21] In Quebec it gave rise to a good deal of disquiet and even anxiety.

For two decades prior to his death in 1959 Maurice Duplessis was the chief spokesman of a brand of autonomy which leveled its sights at the centralizers in Ottawa. Sometimes it seemed little more than a myth which he had concocted to keep his Union Nationale in office. Yet he could not be induced to surrender any of the province's sources of revenue by entering into tax rental agreements, no matter what the loss in dollars, and he was reluctant to conclude cost-sharing arrangements with the Dominion in

19. *Ibid.*, p. 85.
20. Only three amendments have altered the distribution of legislative authority, those having to do with unemployment insurance in 1940, and old age pensions and ancillary matters in 1951 and 1964.
21. Smiley, "Two Themes of Canadian Federalism," p. 85.

matters which had a direct cultural impact on Quebec. He found himself seriously hampered in pressing his views, however, because the same persons who kept voting him back into power usually returned a solid phalanx of Liberals, who became the bulwark of a centralizing government at Ottawa.

Jean Lesage took over a Quebec of quite a different mood. The Royal Commission on Bilingualism and Biculturalism, in its preliminary report, could find no French Canadians who were avowed supporters of the status quo. In varying degrees all of them came out for greatly increased scope for the French language, a greater recognition of the French-Canadian nation, a greater role for "the state of Quebec."[22] Those who spearheaded the Quiet Revolution—a new middle class of youthful university graduates, a young well-educated, elite group of technicians, engineers, and executives—possessed self-confidence far surpassing that of the leaders of Quebec's previous nationalist movements. Their province, they kept reiterating, was not a province *comme les autres* and must be *maître chez soi*. Give it the political emancipation it required or it would have no trouble "going it" by itself.

All who now spoke for Quebec built up a case something like this: Canada consists of two nations largely occupying separate territory; these nations have been forced into a common constitutional straitjacket in which each tries to use a common tool, the federal state, to fulfil diverging aspirations; Quebecers now possess a degree of national identification far different from anything which has existed in the past; a nation which has become fully aware of its existence cannot and ought not to be prevented from achieving full nationhood. But the conclusions which are drawn from this statement of the case vary. The separatist argues that in such circumstances the two nations cannot possibly be contained within the bosom of a single state. Others maintain that the circumstances have made federalism irrelevant and that Canada is headed toward a loose confederation, or at least associate status for Quebec, as a complete solution of the English-French prob-

22. A *Preliminary Report of the Royal Commission on Bilingualism and Biculturalism* (Ottawa, 1965), chap. vi.

lem. Practical politicians like Jean Lesage and Daniel Johnson, on the other hand, have made no attempt to define explicitly the political form which may be required for the fulfilment of their objectives.

Since 1963, therefore, the Canadian federation has been confronted with such questions as: Can Quebec be sufficiently master of its own house within a genuine federal state? Or is Quebec so different that its demands cannot be met unless it is accorded the status of an associate state, or is allowed to go completely its own way? There were no clear-cut answers to these questions in the philosophy of federal-provincial relationships which Premier Jean Lesage elaborated between 1963 and 1966. Basic to that philosophy was his concept of priorities. Depression and war, he said, had given temporary precedence to the Dominion, but now the needs of the province had priority. Accordingly there needed to be "a genuine decentralization of powers, resources and decision making in the federal system of government,"[23] to the end that the government of Quebec would have all the means necessary for the development of a French-Canadian nation mainly concentrated within its borders. Evidently Lesage saw the provinces as the real centers of power within the Confederation, possessing a great measure of autonomy, deciding together the direction of national policy, and leaving the federal authority only a limited role to play. And he was a moderate in the Quebec of those days.

While Lesage did not state precisely what the enhanced powers of the Quebec government ought to be, his ministers conducted a series of probes to see what accretion of power might be effected piecemeal through the political process. The Minister of Education proclaimed the right of Quebec to conclude agreements with foreign countries on cultural matters; the Minister of Municipal and Cultural Affairs talked about assuming full control of the housing programs of Central Mortgage and Housing Corporation, naturally without loss of the federal financial outlay; the Minister of Revenue demanded that the provincial governments have the right to become sharcholders in chartered banks; the Minister of Labour proposed to take over the administration of

23. *Globe and Mail* (Toronto), Sept. 29, 1964, p. 33.

job placement and unemployment services and contested the federal government's authority to implement national manpower policies; the Minister of Family and Social Welfare asked for full administrative control first over the Eskimos and later over family allowances. His latter demand challenged, in effect, the federal government's use of its spending power to enter directly into fields which normally come within provincial legislative competence. Such were the nibblers at the authority and power of the central government.

In dealing with financial resources Lesage regarded any abatements he had already secured in the federal personal income tax as merely the first instalments of more substantial gains to follow. Because the present needs of the provinces had priority, he said their financial capabilities had to be proportionate. During the provincial election of 1966 his minister René Lévesque even hinted that Ottawa might have to cut its defense spending to provide sufficient leeway for the provinces, while Lesage himself suggested more than once that the federal government did not need large sums of money to perform an anti-inflationary and stabilizing role in managing the economy.

In decision-making, Lesage insisted that the provinces have the right to participate in reaching conclusions on some matters which lie exclusively within federal jurisdiction, such as monetary, tariff, and transportation policy. No longer did Ottawa need wide powers to promote economic growth. What was vital now was regional development, and in this area the provinces had the greatest role to play, for they controlled most of the factors through which a true development policy could be developed and have a chance of success.

Such were the demands which faced the Pearson minority government from the very first days of its existence. From then until September, 1966, the question was raised more than once whether Pearson was setting his course for a known destination or according to the force and direction of the wind from Quebec. Pearson himself boasted that he was not on the defensive. "If you play a defensive game," he said, "you are not likely to get so many penalties, but you are certainly not going to score goals." Undoubtedly his government incurred penalties because of the "image of constant retreat and disarray" is presented.[24] But did it also score goals in adopting what it sometimes called "co-operative federalism" and sometimes "creative, co-operative federalism"? Although the Pearson administration rather turned up its nose at the brand of federalism which prevailed after 1945, which political scientists have labeled as "co-operative federalism," as an instrument of discord, Pearson seemed loath to define his own brand of co-operative federalism in anything but the most general terms, and his ministers were equally vague. Maurice Lamontagne, for example, called it a new mixture of interdependence, consultation, and co-ordination, a new means of political decentralization, while Guy Favreau described it as a system in which "le gouvernement fédéral n'est donc pas le seigneur ni le roi de dix gouvernements provinciaux; il ne leur est pas supérieur. Avec eux, il travaille à réaliser les fins de la Confédération."[25]

The dominion-provincial conferences of 1963 and 1964 demonstrated how the Pearson brand of co-operative federalism worked in practice. Included in the Liberal platform of 1963 had been a promise to relieve unemployment through federal assistance to municipalities for public works. Accordingly the Pearson government introduced a bill to establish a federal Municipal Loan Board, which with provincial approval could make loans directly to municipalities for specified purposes. In short order Lesage denounced the bill as an interference with the traditional relationship between a province and its municipalities, and a serious infringement upon the exclusive jurisdiction and autonomy of Quebec. At a federal-provincial conference convened principally to deal with this matter in July, 1963, the Dominion agreed to allow any provincial government, under proper safeguards, to assume the responsibility of the Municipal Loan Board for granting and administering the loans to the municipalities. Lesage exulted over this recognition that Quebec was not a province *comme les autres* and the willingness to find formulas "qui satisfont le point de vue légitime du Québec sans priver les autres gouvernements provinciaux de leur droit d'obtenir des conditions

24. *Canadian Annual Review for 1964* (Toronto, 1965), p. 63.
25. *Canadian Annual Review for 1963* (Toronto, 1964), p. 73.

différentes."[26] Throughout Quebec there was talk of *un nouvel ère* in federal-provincial relations and *La Presse* anticipated "un fédéralisme horizontal qui prendra forme pour remplacer le fédéralisme autoritaire, imposé par Ottawa."[27]

The so-called "Last-Chance Conference" of November, 1963, dealt primarily with Quebec's financial demands. Basically the federal government agreed to increase the provinces' share of succession duties from 50 to 75 per cent and to revert to the practice of using the yields of the standard taxes in the two provinces in which they were highest as the basis for determining equalization grants. It needed little imagination to appreciate why the Pearson government had seized upon these particular devices; of the additional $87 million being made available to the provinces, $43 million would go to Quebec. "To a lot of people," said Saskatchewan Premier T. C. Douglas, this would look "very much like a behind-the-barn deal."[28] Yet it fell far short of meeting the "50–50–100 ultimatum," and René Lévesque labeled it an "apéritif qui tournerait au vinaigre si le repas ne vient pas après."[29]

The conference of March–April, 1964, left Lesage even less happy. It is true that Pearson made known, more specifically than he had done previously, his government's willingness to let the provinces "opt out" of most shared-cost arrangements without financial loss to themselves. But he failed, according to Lesage, to provide a division of the tax revenues which would take into account the priority needs of the provinces, and he indicated his intention to proceed with the provision of student loans and the extension of family allowances which, in Quebec's view, were serious encroachments on the most important sectors of provincial jurisdiction. Lesage even threatened to go to the courts to see that the constitutional rights of the provinces were respected.

It looked as if the conference had been an unmitigated disaster. But in secret behind-the-scenes negotiations Ottawa and Quebec came to terms. Pearson communicated the outcome to the other

26. *Ibid.*, p. 68. But actually three other provinces—Ontario, Manitoba, and Saskatchewan—also availed themselves of this alternative.
27. *Ibid.*, p. 68.
28. *Ibid.*, p. 79.
29. *Ibid.*, p. 78.

premiers who, for the moment at least, chose not to complain about one province exercising bargaining rights for all of them.[30] By the new arrangements, Ottawa consented to make further abatements in personal income tax rates over the next two years and to grant a fiscal equivalent to Quebec for its non-participation in student loans and the extension of family allowances. It also agreed to substantial changes in the Canadian pension plan to make it portable with the Quebec plan, which was designed not only to provide pensions but to build up a large accumulation of funds to be used for provincial development. While Quebec had made a few concessions, the bargain was again heavily weighted in its favor. Premier Lesage refrained from calling it a victory, but in fact that is what it was. "In the past month I have lived a terrible life," he said. "I have worked for my province as no one has ever worked for his province . . . so that Quebec, finally, might be recognized as a province that has a special status in Confederation, and I succeeded."[31]

But despite Lesage's elation he had made only small headway toward having his general case recognized, and even in shared-cost arrangements he had not fully established the basic principle he had been advocating. These arrangements had been a primary ingredient in the co-operative federalism which had developed since 1945. Over the years they had multiplied in helter-skelter fashion until by the sixties there were more than sixty programs costing the federal government a total of $900 million annually. To the poorer provinces, which had often been led by the availability of federal funds into providing services they could ill afford, the programs were not an unmixed blessing. To Quebec they had often been anathema, since practically all of them fell in fields within provincial jurisdiction and conflicted with Quebec's particular concept of autonomy. In 1960 Lesage reluctantly decided to participate in a few of the programs which Duplessis had spurned in order to avoid the financial penalty of staying out. He still contended, however, that any federal move which reduced or

30. But in October, Premier Robarts of Ontario made it known that no satisfactory results would be achieved if arrangements were made with one or more provinces and then presented to the balance as a fait accompli.

31. *Globe and Mail* (Toronto), April 22, 1964, p. 3.

attacked provincial powers even indirectly was a threat to provincial autonomy and constituted a precedent which might later be invoked to justify further threats. But his fears on this score were at least partially met in 1965 by the passage of the Established Programs (Interim Arrangements) Act, which permitted any province to contract out of practically all the existing programs and receive abatements of the federal personal income tax or cash payments in lieu thereof. He indicated almost immediately that he would take full advantage of this option.

Yet Lesage had altered his earlier stand in one respect. Although he intended to permit no further federal initiative in areas within Quebec's jurisdiction, he now had no objection to other provinces' accepting it provided that Quebec was not penalized for non-participation. The other premiers did not receive Pearson's original announcement of the opting out provisions with anything like the same enthusiasm. While they felt that Ottawa had been far too rigid in prescribing the regulations for joint programs, thus limiting their adaptability to differing needs, they were fearful that contracting out might bring the whole structure down and thereby destroy a device which had helped to create something like national standards. Once again English Canada manifested its view that the national government has a moral right to take the initiative in promoting the national good even in matters beyond its jurisdiction.

Had Quebec been accorded a special status by apparently winning the right to different but equal treatment in federal-provincial programs? Legally it had not received privileges which another province might not exercise if it saw fit. In fact, some were a little aggrieved that Quebec alone had not been given the right to contract out and hence had failed to make good its claim that it was not a province *comme les autres*. Nonetheless, since the Established Programs Act was designed to meet Quebec's demands and since Quebec alone took advantage of the act's provisions, it did in fact come to occupy a different position from that of the other provinces. Lesage might keep saying that he was not opting out of the Confederation, but there were at least grounds for the feeling that, if one province did all the contracting out, it would isolate that province from the rest of Canada and would make for division rather than union.

Contracting out also posed the problem of non-participating provinces helping to devise, approve, and run programs for the other provinces through their representatives in the cabinet and Parliament at Ottawa. It was contended that, if both Quebec and Ontario opted out of a joint program, a majority of M.P.'s might be deciding on policies which were to be inoperative in their own provinces. While this already had occurred in a limited way in day-to-day legislation, it was feared that if it were to become a regular occurrence, it would strike at the very roots of the constitution. Actually, however, since an opting-out province agreed to operate the programs substantially in their existing form, Parliament was, in effect, determining their basic nature in all the provinces. That was why Pearson appeared to set a dangerous precedent early in 1966 when he acquiesced in Lesage's treatment of a cash payment in lieu of an increase in per capita university grants as an unconditional grant to his province.[32] But until a premier of Quebec clearly establishes a general right to use abatements or cash payments in lieu just as he pleases, he will not have freed himself fully from federal initiative in these programs.

The three conferences of 1963 and 1964 and their aftermath demonstrated that, as in the past, a process of piecemeal adjustment between the two levels of government was continuing to take place and that these adjustments came about primarily through interaction between federal and provincial executives.[33] But in English Canada, more than ever before, the results of these conferences raised the fear that power had shifted from Ottawa to the provincial capitals, particularly Quebec City, and from Parliament to secret sessions of the premiers and the prime minister, and it was alleged that these procedures had robbed Parliament of supremacy and inaugurated change in secrecy instead of in the cleansing force of public debate.

32. See the correspondence between Pearson and Lesage in Appendix to Canada, *House of Commons Debates, 1966* (unrevised), (Feb. 10), pp. 1063–1065. Premier Lesage called it an "unusual victory."
33. See Donald V. Smiley, "The Rowell-Sirois Report, Provincial Autonomy, and Post-War Federalism," *Canadian Journal of Economics and Political Science,* XXVIII (Feb., 1962), 58.

Be that as it may, had they also ushered in a new brand of co-operative federalism? Not so, said Lesage, unless they were leading toward a state of affairs in which Quebec would at last perform all its constitutional responsibilities with its own financial resources and also participate in the formulation of national economic policies; otherwise, his province was being taken in by a trick in semantics. For his part Premier Robarts expressed fears that the game of co-operative federalism as it was being played would put his province in a continuing series of squeeze plays. If it were a system by which the eleven governments met frequently to exchange points of view, make known intentions, discuss policies, and engage in co-operative decision-making, he approved it without qualification. If it were a system by which any province might opt out of a joint program without penalty, he was equally favorable. But he was insistent that it not become a system in which some provinces might stay out of programs with federal approval and others be accused of breaking up the Confederation if they tried to do the same thing.

Yet under the Pearson brand of co-operative federalism the premier of another province lacked anything like the same bargaining power as his Quebec counterpart. Thus once the federal government had made certain that the Canada and Quebec pension plans were mutually portable it apparently expected him to be a good Canadian and go along with its plan rather than devise his own. Later it instituted the same sort of squeeze play in medicare. Assured by Lesage that Quebec would have a medicare plan in operation by July 1, 1967, which could qualify for federal grants or their fiscal equivalent, the federal government announced that it would go ahead with its shared-cost plan on that date regardless of how many provinces were prepared to sign agreements.[34]

This put Ontario on the spot. Its course had been to adopt a medicare plan alongside but not supplanting existing private

34. At the founding convention of the Quebec section of the Liberal Federation of Canada in March, 1966, Prime Minister Pearson indicated his intention not to opt into further matters within provincial jurisdiction. Within days, however, he assured the Commons that medicare was not the type of matter he had in mind (Canada, *House of Commons Debates, 1966*, March 28, p. 3255). He did not state explicitly what type he did mean.

plans, thereby saving its resources for such high-priority programs as the coverage of tuberculosis and mental health. But unless its plan was made fully public and possessed a high degree of universality it would apparently not qualify for federal grants. This would have meant that Ontario would have provided a large share of the total federal medicare subsidy through its share of federal taxes and would have got none of it back. It might have bargained with Ottawa, arguing that when Pearson agreed that Quebec could spend federal money intended to assist universities for other purposes, he set a precedent which could enable any province to take federal money intended for a particular shared program and spend it as it chose. But if anything was certain in federal-provincial relations as they then stood—and under the circumstances it was understandable—it was that Quebec, not Ontario, called the tune. Ottawa's temporary postponement of medicare was supposedly due to a desire not to add to the inflationary pressures. But a cynic might have wondered if it was not as much due to the realization that the new premier of Quebec, Daniel Johnson, had no intention of embarking on a medicare scheme by July 1, 1967.

The medicare question illustrated another alleged weakness of shared-cost arrangements. It was contended that under pressure Premier Robarts might be forced to spend Ontario money at the direction of Ottawa rather than according to his own judgment. That is the way it always was with conditional grants. By an indeterminable process Ottawa has decided that at a particular time all Canadians ought to be provided with a clearly defined service which is clearly within provincial competence, and the provinces have had to go along with that decision or be penalized financially. The existence of these programs sometimes distorts the order of priority which the provinces would like to establish in their own expenditures.

At any rate, one thing is certain. To contend that a new brand of "creative, co-operative federalism" had been ushered in between 1963 and 1966 was more than a trifle euphemistic. Pearson undoubtedly deserved credit for his diplomatic handling of a difficult situation, but actually his accomplishments were much like those of his predecessors, a series of empirical adjustments which incorporated the federal cabinet's concept of the public interest to the degree that political expediency dictated.[35] In any case, if the Pearson government described its practices before September, 1966, as "creative, co-operative federalism," it should surely conjure up a different designation for the distinctively new course it has followed since then.

Its new philosophy of federalism was first expounded in detail by Mitchell Sharp, the minister of finance, at the fourth meeting of the Federal-Provincial Tax Structure Committee on September 14, 1966. Implicitly then, and explicitly later, Sharp admitted that the government had been letting Quebec develop a special status and that it had erred in this matter. Its new policy, he said, was well within the constitution and avoided a special status for any province. On the one hand, it hoped to fashion machinery which would "permit a strong Federal Government to accomplish the economic and social responsibilities which properly belong to it, but without impairing the fiscal freedom and responsibility of the provinces." On the other hand, it wished to

strengthen the ability of the provinces to provide the greatly expanded and improved public services which are expected of them, but without at the same time hobbling the Federal Government or forcing it to have different laws for different parts of Canada—differences which might have the effect of obscuring or weakening its proper role as a government which governs all Canadians and protects equally the interests of all of them.[36]

Sharp unequivocally rejected provincial demands that he make further substantial abatements in federal income taxes in order to provide the provinces with additional "tax room." If he followed such a course, he said, he would be admitting that Parliament was appropriating funds for purposes which were less important than those undertaken by the provinces, an implication he could not accept. Yet there were even more compelling reasons for rejecting the provinces' demands for further tax room. Corporation taxes,

35. Beck, "New Look in Finance," p. 214.
36. *Report of Fourth Meeting of Federal-Provincial Tax Structure Committee,* Sept. 14–15 (Ottawa, 1966), p. 13.

he pointed out, had "national as opposed to provincial characteristics," in that the profits of corporations were often earned elsewhere than in the province where their head office was located and their profits recorded. But above all, the national government needed "a predominant share of this tax field by reason of [its] importance and peculiar value . . . as an instrument of national economic policy."[37] Accordingly, Sharp made it clear he was not prepared to go beyond the existing abatement of about one-quarter of the federal corporation tax.

Likewise, he argued, the federal government needed to retain a substantial position in the personal income tax field because it was "the principal tax by which equity is achieved between the rich and the poor across the nation" and "one of the central instruments for regulating total demand in the economy."[38] Already, Quebec, by opting out of most shared-cost arrangements and using personal income tax abatements in lieu, was levying this tax at a rate approximately equal that of the federal rate. Sharp again insisted that this was as far as the Dominion might go and still use the tax effectively as equalizer and regulator.

Granted that the retention of income taxes to this degree permitted the federal authority to fulfil its proper economic and social responsibilities, did it put the provinces in an analogous position? Sharp maintained that any province which wished to embark on new or improved services clearly had the right to increase its own income taxes, but that it should be prepared to assume full responsibility for its action and not expect a corresponding abatement in federal taxes. Yet, he conceded that if all the provinces were to perform their constitutional responsibilities properly, new equalization arrangements would have to be introduced. Accordingly he presented an equalization formula which was designed to "measure the whole revenue or fiscal capacity of the provinces—to develop a comprehensive 'prosperity index' if you will—in place of the partial measure now in use." His formula, he contended, took into account all the revenue sources of a province, not an arbitrarily selected few, and provided automati-

37. *Ibid.*, p. 25.
38. *Ibid.*

cally for increases in payments to the eligible provinces as provincial responsibilities grew, not as tax yields increased.[39] Sharp may have claimed more for his proposals than was warranted but they undoubtedly did provide something closer to true equalization than the previous arrangements. Likely too, the cabinet found to its liking a formula which gave $85.8 million (or 61.9 per cent) of an additional $138.7 million in equalization grants to Quebec.

In seeking to put all the provinces back on an equal status vis-à-vis the Dominion, Sharp was confronted with a situation in which Quebec had acquired 47 per cent of the personal income tax and 10 per cent of corporation profits, while the other provinces had only 24 and 9 per cent, respectively. To remove Quebec's special status he simply proposed to give the other provinces the number of percentage points of income tax and the associated equalization needed to compensate them for the loss of the federal government's contribution toward the major shared-cost program. Then, on April 1, 1970, Ottawa would eliminate the conditions with which the provinces were forced to comply under these programs, and the compensation would take on a completely unconditional character. This change would serve to implement the final ingredient in the new philosophy of federalism by increasing the fiscal independence and responsibility of all the provinces in fields which were constitutionally theirs.[40]

Education received special attention at the federal-provincial conference on higher education on October 25, 1966. This time Ottawa announced its intention to eliminate the per capita grants by which it had provided assistance to the universities in the English-speaking provinces in accordance with provisions recommended by the Association of Universities and Colleges of Canada. It indicated also that it would bring to an end the agreements by which it had made substantial contributions to the capital and operational costs of technical and vocational education. To replace the old procedures it proposed the one it had adopted to provide assistance to the universities of Quebec, i.e., permitting the abatement of an appropriate number of percentage

39. *Ibid.*, pp. 15–16.
40. *Ibid.*, p. 20.

points of the income taxes and allowing a provincial government to allocate the proceeds as it saw fit. Past federal programs of aid to education had tended to distort the development in the direction indicated by Ottawa. And this was now recognized as being constitutionally wrong. But at the same time Ottawa made it clear that such programs as the retraining of adults were part and parcel of manpower and employment policy and hence clearly within federal jurisdiction.

This, then, is the new mode by which Ottawa may institute new arrangements and which will be well within the constitution. Mitchell Sharp admitted one possible type of exception, perhaps to justify the federal government's imminent intervention in medicare. Very occasionally the Dominion might intrude itself in provincial matters to insure broad national standards, but once such standards were established, it would get out. In its professed respect for the constitution, the Pearson government's philosophy of federalism might have been calculated to win favor in Quebec. But actually it fell far short of meeting the demands which Premier Daniel Johnson had been making since his advent to office in mid-1966. As an overall solution he had asked that the British North America Act be completely scrapped and replaced by a new document which spelled out explicitly the rights of the French-Canadian nation and the "state of Quebec"; more particularly, he had importuned Ottawa to withdraw completely from the income tax and succession duty fields. For his first demand the Pearson government had evinced little enthusiasm; his second it rejected outright.

Why did it finally decide to stop playing for time and abandon its former reluctance to offend Quebec sensibilities? One reason was that the extremist ardor of 1963 had worn off somewhat, and the "great debate" could therefore be conducted on more moderate, rational grounds than had been hitherto possible. But mainly it was because the Pearson government finally succeeded in finding Quebecers it felt could cope with those who thought like Johnson or even Lesage. It is difficult enough at any time to operate a federal system composed of English-speaking Canadians who generally subscribe to the primacy of the national interest and French Canadians who just as generally place Quebec before Confederation. It became doubly difficult in the early sixties when the only voices which found favor in Quebec were those of politicians who seemed to regard the national interest as nonexistent. In the past Duplessis had not constituted a challenge to Canadian federalism because he was confronted at Ottawa by an equally acceptable figure in the person of St. Laurent. But during the Diefenbaker period Quebec's voice in the counsels of the nation was a still, small one, and by the time the Liberals returned to office in 1963 their federal team from Quebec had disintegrated. Furthermore, Ottawa had not the political attraction it used to have because of the dynamic developments that were taking place in Quebec City.

Not surprisingly, then, the dialogue in Quebec on the status of the province within the Confederation had taken place over only a limited portion of the political spectrum. Without intending it, the provincial Liberals of Quebec caused this situation to be altered. By forcing a separation of their party into federal and provincial divisions, which they had done in the spring of 1966, they enabled the Pearson government to adopt a much stronger stand toward Quebec. For there can be little doubt that the philosophy which dominated the founding convention of the Quebec section of the Liberal Federation of Canada in March, 1966, became that of the Pearson administration six months later.

As Mitchell Sharp was to do in September, the Quebec Liberal convention in March had called for a solution which accorded squarely with the constitution. While it favored the setting up of permanent consulting bodies with provincial representation to insure that all the interests of the country would be taken into consideration in the making of commercial, credit, and tariff policies and to provide a means of bringing provincial policies in these matters into harmony with the economic policy of Canada, it insisted that the central government retain control over the regulation of the Canadian economy and especially jurisdiction over money, banking, tariffs, and foreign trade. On the other hand, it called for the general transfer of social security policy to the provinces with corresponding fiscal powers. Yet even here it tempered its proposition by suggesting that the national government seek interprovincial agreement on minimum standards in social legislation.

At the convention the so-called Three Wise Men who had opted for federal politics as members of the Liberal party— Gerard Pelletier, Jean Marchand, and Pierre Elliott Trudeau— almost went out of their way to take issue with the provincial Liberals. In the proposals to give Quebec jurisdiction over banks, manpower placement, and the like, they professed to see evidence of a distinctly isolationist trend. Quebec, they contended, should not isolate itself, but integrate itself in a larger complex where it would find both markets and competition."

Thus for the first time in three or four years Quebec heard politicians of some stature who spoke for the national (i.e. Canadian) as well as the provincial interest. Trudeau in particular recognized that the indrawn attitudes which had recently dominated Quebec thinking were likely to prevent its full development. He suggested that French Canadians could retain their distinctiveness and be masters in their own house, while making a substantial contribution toward the evolution of what the Fathers of Confederation hoped would be a new nationality. And above all, he insisted it could be done by exploiting the terms of the existing constitution more fully rather than resorting to some brand-new constitutional form.

And so the vital question in Canadian federalism has become: Are proposals based on the Trudeau point of view viable in all the provinces? Undoubtedly the degree of acceptability will be determined in part by their merits and demerits. But the question is primarily political and will be decided mainly by the interplay of forces which may not operate on rational grounds. English Canada's attitude toward federalism has always been based on pragmatic rather than theoretical considerations. Only a few of its political practitioners—like Edward Blake and Oliver Mowat, and more recently, George Drew and Angus L. Macdonald—have ever attempted to raise their views on federalism to the level of principle. For the most part English Canada measures the utility of the federal system by the amount of money it provides for provincial purposes and by the extent to which the federal authority takes action to promote the country's economic and general well-being. Thus at the full-dress federal-provincial conference of October, 1966, most premiers of English Canada concentrated on securing additional tax room for their provinces, especially as the projections of future revenues and expenditures indicated that by 1972 the federal government would have an increasing surplus, while the combined provincial-municipal deficit might rise to as much as $2.4 billion. At the same time Premier Robarts suggested that the federal government could abate 60 per cent of the federal personal income tax and one third of the corporation tax without impairing their use as instruments of fiscal policy.

But it is not the Pearson government's refusal to make additional tax room available to the provinces which threatens the viability of its proposals in English Canada. What endangers their acceptability is the abdication of federal authority which is implicit in the new philosophy of federalism. Certainly English Canada has not received with enthusiasm the Pearson administration's self-removal from the field of university education. A little earlier the English-speaking delegates attending the conference of the Liberal Federation of Canada had called for fresh initiative on the part of Ottawa in several fields, especially that of education, and pleas to adhere to the constitution were coolly received; indeed, the conference relegated French Canada altogether to the background. Why, some observers asked, should a degree of provincial autonomy required only by Quebec be imposed on the rest of Canada? Might it not render the federal government incapable of acting effectively in the areas of economic planning and social reform? What would be its effect on the development of Canada as a nation? Would it remove the will and the means to accomplish national objectives and undertake nationwide projects? Worse still, would it make the federal government incapable of meeting Quebec's next set of demands, should they be made, except by a further step toward decentralization? Certainly, all these questions raised disturbing possibilities for English Canada.

In, Quebec the Pearson-Trudeau solution is likely to be even less viable. For excepting the federal withdrawal from intervention in matters under provincial jurisdiction, it seeks to freeze a status quo which almost every provincial politician in Quebec has rejected. At the fourth meeting of the Federal-Provincial Tax Structure Committee in September, 1966, Premier Johnson reiterated Quebec's general contention that there is in Canada a nation of French speech, whose home is in Quebec and which must possess all the instruments required for its development.

As the mainstay of a nation, it wants free rein to make its own decisions affecting the growth of its citizens as human beings (i.e., education, social security, and health in all respects), their economic development (i.e., the forging of any economic and financial tool deemed necessary), their cultural fulfilment (which takes in not only arts and literature, but the French language as well), and the presence abroad of the Quebec community (i.e., relations with certain countries and international organizations).[40]

Like Premier Johnson, Michel Brunet had been demanding for some time that Anglo-Saxon Canadians change their conception of Canada from a federation of ten provinces to a federation of two national collectivities: the English, which concentrates its national loyalty on the Canadian nation state, and the French, which divides its national loyalty between Canada and Quebec.[41] Opposed to this concept is the English-Canadian point of view, as expressed by Kenneth McNaught, of a Canadian nationality which embraces peoples of all cultures, races, and languages, all equal and all owing allegiance to the Canadian state alone.[42] Is he realistic? Or is it only a dream?

At the very least the stereotype of the national government which has been built up in French Canada stands as an imposing obstacle to the acceptance of both McNaught's views and the Pearson-Trudeau solution. During the Duplessis regime the federal authority was made to appear as something which needed to

---

40. *Report of Fourth Meeting of Federal-Provincial Tax Structure Committee,* p. 50.
41. See "The French Canadians' Search for a Fatherland," in Peter Russell, ed., *Nationalism in Canada* (Toronto, 1966), pp. 47–60.
42. See "The National Outlook of English-speaking Canadians," *ibid.,* pp. 61–71.

be resisted if Quebec's rights were to be preserved. More recently, it has been pictured as a hostile institution which stands in the way of achieving the objectives of the Quiet Revolution. The idea that Quebec might realize at least part of its aspirations through the national government has simply been dismissed. Perhaps the Royal Commission on Bilingualism and Biculturalism may suggest some ameliorative measures, but it will be a long time before the present sterotype of the national government can be effectively sublimated.

Nonetheless, cabinet ministers like Maurice Sauvé and M.P.'s like Jean Chrétien have been making strenuous efforts to sell the new brand of federalism in Quebec. Yet it is undoubtedly Jean Marchand who is expected to do the main job of convincing French Canada of its merits. Whether he will be able to do so remains to be seen.

Is there an alternative other than that of separatism or allowing Quebec to be an associate state? There is Professor Smiley's idea of establishing a new equilibrium in Canadian federalism by instituting "a different sharing of legislative powers, revenue sources, and functional responsibilities between Quebec and Ottawa than between the federal government and the other provinces."[43] Certainly a scheme of this kind could give full recognition to the differing concepts of the functions of the national government in Quebec and English Canada and allow the Quebec government to provide more fully for the French-Canadian collectivity. Yet it would have slight chance of success. For if the stronger of the English provinces have insisted on one thing in recent years it is that all the provinces be permitted the right to accept or reject the special treatment which is accorded any one of them.

Federal Canada will likely survive because Quebec cannot presently afford to get out. But the Pearson-Trudeau solution, subjected as it will be to pressure from both English and French Canada, will not survive. Before long there will be a return to the practice of meeting the pressing needs of Canadian federalism through empirical expedients which accord with no recognizable

43. Smiley, "Two Themes of Canadian Federalism," p. 93.

philosophy. The most that can be said is that, if Canadian federalism endures, the French-Canadian fact will have molded it significantly. Because of it, the national government will be cast more in the role of equal partner with the provincial government rather than that of dominant member as in American and Australian federalism.

8

Canadian Education Today

Claude T. Bissell

Nothing is more conspicuous about the early development of Canadian society than the high place given to education, particularly education at an advanced level. The Tory loyalists, who largely determined the nature of society in the Maritimes and Upper Canada, were deeply conscious of the importance of the university tradition. Their motives, it is true, were as much political as educational. Universities, they believed, were institutions embodying principles of order and authority and thereby providing a bulwark against republican ideas. In addition, a nascent society needed lawyers and clergymen, who alone could provide the necessary leadership. The Tory loyalist tradition thus gave one powerful impetus to the establishment of educational institutions. Sectarian zeal provided an even more powerful impetus, so that the young nation could soon boast of quantity, if not of quality. In Ontario alone in 1867 there were no less than seven degree-granting universities. One recalls that in England at the same time there were only four degree-granting universities, Oxford, Cambridge, Durham, and London. The progress on the primary and secondary school levels was somewhat less rapid. But again the comparison with England was favorable. In England there were no publicly supported elementary schools until 1870, and no publicly supported secondary schools until 1902. In Ontario, by acts of 1846 and 1871 respectively, an integrated system of publicly supported elementary and secondary schools was provided for, and there were parallel developments between 1840 and 1890 in New Brunswick, Nova Scotia, and, within the context of a much smaller population, Prince Edward Island. In the West, systems of public education, essentially modeled on those already provided for in eastern Canada, were introduced by legislation within months of the creation of each province. The provincial universities of Manitoba, Saskatchewan, and Alberta are almost as old as the provinces themselves. In French Canada the claim for relative antiquity is even greater, since Laval University traces its origin back to the Jesuit College established at Quebec in 1635, the year before the founding of Harvard. The connection, however, is a tenuous one, and the University of Laval did not emerge until 1850. In the meantime, however, there had been a substantial beginning in the growth of the *Colleges Classiques* which correspond in a general sense to the Faculty of Arts and Sciences in North American universities.

The founding of universities and the development of schools in the early part of the nineteenth century coincided with intense discussions and sometimes bitter controversy. Education, particularly in its relationship to religion and to democratic theory, was a dominating subject in the legislatures and, one presumes, in the homes. By the end of the century, with the emergence of most of the principal universities and the full articulation of the system of primary and secondary school systems, education yields its place to other subjects. Not until the fifties and sixties of this century did it reassume a central place in the public consciousness and on the order paper of debates in both provincial and federal houses of Parliament. The reasons for the revival in Canada are the same as the reasons for revival elsewhere in the industrialized world, namely, the atmosphere of tough technological competitiveness symbolized in the space rivalry, the great increase in leisure time in an increasingly automated society, and the growth of the communications industry with resulting speed and sophistication in the gathering and spread of knowledge. In Canada there is a special problem that has given a clamorous urgency to educational problems. It is the problem that now squarely confronts us—the nature of national unity and even, at times, of national identity. It was concern about these matters that led the federal government, rigidly restricted by the terms of the British North

America Act from active participation in formal education, to
move into areas of informal adult education, with the establishment of the Canadian Broadcasting Corporation in the thirties,
and of the Canada Council in the fifties. Now the problem and
the federal responsibility for its solution have been brought even
more sharply before the nation by the current disquiet with respect to the relationship between the two founding races. The
establishment of the Commission on Bilingualism and Biculturalism is another attempt to move into this area of informal adult
education. That commission is, first of all, a research organization
staffed by members of Canadian universities. In these ways the
federal government has tried to answer the question: How does
one achieve an educational goal if one is denied normal means to
achieve it?

To all these reasons for educational concern has now been
added an even more compelling one, namely, the demonstration
that the Canadian educational system, far from being able to meet
these extraordinary pressures, is not even adequate for normal
growth. The arresting document here is the Second Annual Review of the Economic Council of Canada, entitled *Towards Sustained and Balanced Economic Growth,* which appeared in December, 1965. An essential part of the argument is that Canadian
economic growth as compared with that of the United States has
been slow because of failure to maintain proper acceleration in
education. The most convincing evidence of this is provided by a
table using 1961 figures showing the minimum years of educational attainment for the male labor force in two age groups, one,
25 to 34, and the other, 55 to 64. The percentage of those completing eight years of elementary school in both countries is moving
closer together, but for those completing four years of high school
or possessing a university degree, the relative Canadian position
is weakening. For instance, in the latter category, the percentage
of the Canadian group 55 to 64 is 4.2, and of the group 25 to 34,
6.0. Comparable percentages for the United States are 7.0 and
14.7. In other words, for the older group the percentage by which
the United States exceeds Canada is 67, but for the younger group
who belong to the immediate postwar educational period, the per-

centage is 145. The report concluded its discussion of education and economic growth with five strong recommendations: (1) that there be an immediate considered effort to close the remaining gaps in secondary school facilities, which are seriously inadequate in many sections of the country; (2) that there be a considered attempt to reduce the drop-outs in high school; (3) that there be a deliberate policy of increasing the ratio of attendance at university and postsecondary technical schools; (4) that the facilities for professional education at the postgraduate university level be greatly expanded; and (5) that vigorous efforts be made to improve the quality and methods of education.

The current mood in Canada, then, is one of deep concern for the educational system with respect to both scope and quality. The nation is engaged in a process of self-reassessment, of which the external signs are reports of royal commissions, newspaper editorials, and speeches by politicians. I should like now to examine the reassessment that is going on in three general areas in education, relating current problems to past traditions.

I begin with the problem that attracts most public attention, namely, education as a political and social force. I have already referred to the conservative milieu in which the early Canadian universities emerged. Education was not conceived of as an extension of the eighteenth-century Enlightenment but rather as a means of containing it. It was, as Frank Underhill would suggest, part of "the great refusal," of Canadian reluctance to drink "from the invigorating fountain of eighteenth-century Enlightenment."[1] The toryism of the first few decades of the nineteenth century was, however, gradually modified. The Protestant sects, armed with radical political and social ideas, became stronger and demanded their right to establish institutions of learning. If Canada lacked the kind of intellectual boldness of men like Jefferson and Franklin, it acquired something of a substitute in the earnestness and humanitarianism that accompanied religious dissent. Moreover, the increasingly strong Scottish element in Canadian society brought with it a democratic flavor that ran counter to the tradi-

1. "Some Reflections on the Liberal Tradition in Canada," in *In Search of Canadian Liberalism* (Toronto, 1960), p. 12.

tion of Tory authoritarianism. Sir Daniel Wilson, who came from Edinburgh in 1853 to teach history and English literature at University College in Toronto and succeeded to the presidency of the college in 1887, had this to say about English and Scottish models: "The English universities under their old rigid system turned out a class of educated men with whom too frequently the people found little sympathy; but the Scottish University system . . . has made an *educated people,* and the latter, I conceive, is what Canada desires."[2] But in Canada one looks in vain for such educational radicalism as is contained in these words of Ira Allen who, at the end of the eighteenth century, pledged a large sum to found the University of Vermont: "It is not the rich man that I am calculating to assist, as the poor; the rich may send their sons to what college they please, but the poor have it not in their power. Yet they may have the most promising posterity, and if they can obtain good education may be in time rulers of the land."[3]

There is nothing comparable in Canada to the land-grant discussions and legislation in the United States in the 1860's with its ideology of egalitarianism. The Canadian West was still a vast hinterland awaiting settlement and political organization; the impact of western radicalism did not come till later on. Another factor hindered the development of Canadian educational radicalism: Canada had no substantial private benefactions to universities, certainly none on a scale sufficient to endow an entire university. There did not emerge then the sharp distinction between public and private universities that characterized the American system, with the assumption that the public universities would have a special responsibility for those less favored economically. Although almost all Canadian universities have become public institutions in the sense that they are dependent upon public funds, they have retained a good deal of the ethos of the private institution. There still remains stubbornly entrenched in the Canadian mind the conviction that university education is a precious commodity to be purchased by the individual in accord-

2. *Address Before the Select Committee of the Legislative Assembly* (Toronto, 1860), p. 19.
3. Quoted in Allan Nevins, *The State Universities and Democracy* (Urbana, 1962), pp. 17–18.

ance with shifts in the market; the idea that education is a social resource to be developed for the benefit of the country is now certainly widespead, but it is yet to be embodied in specific legislation.

The Canadian attitude was illustrated in a paper delivered by Principal James of McGill University at a national conference of Canadian universities in 1957. He was comparing and contrasting university financing in Canada and the United States and the United Kingdom, and his concluding point had to do with the relative strength of student aid in the three countries. At British universities over 70 per cent of all students were in receipt of some kind of scholarship or bursary. A comparable figure was more difficult to establish for American universities. James pointed out, however, that about 60 per cent of all university students were enrolled in state universities, where fees were markedly lower than those charged in any Canadian university, and even in the private institutions it was estimated that about 20 per cent of the students were on scholarships carrying at least the cost of tuition. In Canada the contrasting percentage was 14. A great deal has happened since 1957, and the Canadian picture would now be far brighter. But the major increase in student aid has come through student loans instituted in large part by the federal government, reinforced by provincial policy. It is doubtful whether a system of this nature will increase mobility of Canadian society and do much to alter the rigidities of the "vertical mosaic" which has recently been described by John Porter.[4]

In French Canada the inadequacy of student aid reached into the secondary school area. Under the old system the *College Classique* took the student at the age of thirteen and put him through an eight-year curriculum culminating in the award of the baccalaureate, which gave admission to specialized professional courses at the university. These colleges charged fees so that the economic problem for the French-Canadian student began much earlier than for the English-Canadian student. It is true that public high schools existed, but these were not normally the

4. *The Vertical Mosaic* (Toronto, 1965).

channel by which one entered university. Now, with the adoption
in Quebec of the recommendations of the Royal Commission of
Inquiry on Education (called after its chairman, the Parent Commission), this economic barrier will disappear. The Parent Report
has outlined a system of public secondary school education which
in effect eliminates the traditional role of the colleges. In many
respects this is the most far-reaching act in the Quiet Revolution
and should, over a period of time, release the talents and energies
of thousands of young students who were, under the old system,
denied their full expression. The problem of extending secondary
school education in other areas of Canada is still perplexing,
especially in those areas where provincial resources are not adequate for the task.

The second area of reassessment is in that of the administration
and government of educational institutions. In general, the tendency on the primary and secondary school levels, where the provincial responsibilities are complete, has been toward centralization and control by a professional administrative bureaucracy. As
yet there is little strong evidence that this will change greatly,
although sheer physical growth and the abandonment of elaborate centralized examination systems will very likely lead to a
degree of regionalism and decentralization. It is difficult to see
how the power of the professional educator and the administrative bureaucrat can be decreased. In 1960 Frank MacKinnon,
principal of Prince of Wales College in Prince Edward Island,
wrote a provocative book called *The Politics of Education* in
which he urged the setting-up of public trusts of large schools
and units of small schools administered in a way similar to that
now used in universities. A lay board would be in charge of
financial matters and academic affairs would be left to a council
made up of active teachers. The idea had its attractions but
obviously created enormous problems in implementation.

The really vexatious problems in administration and government have appeared at the university level. In the nineteenth
century a tradition of active governmental control of the universities grew up, with no interposing body between the universities
and the raw arena of politics. The University of Toronto Act of

1906 was a turning point, since it established the lay board as essentially a buffer between the government and the universities and gave to the president sole responsibility for recommending academic appointments. That act was a bulwark of freedom as long as governmental concern with the universities was minor. Now, however, the environment has radically changed. The enormous sums required by universities to take care of expansion have attracted a lively and necessary interest on the part of the provincial government. When, as in Ontario, Quebec, and the Maritimes, appropriations must be apportioned between a number of universities, the necessity for centralized control and direction is obvious even to the most eloquent apologist for university autonomy. The problem has now shifted from the individual university to the collective group. How can one provide on a provincial basis some of the same safeguards that were provided in 1906 on an institutional basis? I shall use Ontario as an example of the working-out of this problem, since it is a province with which I am familiar, and it is the province, moreover, where the number of universities (now sixteen) compels an immediate solution. In 1964 the province set up a Department of University Affairs, with a minister and deputy minister and a small group of civil servants, and at the same time reconstituted a lay advisory committee so as to give representation from the academic community. The problem was to make the committee at one and the same time a buffer between the government and the universities, a co-ordinating and policy-making committee with adequate power to enforce its decisions, and a sympathetic and persuasive spokesman for the universities in the annual division of the taxpayer's dollar. The universities believe that they have a chance to work out a pattern that is distinctive and effective. Like the Grants Committee in the United Kingdom, the committee would have an academic bias but, unlike the British pattern, it would have a lay representation strong and authoritative enough to command the attention of government. It would not work in secrecy, as is the tendency of the committee in Britain, but would accept as the very essence of its procedures the principle of open and frequent consultation with the universities. To accomplish these purposes the committee must be intrusted by the government with real power under strong full-time leadership. The policy of consultation demands time and patience and a willingness to see not only that justice is done but that it appears to be done. If these conditions are not fulfilled, the committee may well perish from self-doubt and frustration or at best become a façade behind which the government determines educational policy in isolation.

The emergence of the problem of government relationships on a provincial scale coincided with increasing concern for the nature of university government itself. The lay board had been established, as we have seen, as a means of preserving the independence and the freedom of the university against external pressure. But now doubts began to be expressed whether a board so composed can adequately represent an increasingly complex academic society which has become sharply conscious of its power. In 1964 a group of Canadian scholars, all active in the Canadian Association of University Teachers, published a series of essays under the title *A Place of Liberty,* in which the doubts, misgivings, and active irritations of the academic community with respect to university government were set forth with various degrees of eloquence and decisiveness. This book provided a good deal of the intellectual background for the appointment of a commission to examine the government of Canadian universities. The commissioners, Sir James Duff, retired vice-chancellor of the University of Durham, and Professor Robert Berdahl of San Francisco State College, have recently issued their report, which in essence recommends that the heart of university government be an elected academic senate and that the board, still given large theoretical powers, be a mixed lay and academic body with the former group drawn from various areas of society and not, as in the past, almost exclusively from business and law.

I think it is likely that the principles recommended by the Duff-Berdahl Report will be implemented. In this area Canadian universities have transcended their conservative origins and are more radical than their American counterparts. If one speculates why there is a greater willingness in Canada than in the United States to accept an academic bias in university government, I would put forward the suggestion that Canadian universities have been closer to political power by reason of the movement back and forth between the universities and the civil service. If the Canadian academic has not provided the intellectual or political leadership of his American colleagues, he has perhaps played a more important role behind the scenes.

The final area of reassessment that I should like to consider is that of the quality of education itself. We are here, of course, in a world of imponderables where one must deal largely in opinions. It used to be the opinion espoused by most Canadians and by a good many Americans that Canadian education on all levels outside the postgraduate had a certain austere quality that made it a superior product. Perhaps this idea was generated by the strong religious and moral emphasis that education on all levels has been given in Canada. The American schoolchild begins his day by saluting the flag; the Canadian begins his by invoking his Creator. A good deal of the opposition in Canada to the so-called progressivism in contemporary education is prompted by a latent feeling that it is secular and materialistic in its emphasis, that it emphasizes human happiness and material comfort at the expense of discipline and a realistic acceptance of man's inherent sinfulness. It was believed that the best education is difficult and frequently painful; in Canadian popular educational theory the insistence on academic content is often a means of underscoring moral principles. This moral and religious emphasis prevented the stampede of Canadian education into some of the more exuberant forms of modern educational progressivism, but it also impeded genuine experimentalism. Only recently have we been turning our thoughts toward a re-examination of the curriculum in terms of changes in knowledge and in the light of new insights into the working of the human mind. At the university level we have until recently been reluctant to take seriously the evangelical vogue of general education and have persisted in our preference for the honors course which emphasizes mastery of a limited number of subjects studied historically and systematically.

It is on the postgraduate level that the real qualitative problems appear in the Canadian university. Canada did not participate in a great outburst of postgraduate education like that found in the United States in the 1880's and 1890's for the simple reason that at that time it lacked the resources to embark upon such an expensive undertaking. Concerted efforts in postgraduate education were not made for a number of decades. An indication of the temper of Canadian academic life with respect to postgraduate education was given in a speech by Dean George S. Brett at the National Conference of Canadian Universities in 1934. Brett was at that time dean of the graduate school of Toronto, and he was the most distinguished philosopher in Canadian academic life. In that speech he suggested approvingly that Canadian universities had "looked upon more advanced studies as a luxury, a hobby or even an eccentricity." He concluded his remarks with this statement: "The fundamental question is whether we are in any significant sense graduate-minded or whether in our hearts we think that it is enough to give Canadians a sound education and let them go to Harvard or Columbia or Chicago, to London or Paris or Berlin, for anything more that they want."

The temper has changed since Dean Brett spoke. The chief factor here has been the realization that Canada can no longer depend so heavily upon the importation of staff who have received their postgraduate education elsewhere and that it must more and more rely upon Canadian graduate schools for university teachers. In 1964/65, out of a total enrollment of 178,000, there were 13,000 graduate students. By 1970/71 the estimate is for 32,000 graduate students as against an undergraduate enrollment of 325,000. This involves a growth of graduate enrollment from approximately 7 per cent in 1964/65 to 9 per cent in 1970/71. In the United States at the present time the proportion is almost 13 per cent.

The growth of the graduate schools results also from an increasing awareness of the university responsibility for research. The responsibility of Canadian universities is even greater, relatively speaking, than in the United States, since there is far less research done in business and private corporations in Canada than in the United States. The need for research applies to all areas, particularly to the physical sciences and the medical sciences. In the last field there is an enormous backlog to be made up, since Canadian medicine for many years was content to separate the training of doctors from the active prosecution of research. The nature of the problem in Canada can perhaps be illustrated by a comparison of American and Canadian accomplishments: The differences in magnitude in support of research between the United States and Canada are truly gargantuan. There are, for instance, nine American universities whose annual research expenditure exceeds the total operating budget for all purposes of the University of Toronto, the largest operating budget in Canada. Many of these universities are much smaller than the University of Toronto. A colleague has compared the per capita contributions to mathematical research of the National Science Foundation in Washington and the National Research Council in Ottawa; the ratio on this basis is 50 to 1. A similar comparison holds in nearly every other area. In the vital area of research this country has elected to stand uncertainly on the threshold of the twentieth century.

This reassessment of the basic Canadian educational tradition will inevitably call for a partnership between the federal and provincial governments that hitherto has been denied or only coyly recognized. The problems on the elementary and secondary school level are particularly complex, and they demand the development of interprovincial policy apart from any direct federal involvement. On the level of postsecondary education, however, there is precedent, particularly in the area of research and professional and postgraduate studies, for federal support. This has been accomplished through such intermediary bodies as the Canada Council and the National Research Council and, since 1951, somewhat hesitantly, through a program of per capita grants. That program was, however, conceived of almost absentmindedly, apart from any coherent philosophy of federal assistance. Such a coherent philosophy has now been supplied by the most important of the recent educational commisions, namely, the one on financing higher education in Canada, of which Dean Vincent Bladen of the University of Toronto was the chairman. The commission gives a clear elucidation of federal responsibility and recommends an apportionment of financial aid between the

federal and provincial governments. The report recommends that
in the operating field the federal government should pay 30 per
cent of the costs and in the capital field 50 per cent, and that the
program should be co-ordinated under a federal minister of the
Crown. It is thus proposed that there be a deliberate movement of
the federal government into higher education in accordance with
certain specific procedures. Canada thus parallels developments
in the United States, except that in the United States the movement has been by special *ad hoc* legislation in a variety of areas
rather than by a specific co-ordinated policy. In education, as
elsewhere, Canada realizes that if it is to survive it must accept
state action on a large and comprehensive scale.[5]

To summarize my argument so far: there has been a revival of
interest in education, brought about by general factors that are
common to all industrialized society but given a special urgency
in Canada by reason of its concern with national unity and national identity. The Canadian consciousness of inadequacy to
meet both these general and specific needs has led to a reassessment of its major traditions, and Canada is now in the mood for
radical revision and action. A good deal has been heard recently
about economic nationalism in Canada. There are at least substantial doubts whether this is an acceptable doctrine, whether,
indeed, it will result in the kind of national strength that its
proponents promise. I think a far better case could be made out

5. Since this passage was written there has been a federal-provincial meeting at
which new arrangements were worked out for the sharing of the costs of higher
education. In a speech to the meeting on October 24, 1966, the Prime Minister
of Canada, Lester Pearson, enunciated a new policy. In essence the policy is that
the federal government will make available to the provinces resources estimated
on the basis of one-half of the total operating costs of institutions of higher education. "The federal government's fiscal transfer," said the Prime Minister, "is made
unconditionally, but will assist the provinces to discharge their increased responsibilities in respect of post-secondary education." It is difficult to assess the implications of the policy. By many it was regarded as a withdrawal from a position of
direct federal interest in the universities and an acceptance of the French-Canadian
theory of strict provincial autonomy in all areas of education. But later on in the
speech the Prime Minister categorically declared that the federal government has
a right to support cultural activities: "culture as such should be of interest to every
level of government and the monopoly of none." It has also a right "to assist Canadians in their personal acquisition of knowledge," in short, to award scholarships
and bursaries. And, above all, the federal government has a solemn obligation to
support research without any restriction of subject matter. When, therefore, the
total federal contribution is known, it may well exceed that recommended by the
Bladen Commission.

for intellectual nationalism, of which the core would be the development, even in what might appear to be a disproportionate way, of the nation's educational resources. Such nationalism, for instance, would do a good deal toward dissolving the tensions between the French and the English. The recommendations of the Parent Commission are in the direction of an educational system close to the American and English-Canadian models. In education Quebec is reaching out toward English-speaking Canada, providing an area of common concern where the two races can easily work together. The strengthening of the educational system will assist in solving internal problems of cohesion and will also strengthen relationships to the United States. Canada is currently obsessed with the "brain drain" to the United States. But the movement of Canadian academics and professionals to the United States has always been a characteristic of Canadian society and will continue to be so. There is no need for alarm provided that the movement is not all in one direction, and that there is a compensating movement back to Canada of American academics and professionals. The latter will not occur, however, unless the Canadian educational system is strong enough, particularly in its more advanced stages, to attract good students and first-class scholars and research scientists. The surest way to return to a position of colonial status is to permit the gap in educational facilities between Canada and the United States to widen so that the relative equality that has prevailed in the past is upset. Finally, this intellectual nationalism is needed in order to maintain Canada's position abroad as a nation capable of exercising influence in the councils of the nations. There are limits to Canada's powers of economic influence. Canada cannot forever ride on the crest of a wave of wheat but must rely increasingly for its position and its right to influence world opinion on the authority of its diplomats and civil servants, of its scholars and scientists, and of its artists and writers. It may be that a few of these will develop by reason of the nation's sobriety and devotion to the simple virtues; but it is more likely that such people will emerge only if Canada decides to make its schools and universities the strongest element in its national life.

9

Canadian Social Welfare Policy

Irving J. Goffman

Introduction

When classical and neoclassical economic writers proposed their non-interventionist models, they meant this principle to be applied much of the time, and perhaps most of the time, but certainly not all of the time. This is easily demonstrated by noting the number of exceptions to this rule made by Smith and his successors. They were not unaware of the possible deleterious effects of relying solely on the market system for both production and distribution. As Professor Lionel Robbins has ably argued, the founders of economic liberalism were clearly concerned about the "conditions of the people."[1] Adam Smith, for example, stated that "no society can be flourishing and happy, of which the far greater part of the members are poor and miserable. It is but equity, besides, that they who feed, clothe, and lodge the whole body of the people, should have such a share of the produce of their own labour as to be themselves tolerably well fed, clothed and lodged."[2] And in his *Principles*, Malthus said, "If a country can only be rich by running a successful race for low wages, I should be disposed to say at once, perish such riches."[3] It is worth

1. *The Theory of Economic Policy in English Classical Political Economy* (London, 1961), pp. 68 ff.
2. *An Inquiry into the Nature and Causes of the Wealth of Nations* (Cannan ed.; New York, 1937), p. 79.
3. T. R. Malthus, *Principles of Political Economy* (2nd ed.; London, 1836), p. 214.

noting that Ricardo, annotating Malthus' book, made the entry "So would I" against this sentiment.[4]

It is too naïve, therefore, to regard the classical economists simply as protagonists of the capitalist interest. They were certainly aware of and concerned about the existence of poverty. The transformation, however, from concern to massive policy action did not really occur until after the twentieth century had been well on its way. Perhaps this was due to the fact that the problem areas are expanded as society becomes more affluent, and at the same time, this affluence enables that society to deal with these magnified problems. In any case, it does appear that a positive awareness of the need to complement market decisions by means of massive action traveled from the continent to England and then out to younger members of the English-speaking union. Once it had crossed the various oceans, this social awareness of the plight of the less fortunate members of the society was absorbed into the prevailing cultures and was expressed in policy measures which differed significantly among countries both in terms of quality and quantity. In New Zealand, for example, the acceptance of social responsibilities proceeded at a very rapid pace, while in North America, there appeared to have been a much greater reluctance on the part of legislators to act. In the United States the process began to accelerate during the thirties, but since the mid-forties, and until only very recently, further social action of the types which we shall discuss has hardly occurred. On the other hand, since the end of World War II, the Canadians have been moving very rapidly into all of those areas which most social scientists interpret as characteristic of the modern welfare state. It shall be my basic purpose to trace and analyze some of the developments which have taken place in Canada and to suggest some of the issues, economic and otherwise, which have been raised.

4. D. Ricardo, *Notes on Malthus* (Hollander ed.; Baltimore, 1938), p. 115.

Social Welfare Policy

There is more than one instrument which the state employs in carrying out its welfare policies. Broadly speaking, the various methods can be grouped into three categories, classified by R. M. Titmuss as occupational welfare, fiscal welfare, and social welfare.[5] The first type has to do with the improved condition of workers in their role as workers. While undoubtedly much of this has been due to more enlightened management-labor relations, it has also been influenced by a host of health, safety, and wage regulations emanating from government. The second class, fiscal welfare, includes those welfare policies which operate through taxation, particularly through the income tax. Tariffs, exemptions, and other tax relief measures yield benefits to individuals which are not too different from more direct subsidies. As A. M. Cartter observed, "By reducing the tax liability of a person with dependents, the State is sharing in the responsibility of caring for each taxpayer's family just as certainly as if it were paying cash allowances in each case."[6]

The third category of welfare instruments has been referred to as social welfare and includes all those public welfare activities which operate primarily and directly through the public spending mechanism. The expenditures may be in the form of direct cash transfers to persons, or expenditures for the production and acquisition of goods and services which are then rendered to individuals. Here we are concerned only with this third category of welfare policy, that is, those programs which involve sizable outlays of public funds for the main purpose of obtaining at least some minimum living standard for all Canadians. This choice is not intended to suggest that occupational and fiscal welfare approaches are of no importance. It does appear, however, as if more intensive use has been made of social welfare instruments in

5. *Essays on the Welfare State* (London, 1958), chap. ii.
6. "Income Tax Allowances and the Family in Great Britain," *Population Studies,* VI (March, 1953), 219.

carrying out welfare objectives in recent years. From all indications, there does not seem to be any movement toward new uses of these other two categories, while there has been much evidence of a trend toward increased welfare activities which operate via the spending mechanism.

The Early Years: 1867–1930

From the first days of Confederation, governments in Canada played an active role in the economic affairs of the nation, despite the laissez-faire orientation of the British North America Act. Public participation in the fields of transportation and resource development had been present prior to Confederation. Protectionism began to flourish before the end of the nineteenth century, and Canada has consistently remained a high-tariff nation. The massive area of the country and its birth as a nation in the midst of a rapidly industrializing world lent support to the arguments for state intervention of the type that might be expected to contribute to its economic development. As a rural frontier nation, it could not effectively compete and develop without such intervention, or so it was believed.[7]

On the other hand, as a rural people, so widely dispersed, problems of a social nature were considered to be personal or at most communal, and hence such problems were dealt with at the family or community levels. Such an attitude is not at all surprising in an early frontier state where self-reliance is an accepted and expected trait. It is no wonder that any talk of social legislation was bitterly criticized as being outside the prerogative of government, particularly the central government. While the social policies in Germany under Bismarck and the cries for social reform among Fabians led to some support for social welfare legislation in Canada, especially among new immigrants, generally the environment remained rather hostile toward such a move. One leading Canadian historian has stated, "For most people in the

---

7. For a discussion of economic policy thinking in Canada during the nineteenth century, see Craufurd D. W. Goodwin, *Canadian Economic Thought* (Durham, N. C., 1961), esp. chap. ii.

colonies, good government was little government—simple, inexpensive and non-interfering government."[8]

This attitude was consistent with the constitutional provisions for welfare functions as set out in the British North America Act. While the federal authorities were assigned the major state functions of the day, public welfare was left to provincial governments, to do with as they wished. Anything which was to be done in the welfare field by the provinces was not mandatory but only permissive. "The fathers of Confederation clearly thought they were assigning the provinces the unimportant and inexpensive functions of government, among which education, hospitals, charities, and municipal institutions were then reasonably numbered."[9] In fact, the terms health and welfare do not even appear in the relevant sections of the constitution (Sections 91 and 92 of the British North America Act), but other provisions implied that such functions were the responsibility of the provinces. The Royal Commission on Dominion-Provincial Relations affirmed this in 1940: "In general, provincial jurisdiction over social welfare and hence responsibility for policy and finance, has been deemed a basic feature of the Act, and any Dominion jurisdiction merely an exception to the general rule of provincial responsibility."[10]

While the provinces and local communities rendered some assistance to the poor, in general poverty was regarded as a symptom of laziness and weakness, and public aid was often opposed on the grounds that it "would remove opportunities for the exercise of moral virtues such as parental devotion, filial piety, and Christian benevolence, and might also have the unfortunate result of discouraging private alms-giving."[11] The problems of the aged, widowed, sick, and unemployed were thought to be better left to the religious and private sectors.

8. D. G. Creighton, *British North America Act at Confederation,* Royal Commission on Dominion-Provincial Relations, 1939 (Ottawa, 1963), p. 70.

9. Elisabeth Wallace, "The Origin of the Social Welfare State in Canada, 1867–1900," *Canadian Journal of Economics and Political Science,* XVI (Aug., 1950), 384.

10. *Report* (Ottawa, 1940), Book II, p. 15. This commission will be referred to as Rowell-Sirois.

11. Wallace, "Origin of the Social Welfare State in Canada," p. 387.

An application of this belief was the enactment of the Children's Protection Acts of Ontario in 1893, under which the province granted the major responsibility for child protection to private Children's Aid Societies. This function was to be administered and financed primarily by the private sector. Such an arrangement was prevalent in all of the English-speaking provinces. Since these were settled primarily by Anglo-Saxon Protestants, John S. Morgan has argued that their laissez-faire attitude toward the needy is a reflection of the morality of self-dependence inherent in their Protestant ethic.[12] In Catholic Quebec, on the other hand, a much different attitude toward social justice and charity was in evidence, reflecting the doctrine of the prevalent church. In general, most of the social programs which might be dealt with through governmental action or private secular agencies were handled by church-related institutions.[13] Thus, social welfare expenditures were objectionable to Protestant social morality and conflicted with existing Catholic social institutions.

But the problems and their magnitudes were in the process of change. With industrialization, mass immigration and urbanization, the old social relationships of the frontier state were beginning to break down. The degree of independence possible in an agrarian society oriented toward self-sufficiency could not be expected to persist in an urban-industrial society. As the shift from rural to urban living accelerated, and as the new immigrants settled in the cities, social problems related to city as contrasted with country living appeared on the scene. Not only was the city far less personal in its social relationships, but also in this new environment, the individual depended for his livelihood on the availability of employment. No longer could he be as certain of a sufficient food supply for his family. If general economic conditions were satisfactory, then urban-industrial living had many

12. "Social Welfare Services in Canada," in Michael Oliver, ed., *Social Purpose for Canada* (Toronto, 1961), p. 134. This relationship between Protestantism and laissez faire was clearly expounded by Max Weber in his *The Protestant Ethic and the Spirit of Capitalism,* trans. Talcott Parsons (New York, 1956).

13. For a statement of the position of Quebec, see Esdras Minville, *Labour Legislation and Social Services in the Province of Quebec,* Royal Commission on Dominion-Provincial Relations (Ottawa, 1939), p. 45.

material benefits; but as activity declined, as it did at least three times between Confederation and the turn of the century (1873–79, 1884–87, 1893–96), then urban-industrial workers were subjected to unemployment and serious economic hardship. This describes the plight of many of the inhabitants of Canada before 1900, particularly the new immigrants. Urban poverty, though a relatively new Canadian problem then, was beginning to exert itself.

As had been the case in Great Britain and the United States (both of which had been urbanized and industrialized before Canada), the Industrial Revolution brought on new public issues and new attitudes. Motivated by concern for the social problems of the industrial worker, but no less motivated by his potential voting strength, attempts were made to adopt federal legislation to improve his lot. Several times during the 1880's, for example, factory bills were introduced in Parliament but failed to pass or else were declared *ultra vires* by the courts.[14] Nevertheless, they did indicate a degree of concern and led to much public discussion. In 1889, the Royal Commission on the Relations of Labor and Capital was appointed, and it is believed that its report contains the first official discussion in any country of the problems of federal participation in the social welfare field.[15] In general, it recommended greater federal participation, though nothing came of this.

At the turn of the century, then, problems related to urban poverty were on the rise, yet federal action was limited by the constitution and by the traditional reliance on local authorities. At the same time, municipal governments, which were explicitly delegated the responsibility of caring for their "poor and destitute," or at least were expected to do so, found themselves increasingly hard put, financially and otherwise, to deal with the growing complex social problems of the time. As a result, the provinces themselves undertook some of the social welfare functions

14. Eugene Forsey, "A Note on the Dominion Factory Bills of the 1880's," *Canadian Journal of Economics and Political Science*, XIII, (Nov., 1947), 580–585.
15. A. H. Birch, *Federalism, Finance and Social Legislation* (Oxford, 1955), p. 179.

during the first two decades of the twentieth century. In 1914, workmen's compensation legislation was adopted in Ontario and subsequently in all the provinces. In 1916, Manitoba adopted a Mothers' Allowance Act which provided public assistance to families deprived of a breadwinner. This, too, was later enacted by the rest of the provincial legislatures. Similarly, other indigent groups were granted provincial relief under public assistance schemes.[16]

Despite the constitutional and other restrictions originally imposed on the extension of federal activity in the welfare field, subsequently that level of government was able to overcome these objections, at least in certain areas. The debates over old-age pensions in the British elections of 1893 and the passage of such a measure in New Zealand in 1898 led to much public discussion in Canada over such social policies.[17] But opposition to policies of this sort was still strong. One opponent wrote in 1907: "No measure could be more thoroughly demagogic than this [British scheme] of Old Age pensions. . . . universal suffrage, and female suffrage will probably follow. Then where will . . . [the] Empire be?"[18] On the other hand, Prime Minister Sir Wilfrid Laurier was somewhat favorably disposed toward pensions but doubted whether they were within the powers of the federal government.[19] However, action was taken by his government with the passage of the Annuities Act in 1908 under which the government made pensions available on a voluntary basis which were somewhat cheaper than those provided by private insurance companies. But as one writer has stated, "it was viewed as a species of insurance

16. Not much study has been carried out on the development of public welfare services in the various provinces. In his study for the Rowell-Sirois Commission (cited in n. 13, above), Minville provides some background for Quebec. For the development in Nova Scotia, see George F. Davidson, *Report on Public Welfare Services, Royal Commission on Development and Rehabilitation* (Halifax, 1944). Also, R. B. Splane, *Social Welfare in Ontario 1791–1893* (Toronto, 1965).

17. For example, during the period 1885 to 1910, *Queen's Quarterly* continually featured articles by leading Canadian thinkers on the role of the state in the social welfare field.

18. Quoted in Elisabeth Wallace, "Old Age Security in Canada: Changing Attitudes," *Canadian Journal of Economics and Political Science*, XVIII (May, 1952), 126.

19. Canada, *House of Commons Debates*, 1906/7, pp. 3374–3396.

and a means of promoting thrift rather than as a type of social legislation or state aid."[20]

The issue of old-age pensions waned during the second decade of the twentieth century, but in 1919 it was included in the recommendations of the Royal Commission on Industrial Relations and was supported by the Liberal party in its election platform. These stands rekindled public interest in such a scheme so that by 1920, federal participation in old-age insurance was a live issue once again.

The same was true of federal participation in the area of health care. The 1919 Liberal party platform also contained a reference to the desirability of a national health insurance scheme, and while such a scheme was not to be seriously considered until almost thirty years later, the question of federal participation in such a plan was now out in the open. Perhaps even more significant, a federal Department of Health was established in 1919 to look after problems of health which were international and inter-provincial in scope, especially the health of new immigrants. This new department gave formal recognition to a federal role in health matters.

Throughout the twenties there occurred further developments which increased the Dominion government's participation in the social welfare area. After earlier rejections of old-age pensions by the Canadian Senate, legislation in 1927 provided for federal grants to those provinces which would enact a provincial non-contributory old-age pension plan.[21] This act was the first *significant* social welfare program adopted by the federal government; and the technique involved, namely to induce the provinces through grants to adopt legislation, was to set the pattern for the subsequent development of other welfare programs.

In addition to old-age pensions, the Dominion government in the twenties authorized grants to co-operating provinces for mothers' allowances and for the improvement of public health

20. Wallace, "Old Age Security in Canada: Changing Attitudes," p. 127.
21. J. A. Maxwell, *Federal Subsidies to the Provincial Governments in Canada* (Cambridge, Mass., 1937), pp. 228–230

standards. Also in 1928 it authorized the establishment of a select committee to investigate health and unemployment insurance. By 1930 it was quite clear that all levels of government in Canada could become involved in social welfare expenditure, and if it were deemed necessary, would further commit themselves to social legislation.

The Great Depression

The worldwide depression of the thirties was particularly severe in Canada. The collapse of world export prices as well as the increased trend toward economic isolationism had a serious impact on the nation's trade position, and in particular the Canadian agricultural, newsprint, and fishing industries. The result was a sharp decline in income from abroad for a nation which had earned over one-third of its national income in that sector. Within four years following 1929, GNP in real terms declined from $9,061 million to $6,359 million, or by about one-third.[22] Unemployment rose from 116,000, or 2.9 per cent of the labor force, to 826,000, or 19.3 per cent of the labor force.[23] The situation called for far more massive government action than had ever before been contemplated, not only in the monetary-fiscal fields, but also in that of public welfare. The traditional reliance on municipal and community ventures could hardly suffice, and the involvement of the federal government was a certainty.

Because of the unequal incidence of the depression, large interregional transfers of income were called for. On their own, the individual provinces, particularly the hard-hit western and Maritime provinces, were not fiscally capable of alleviating the economic hardships.[24] The functions which were originally conceived of as being "minor and inexpensive" and therefore provincial, now took on very large proportions, just at the time when the provinces were hard pressed for funds. There were often large

22. Dominion Bureau of Statistics, *National Accounts-Income and Expenditures 1926–56*, Table 5.
23. *Ibid.*, Appendix Table II.
24. See, e.g., E. J. Hanson, "Public Finance in Alberta since 1935," *Canadian Journal of Economics and Political Science*, XVIII (Aug., 1952), 322–335.

budgetary deficits even before anything had been provided for relief. In not one province in any one year following 1930 did the municipal-provincial revenues left over after provision for ordinary services meet the total cost of relief. "The amount of borrowing necessary to pay for the whole of the remaining requirements would have bankrupted most of the provinces and municipalities in the country."[25]

But the constitutional question of federal participation in welfare activities still loomed large. In order to adhere to the original jurisdictional division of functions, at least in form, the federal government assisted the provinces and municipalities by means of "temporary" arrangements. Between 1930 and 1940 eleven such temporary emergency acts were passed.[26] There was aid for relief works, single homeless men, unemployed farm workers, western farmers, youth, and other groups. In fact, federal grants for relief amounted to over $393 million during the decade—over 40 per cent of total relief expenditures.[27] The provinces contributed another 40 per cent, while the municipalities paid the rest. This tripartite scheme for relief to the unemployed came to an end in March, 1941, when wartime conditions virtually eliminated the problem of severe national economic distress.

As has been stated, the provinces just about matched the federal contributions (though this sometimes required short-term federal loans) and in addition administered many of the new relief programs. Where municipalities went bankrupt, provincial authorities often handled the traditional forms of direct relief as well as the new ventures. But the increasing cost of relief during the thirties and the growing debt charges as a result of the rapid provincial debt accumulation reduced considerably the revenue remaining for other governmental functions. Education and road maintenance bore much of the brunt. In fact, per capita expenditures on education declined by about 16 per cent so that by 1937

25. Rowell-Sirois *Report,* Book I, p. 163.
26. H. M. Cassidy, *Social Security and Reconstruction in Canada* (Toronto, 1943), p. 29.
27. From 1931 to 1937 total relief expenditures amounted to $813 million. A. E. Grauer, *Public Assistance and Social Insurance,* Royal Commission on Dominion-Provincial Relations (Ottawa, 1939), p. 15.

total expenditures on education had declined to the level of 1926. Of course, price declines ameliorated this somewhat, but even in real terms, the sums devoted to education were insufficient, and in several western provinces, they were too low to maintain acceptable standards.[28]

Even though the first western reaction to the Great Depression was simply to extend a helping hand to those who were in need, this period did have some deep and profound effects upon society. It was not long before Canadians, along with others, began to question the adequacy of a laissez-faire capitalist state with its apparent antisocial welfare attitudes. The somewhat superficial sense of order of communism, fascism, and other forms of authoritarianism was enormously attractive at a time when much of the free world was in economic chaos. The acceptance by some of assorted new schemes such as Technocracy, Social Credit, and the Townsend Plan indicates the deep and widespread dissatisfaction with the traditional approaches to economic and social organization in Great Britain, Canada, and the United States. It began to become evident that either a major reconstruction of the institutions and arrangements of society would have to be carried out or the individualistic system completely abandoned.

In both Great Britain and the United States, the recognition of and official reaction to this fundamental social issue were much more rapid than in Canada. Not only did the thirties lead to massive increases in public welfare spending, but in these two countries it also gave rise to the complete reorganization of welfare services into integrated systems of social insurance. The basic frameworks were laid down in the British Unemployment Assistance Act of 1934 and the American Social Security Act of 1935. In Canada, however, while the depression did lead to much more public welfare spending, there was no accompanying change in the *basic* pattern of welfare services. These remained relief-oriented and basically provincial in jurisdiction. This is not meant to imply that the government of Canada was oblivious to the need for radical social legislation. Indeed, the Conservative govern-

28. Rowell-Sirois *Report*, Book I, p. 175.

ment under Bennett announced some very far-reaching proposals in 1935. In describing his "New Deal" platform, Bennett publicly admitted that "it means the end of *laissez-faire*."[29] But the mandate that he was seeking was not granted by the Canadian people. A multiplicity of factors was responsible for his Conservative Party's defeat in 1935, not the least of which was the growth of "third" parties. As one writer has observed,

this defeat does not prove that the New Deal was rejected by the great majority of the electorate, for the peculiarities of the party system have to be taken into account. . . . His legislation was radical enough to frighten his supporters among the business classes . . . but not radical enough to attract voters who favored the dissident parties.[30]

The victorious King government proceeded very slowly and most cautiously. It was not at all willing to take over the responsibility for relief, but preferred to rely upon the traditional device of granting aid to the provinces despite the almost continuous intergovernmental haggling which accompanies such a scheme. As a result, there was no enactment of social legislation which resembled the British or American development. Indeed, it must be noted that not until 1944, with the creation of the Department of National Health and Welfare, did the federal government even acknowledge formally that welfare was a federal responsibility. The lack of action was made up in part, however, by a great deal of discussion and ferment about social welfare issues.

World War II and Its Aftermath

Though the immediate problem of unemployment and relief was considerably reduced soon after the outbreak of hostilities in 1939, considerable dissatisfaction was expressed over the haphazard way in which social welfare services had been developed, and particularly their continued emphasis upon a relief concept rather than social insurance. Criticism of the system mounted throughout the forties and widespread support for a complete revision was in evidence. Perhaps the most outspoken critic was H. M.

29. *Round Table*, XXV (1935), 392.
30. Birch, *Federalism, Finance and Social Legislation*, p. 186.

Cassidy, dean of Canadian social work.[31] Nor were the social workers the only ones anxious for major policy changes. From very early in the war, there was much speculation among economists and others concerning the extent of unemployment which would ensue after the defeat of the Axis powers. Spurred on by the framework provided by John Maynard Keynes in his *General Theory*,[32] a great many knowledgeable Canadians, particularly among those in policy-influencing positions, urged the adoption of various counter-cyclical instruments. In 1940 the Unemployment Insurance Act was passed as well as the necessary constitutional amendment, replacing much of the federal and provincial unemployment assistance program. By 1944, a national housing policy was adopted which was to provide relatively low rates for financing construction in order to spur investment in this area. Similarly, public investment, fiscal policy, and monetary policy were all expected to operate in the manner which would contribute to the improvement and stabilization of employment.[33] This objective was most explicitly and undeniably stated in the declaration on employment policy in the White Paper on Employment and Income of April, 1945, which showed clearly the influence of Keynesian thought.

This same influence was observable at the Dominion-Provincial Conference of 1945. This conference was devoted to several of the leading domestic issues in Canada, some of which had been the subject of debate since Confederation. In support of its position for an extension of social welfare activities, the federal representatives argued:

During the war years we have been obligated to keep this consumer purchasing power under control as far as possible. But as scarcities disappear and wartime demand falls away, it becomes essential to encourage a freer use of consumer purchasing power in order to take up the slack that will otherwise develop. It is in this connection—namely, the maintenance of a high degree of consumer purchasing power—that large-scale social security measures can and do play an important role.

31. Cassidy, *Social Security and Reconstruction in Canada*.
32. *The General Theory of Employment, Interest and Money* (London, 1936).
33. T. N. Brewis *et al.*, *Canadian Economic Policy* (Toronto, 1961), chap. vii.

A significant volume of social security payments, flowing into the consumer spending stream, will stabilize the economy of the country as a whole and work against a fall in the national income. Social security payments, therefore, become, in these circumstances, a powerful weapon with which to ward off general economic depression.[34]

Among the major questions on the agenda were tax agreements, public investment, and social welfare, and in all cases the federal government presented very elaborate proposals. Unfortunately, all of these were presented as if they were completely interrelated so that if the provinces chose to reject any one part, they would in effect reject the whole. This was particularly true of the tax-rental agreements which the federal government was most anxious to negotiate and which very quickly became the main subject of debate. As soon as it became evident that some of the provinces (especially Ontario and Quebec) were unhappy over these tax proposals and were unwilling to enter into the proposed agreement, the conference collapsed. The social welfare proposals did not, therefore, receive serious consideration. Nevertheless, this Dominion-Provincial Conference is an important landmark in the historical development of social welfare policy in Canada.

For the first time, a comprehensive and integrated plan which included national health insurance, universal old-age pensions, and unemployment assistance was proposed by the Dominion. Unfortunately, it was presented on a "take-it-or-leave-it" basis which aroused the ire of the two largest provinces, Ontario and Quebec. The former objected to the proposed financing arrangements which would have required increased taxation at both the federal and provincial levels, while the latter resented the federal intrusion in an area which was traditionally and constitutionally provincial. Without the support of these two provinces, which together comprised more than half the population of Canada, no program could be considered national in any meaningful sense.[35] Despite its failure, this conference did indicate that the prevailing

34. *Proposals of the Government of Canada,* Dominion-Provincial Conference on Reconstruction (Ottawa, Aug., 1945), pp. 27–28.

35. The positions of the various provinces are contained in *Dominion and Provincial Submissions and Plenary Conference Discussions,* Dominion-Provincial Conference on Reconstruction, 1945 (Ottawa, 1946).

view in Canada concerning the state's role in welfare matters had been permanently changed by the depression and the war. What had previously been objectionable philosophically and entertained only reluctantly in the face of emergencies was now regarded as a desirable long-run course of action. Such a conclusion has been supported by subsequent developments, particularly in three major social welfare areas—family allowances, old-age pensions, and health care.

Family allowances. Whatever its original purposes, disregarding any other reasons for its existence, the most important rationalization for family or children's allowances is that the size of the family has a direct bearing upon the economic needs of the family.[36] Not only are children usually born to families of *younger* adults at a time in their lives when incomes tend to be low, but an unusually large number of children are born to families which are poor. This is not the place to trace the order of causality, but undeniably each additional child places additional demands on family income, and there is no significant connection between the number of dependent children and the family income, at least not in an industrial environment. In a market system, wages are related to productivity in recognition of one's contributions to the nation's material wealth. While such a distributive system is defensible on grounds of efficiency, it does present a problem in that no recognition is granted to the contribution made by parents in rearing a generation of future citizens. Thus it has been recognized for some time that a dilemma exists between the industrially determined wage and the needs of the varying sizes of families. It is not at all surprising, therefore, that Lord Beveridge considered children's allowances an essential component of his social security proposals for Britain, or that L. C. Marsh considered such allowances the "key to consistency" in his report to the Canadian government on social security.[37]

These arguments for family allowances were well-grounded.

36. J. C. Vadakin, *Family Allowances, An Analysis of Their Development and Implications* (Coral Gables, Fla., 1958).
37. *Report on Social Security for Canada* (Ottawa, 1943).

Unlike an agrarian society, where children are often an important economic asset, in advanced industrial societies they often result in heavy economic burdens to their parents. They are usually required to attend school until well into their teens, so that they are not in a position to pay their own way; and even if they are permitted to work, children are not as likely to fit readily into industry as they might into agriculture. This dilemma has long been recognized and is reflected in child assistance programs as well as in the dependent exemptions in the personal income tax laws. But such measures were not by themselves enough to solve the problem. Child assistance benefits are normally restricted to families without a normal breadwinner, while income tax exemptions are of real benefit only to those with high taxable incomes. Something more was needed to give the economy the boost it needed. Indeed, it was the alleged economic aspects which gave a sense of urgency to the passage of this program. Presumably family allowances would redistribute income in favor of those who would consume rather than save and therefore would contribute to aggregate demand. Prime Minister Mackenzie King expressed this succinctly when he first introduced the legislation:

. . . the expenditure of money paid out for family allowances will create a demand for goods and, thereby a demand for labour for the production of those things that are in daily use in all parts of the country. The importance of the stimulus to employment cannot, I think, be too greatly emphasized. The one supreme object of all our work of reconstruction is to prevent the possibility of lack of employment by seeing that we have maximum production and, as a consequence, a large national income. . . . this instrument will help prevent anything like the depressions that have followed in previous periods in the wake of wars.[38]

Accordingly, the act passed in 1944 provided that a monthly allowance be paid to all children under sixteen, irrespective of need. The benefit at the present varies from $6.00 to $8.00, depending on age. In fiscal 1965, family allowance expenditures amounted to almost $550 million or a little more than 25 per cent of total federal expenditures for security. The average annual

38. Canada, *House of Commons Debates, 1944,* p. 5333.

family allowance in March, 1965, was $200.16 per family and $80.64 per child. Over 2.7 million families with some 6.8 million children received these allowances.[39] To the extent that many needy families contain a greater than average number of children, these allowances constitute a significant part of the family's cash income. Conversely, to small families with higher incomes, the allowances are likely to be less relevant. One study, for example, showed that family allowances amounted to 12.8 per cent of net income for families of five or more children and less than 2.2 per cent for one-child families in 1948, and while these benefits accounted for 11.0 per cent of the income for families receiving less than $1,500 a year, they amounted only to 3.1 per cent for those families earning $4,000 or more. On the basis of these figures and information on the geographical distribution of family allowances, J. W. Willard has argued that this family allowance system has had measurable income redistributive effects.[40]

Old-age security. Just as the family allowance program attempts to deal with income inadequacies by identifying and associating itself with vital and clearly observable causal characteristics of poverty, in the same way programs which provide support for the aged members of a population are a proper response to a universally recognizable social need. There is not a single important study of the characteristics of poor families which fails to identify old age as a leading one. While local and provincial old-age welfare programs had been adopted in Canada on and off since Confederation, a national pension plan which provided income to those above the age of seventy was only inaugurated in 1927, and then with great difficulty.

After sporadic debate for a quarter of a century, the old-age pension became a central issue during the 1926 legislative session. Depending upon the support of Progressive and Labour party members for his continuance in office, King proposed a program to the House. The opposition was lively, and their arguments

39. Canadian Tax Foundation, *The National Finances, 1965–66* (Toronto, 1965), p. 111.

40. "Some Aspects of Family Allowances and Income Redistribution in Canada," *Public Policy*, V (1954), 225, 227.

ranged from the issue of constitutionality to an expressed concern over the future of poorhouses if old-age pensions were to enable people to stay out of them.[41] Though finally passed by the House, it was defeated in the Senate and contributed to the fall of the government. King's re-election, however, assured the enactment of the Old-Age Pension Act in 1927. Under the act the federal government would grant one-half of the cost of such pensions to all Canadians over seventy years of age. The scheme provided a maximum benefit of $20 a month and was applicable only to those who received less than $125 income per *year,* and by modern standards, it was hardly a liberal program. But it was the first major welfare program passed by the federal government, and for this reason it is most significant.

The inadequacy of the pension (even in 1927 terms), the strictness of the means test, and the high eligibility age led to continuous pressure for a review of the pension plan; but resistance by the provinces and the high levels of wartime and postwar employment and incomes resulted in the postponement of further action until the early fifties. By then the pressures from trade unions and the experiences of other countries persuaded politicians of all parties of the desirability of greater income security for the aged, and the provinces unanimously agreed. Within a short time during 1951, a constitutional amendment was adopted which permitted direct federal action in this area, and by December, 1951, the Old-Age Security Act had been enacted. The act provided a flat benefit, presently seventy-five dollars a month, to all Canadian residents aged seventy and over as a matter of right. By 1970 the eligible age will be reduced to sixty-five, and the benefits will be increased to reflect price level changes.

This shift in the structure of the old-age security system from one limited to those who could satisfy certain criteria to the presumption that need is *likely* to exist among all the nation's senior citizens was widely acclaimed in Canada. First of all, it relieved the recipients of embarrassment and humiliation and of the necessity of submitting to an examination of their private

41. Canada, *House of Commons Debates, 1926,* II, 1950–1953 and 1979.

affairs. Second, the non-direct contributory nature of the plan meant that benefits were not restricted to certain groups. Since coverage has always been universal, none of the problems of phasing-in or lack of coverage have arisen as they have in the United States. Third, and perhaps most important, such a program reflected the widespread belief that society was responsible for the plight of its older citizens not because they contributed to a trust fund while they worked but simply because they contributed to society.

This is not to be interpreted to mean that there are no pitfalls involved in a non-contributory universal scheme. On the contrary, a real problem may result if citizens begin to regard such a program as being gratuitous. Politicians would then be under constant pressure to increase the benefits. This danger led Edwin Witte to reject universal flat-rate pensions and to conclude: "No matter how high the age and how low the pensions at the outset, it can be taken for granted that ere long the minimum age will be reduced and the pension increased; and this is apt to be repeated many times."[42] In addition, because such a scheme is financed out of current revenues only, there is no attempt to recognize that the shifting demographic composition of a population will result in fluctuating demands upon the public purse. Instead of anticipating this through the establishment of special reserves, costs are left to be handled as they arise. There can be no assurance whatever that economic activity will fluctuate each year in the same way as the outpayments for pensions or allowances, so that the tax burden required will in fact be a fluctuating one.

But, what is more serious, the fact that benefits from such programs depend completely upon current income may jeopardize their existence, particularly in the case of old-age pensions. If the outpayments grow too large, then the tax burden may be regarded as objectionable by the younger workers who must pay for them. There is, therefore, a possibility that they will not be willing to carry such a burden and that the promised pensions may not be forthcoming indefinitely.

42. Robert J. Lampman, ed., *Social Security Perspectives: Essays by Edwin E. Witte* (Madison, Wisc., 1962), p. 146.

Recognizing some of these difficulties and mindful of the demands for higher benefits, particularly from those accustomed to higher levels of living, a strong movement began in the last years of the fifties for a supplemental contributory wage related portable pension system, which culminated in the enactment of the Canada Pension Plan in April, 1965. Though not unlike Old-Age and Survivors Insurance in the United States in format, there are some features which are different. In the first place, this pension is not to replace the Old-Age Security Benefits, which are universal; instead, it is supplemental. In the second place, the benefits are tied to a cost-of-living index so that their values are not as likely to be eroded by inflationary tendencies. In the third place, the anticipated reserves (over $2 billion by 1975) are to be made available to the provinces in proportion to amounts paid into the fund by contributors in each province. These provincial borrowings from the fund are not restricted as to use and will be interest-bearing. It should be noted that Quebec is not included in this total program, but instead has established an identical plan of its own.

Hospital and medical benefits. We turn now to the third and final policy area which is indicative of the trend of social welfare developments in Canada. The attitudes and experiences of Canada and the United States are often considered to be similar, and most often this is quite valid; but in the realm of health and medicine, a very clear difference has been emerging. While Americans have for years been debating the merits of medicare—that is, hospital services for the *aged*—Canada adopted a national hospital insurance plan for all Canadians *regardless of age* in 1958. Interestingly enough, though the doctors' strike in Saskatchewan of some years back was fully publicized, the hospital insurance program has received very scant attention in the United States. Incidentally, that strike had nothing to do with the national scheme, but was a result of the enactment of a provincial and all-inclusive socialized health scheme. The plan which was adopted was, however, the subject of much public discussion in Canada for many years and had the blessings of every important professional health association, including the Canadian Medical

Association. Included in the Liberal party's platform in 1919 and the CCF's platform since that party's inception in 1932, the enactment of comprehensive health care was impeded by the lack of federal jurisdiction in this area, although some provincial prepayment plans did exist even prior to the twenties. In 1941, a report on national health deficiencies served to stimulate public and private investigations into the matter of health insurance, and by the mid-forties, every major health-related professional organization had endorsed the principle of public comprehensive health insurance. Indeed, as early as 1914, the president of the Canadian Medical Association suggested the study of health insurance, and after many years of considering the problems involved, the council of the association in 1943 issued a precedent-shattering statement approving unequivocally the adoption of a public insurance program.[43]

At least for the past twenty years, the issue in Canada has thus not been whether there should be some type of publicly financed health scheme, but rather how the national government could become involved in an area which was unquestionably of provincial jurisdiction.[44] The issue was resolved in 1958 by the adoption of a program whereby the federal government contributes approximately 50 per cent of the cost of a provincial hospital insurance plan.[45] Provinces were free to enact a co-operating plan whenever they wished and could finance their half in any manner. The main condition was that the provincial plan had to extend its coverage to all residents (though phasing-in for some groups such as the self-employed was permitted). By 1961 all of the provinces and territories had adopted satisfactory schemes,

---

43. For an illuminating discussion of the CMA's views on social and political issues, see M. G. Taylor, "The Role of the Medical Profession in the Formulation and Execution of Public Policy," *Canadian Journal of Economic and Political Science*, XXVI (Feb., 1960), 108–127.

44. See Irving J. Goffman, "The Political History of National Hospital Insurance in Canada," *Journal of Commonwealth Political Studies*, III (July, 1965), 136–147.

45. Specifically, the amount granted by the federal government is derived as follows: 25 per cent of per capita hospital costs in Canada as a whole, plus 25 per cent of per capita costs in the particular province, multiplied by the number of insured people in the provinces.

and by 1966 hospital insurance coverage had been extended to better than 95 per cent of the population.

The hospital program is not without weaknesses, and criticism has been abundant since its inception. But the most articulate criticism was that a hospital scheme was only a partial solution to the health problem. Pressure for further extensions thus mounted throughout the fifties. Finally, a royal commission was established in 1961 for the purpose of investigating fully the health sphere. It is important to note that this body was set up and its composition determined by the Conservative party of Canada when it was in power. The members of the commission consisted of two physicians, one dentist, and one nurse (all having served as heads of their respective professional associations), a Supreme Court justice, a leading Canadian economist, and a prominent financier. After several years of hearings and volumes of studies, the commission published its recommendations in 1964,[46] and these were far more inclusive than most people had expected, especially since the commission was often criticized as being overly conservative in its composition. It is not at all possible to do justice to the commission's report in a summary sentence, but among its proposals was the establishment of a federal grant system for the construction of new medical schools and hospitals, extension of national hospital insurance to mental hospitalization and nursing homes, and a complete national medical insurance scheme, subsidized by the federal government, to be instituted by 1971. The response to this report has been quite varied, but among the critics, the major issue has not been the question of the desirability of a publicly sponsored medical program, but the speed with which this program is to be instituted and the proposed financing arrangements. Even the Canadian Medical Association did not oppose the fundamental principles involved, although this group has had some important points to make concerning some of the details. One cannot help but observe the very basic differences in the official attitudes toward such proposals of the Canadian and American medical communities.

46. *Royal Commission on Health Services,* Vol. I (Ottawa, 1964).

In the discussion of the major facets of contemporary Canadian social welfare policy and how it has evolved, it has been shown that attitudes toward collective responsibility have exhibited significant changes during Canada's first century and that the resulting legislative responses have established a comprehensive but still developing system of social security. While its comprehensiveness may not be as full as those systems existing in Western Europe, Canada is undoubtedly further along the road to modern welfare statism than is its southern neighbor. It is not our purpose here to evaluate the philosophical implications of this trend, but in the remainder of this essay to make some suggestions concerning the major issues surrounding social welfare policy in Canada as that nation enters its second century.

Social Welfare Policy: The Major Issues

It has not been uncommon to hear condemnation of the trends in Canadian welfare activities on the grounds that they are to blame for the growing national debt, the balance-of-payments problem, the sluggish performance of the economy, inflation, the demise of the empire, and the threatened dissolution of the federation. Some of this criticism is not without basis, but a good deal of it stems from the myriad of frustrations which are being experienced by Canadians as their nation moves from adolescence to adulthood. To hear some of the comments about welfare costs could easily lead one to the conclusion that an abnormal and oppressive burden has been imposed upon the Canadian populace.

What are the facts? The increased scope of social security in Canada is readily indicated by an examination of the fiscal picture.[47] From $307 million in 1945, social welfare programs presently cost in excess of $4 billion annually, which amounts to almost one-third of total public spending. While much of this increase has been due to the inauguration of new programs, de-

47. See Irving J. Goffman, *Some Fiscal Aspects of Public Welfare in Canada* (Toronto, 1965), esp. chap. iv.

mographic changes as a result of higher birth rates and extended life spans have also played a role. Similarly, the movement of the population has created a need for greater capital expenditures on social welfare facilities such as hospitals. Finally, it must be recognized that for all programs, the benefits have been continuously expanded, particularly under the pressures of the postwar inflation.

Yet the absolute and relative increases in the expenditures related to social welfare cannot be characterized as having caused any dramatic change in the nature of the Canadian economic system, except to the extent that they have led to greater transfers of funds from the central government to the provinces. Nor have Canadian welfare expenditures been unfavorably high in comparison with other nations.

It appears from the figures in Table 1[48] that the more highly industrialized nations usually spend a larger proportion of their national income for welfare purposes than less-developed nations. The top fifteen countries on the list are all Western industrialized nations, while the African, Asian, and Latin-American countries constitute the smaller spenders. Canada places somewhat lower than the European nations, though higher than the United States, in terms of the proportion of income spent for public welfare. Between 1957 and 1960, Canada's proportion climbed from 8.7 per cent to 11.8 per cent, reflecting mainly the cost of the hospitalization program.

One explanation of the relatively poorer performance of Canada in contrast to most other Western industrial nations may have to do with the fact that Canada is a newcomer to the field of social security. Margaret S. Gordon suggests that countries with the oldest social security systems (of the modern type) tend to pay out much higher benefits.[49] Thus, for example, she found a high correlation between the date of the establishment of old-age programs and the levels of benefits. This hypothesis would help to explain the relatively low expenditures in North America. More-

48. International comparisons such as the one presented here are not without deficiencies. For a discussion of these problems, see *ibid.*, Appendix to chap. iv.
49. *The Economics of Welfare Policies* (New York, 1963), p. 16.

Table 1. *Public welfare expenditures as a percentage of national income, selected countries, 1960*

Rank	Country	Percentage
1	West Germany	20.7
2	France	18.4
2	Luxembourg	18.4
4	Austria	18.1
5	Belgium	17.2
6	Italy	16.1
7	New Zealand	15.3
8	Sweden	13.9
9	United Kingdom	13.7
9	Denmark	13.7
11	Netherlands	13.4
11	Norway	13.4
13	Finland	12.0
14	Canada	11.8
15	Ireland	10.9
16	Iceland	10.3
17	Australia	9.8
18	Switzerland	8.9
19	Israel	8.7
20	United States	7.7
21	Panama	7.1
22	Japan	6.6
23	Portugal	6.3
24	Ceylon	5.0
25	Spain	4.9
26	Union of South Africa	4.5
27	Cyprus	3.9
28	Malaya	3.8
29	Guatemala	3.5
30	Venezuela	3.4
31	El Salvador	2.6
32	China (Taiwan)	1.6
33	Turkey	1.5
34	India	1.4
35	Philippines	1.3

Source: International Labor Office, *The Cost of Social Security, 1958–1960* (Geneva, 1964).

over, it would lead one to expect that over time, public welfare spending in Canada will continue to increase not only absolutely, but also as a proportion of the national income. In fact, the developments since 1957 conform to this hypothesis.

The significance of this past trend and future expectation cannot be identified simply by referring to the costs. What *is* important is the effect this aspect of public policy has had on the relevant goals of the society. To what extent has social welfare policy in Canada modified the market-determined distribution of income in a direction which is socially desired? To what extent has it resulted in a more equitable and economically efficient provision of certain goods and services, such as those connected with health care? Have these policy developments contributed to higher levels of employment, and what are their influences on the index of prices and the rate of growth? None of these questions has yet been fully answered within the Canadian context, but some suggestions are presented here in order to indicate some avenues for future research.

The tendency for Canadian social welfare programs to provide universal flat per capita benefits, as in the cases of family allowances and old-age payments, contains some elements which could contribute to a more equitable income distribution. Much depends upon the taxing schemes which are used to finance such programs. If we first examine the family allowances program, we find that the total resources of this program are distributed on the basis of family size on the presumption that unmet needs increase with the number of eligible children. There is certainly some evidence to suggest that this presumption is valid. Larger families are in evidence among the lower-income groups and also in those regions of the country with relatively lower economic activity. If this characteristic is sufficiently widespread, then the present family allowance system does get disposable income to the needy, and it does so with a consistent financing device. While family allowances are paid out of the general revenues, which are after all raised by a moderately progressive tax system,[50] at the time this act was passed, a provision was introduced

50. Irving J. Goffman, *The Burden of Canadian Taxation*, Canadian Tax Paper No. 29 (Toronto, 1962), p. 15.

into the Income Tax Code reducing the personal deduction for all those dependents who are eligible for family allowances. Thus the tax burdens on those in higher income brackets were increased considerably, while it made much less difference for those in the lower brackets. But while this program probably does alleviate the circumstances of those it is supposed to help, it could be made more effective without any increase in cost. One method would be to apply a version of the negative income tax, whereby these benefits would be limited to families who earn less than some predetermined amount, with the income ceiling increasing with family size. Another method would be to exclude from benefits all first-born children in order to provide greater benefits to families with two or more children. Presumably these are the families with the greater needs, or so it is assumed under the family allowances program. In 1965 this latter proposal would have increased the benefits to be eligible children by almost 40 per cent and hence would have redistributed income somewhat more effectively.

The old-age security program is probably not as redistributive as intended because of its financing arrangement. From the beginning, it has depended upon an earmarked tax levy, at the present 3 per cent on each of sales, personal income, and corporate income. I would expect that on balance these three taxes in the aggregate are somewhat regressive, so that a serious question concerning equity may be raised as this program transfers income from the poor young to the less poor aged. A careful statistical study of the matter would be most useful.[51]

To the extent that social welfare policy in Canada redistributes at all, it invariably has some impact upon the allocation of resources. But it is not readily arguable in economic theory that one method of redistribution of income leads to a more efficient resource allocation than any other.[52] In the case of health care, however, some arguments can be made. It has long been recognized that certain facets of health care, particularly those related to

51. For an early discussion of this problem see Monteath Douglas, "Welfare and Redistribution," *Canadian Journal of Economics and Political Science,* XIX (Aug., 1953), 316–325.

52. See P. A. Samuelson, "Diagrammatic Exposition of a Theory of Public Expenditure," *Review of Economics and Statistics,* XXXVII (Nov., 1955), 350–356.

contagious diseases, possess certain ecenomic characteristics which are somewhat different from the typical good or service. Ordinarily, the benefits of a good accrue only to the individual who purchases the particular good (as do any deleterious effects as well). This is often referred to as the "exclusion principle," since utility (or disutility) is reserved only for those who choose to purchase the good; all others are excluded from its enjoyment.

However, in some cases, this principle may not apply. This may well be the case for certain types of health care where extensive external economies of consumption may exist. The prevention, elimination, and rapid cure of diseases which may be transmitted from one to another may be considered to yield such externalities. Inoculations are often cited as examples of health care expenditures with spillover benefits. If *A* is vaccinated against polio, he reduces the risk of his contracting this disease; but in addition, he also reduces the risk of communicating it to *B*. Hence, not only does *A* benefit from his own expenditure, but *B* does as well. It is therefore of interest to *B* that *A* makes this expenditure. To the extent that *A* does not include *B*'s utility (benefits) in his demand price, the economy will not as likely allocate a sufficient quantity of resources to polio inoculation. In more technical language, these external economies must be internalized in order for efficient resource allocation to be achieved. Whether or not the private market can and will carry this out depends on several circumstances.[53] However, when it fails to do so, public provision or at least subsidy becomes desirable. It is on the basis of this kind of argument that traditional Pigouvian welfare economics concluded that where external economies of consumption existed, private provision underutilized resources, and hence collective action would lead to a greater devotion of resources to that particular good or service. This was certainly widely expected at the time of the British medical scheme.[54]

53. For a theoretical account of how this might occur, see Murray Kemp, "The Efficiency of Competition as an Allocator of Resources, II: External Economies of Consumption," *Canadian Journal of Economics and Political Science*, XXI (May, 1955), 217–227.

54. For example, see Seymour Harris, "The British Health Experiment: The First Two Years of the National Health Service," *American Economic Review*, XLI (May, 1951), 652–666.

More recently, however, there has been a withdrawal from this view. Total outlay on health services has been increasing more rapidly in the United States under private medicine than in Great Britain under public medicine,[55] with the effect on casting some doubt on the validity of the traditional "secondary benefits" hypothesis. Rather than resulting in underproduction, economic analysis may be able to show that the private mechanism, in its efforts to reflect these secondary benefits (that is, in economists' jargon, to internalize these external economies), may actually overproduce.[56] Also, a socialized scheme may result in more preventive medicine, or at least in earlier medical diagnosis, and thus reduce the ultimate incidence of sickness. In other words, there is some possibility that public provision will actually result in fewer resources being needed for health care. However, it might be that the different British and American experiences do not merely reflect the different financing arrangements in these two countries, but more important, that they are based on the income elasticity of demand for health services. It may be that a given percentage increase in income results in an even greater percentage increase in the amount spent on health services in the United States than in Britain. That is, the income elasticity of demand for health services is higher in the United States than in Great Britain. This may be a result of the higher per capita income in the United States. In the first place, the demand for services of all kinds, including health services, has shown a tendency to rise with incomes.[57] Secondly, with higher incomes, the price of sickness is higher so that it becomes economically rational to spend more on avoiding sickness. Third, some aspects of health services are regarded as "snob goods," and the demand for these rises with affluence. Capped teeth, plastic surgery for aesthetic purposes, and even some psychoanalysis may be cited as examples. A fourth

55. For an examination of the comparative record, see John and Sylvia Jewkes, *The Genesis of the National Health Service* (Oxford, 1961).

56. Some very interesting preliminary theoretical discussions along these lines have recently appeared. See J. M. Buchanan and M. Z. Kafoglis, "A Note on Public Goods Supply," *American Economic Review*, XLIII (June, 1963), 403–414; and W. J. Baumol, "External Economies and Second Order Conditions," *American Economic Review* XLIV (June, 1964), 358–372.

57. Colin Clark, *The Conditions of Economic Progress* (London, 1957), p. 379.

possibility is that affluence may lead to an increase in the frequency of certain diseases (such as ulcers) which require costly medical care.

How much these income-related factors will affect the demand for health care cannot be determined yet. Much more intensive investigation is called for. In light of observations that the total outlay on health services has been increasing more rapidly in the United States under private medicine than in Great Britain under public medicine, such investigations might also include re-examination of the supply side of health services. Particular forms of socialized medicine may introduce inflexibilities which inhibit desirable growth in the supply of health services. For example, resistance to tax increases and the possible reluctance of people to enter health service professions under socialized conditions may account for some of the differences in health care outlay growth rates under public and private medicine. Such an investigation would have to include an assessment of qualitative as well as quantitative changes in health care over the period under the two systems.

So far in the Canadian experience, it appears that for the first few years after the introduction of the hospitalization plan, hospital costs exhibited a sharp rise which then stabilized on a higher plateau.[58] This may reflect malingering and hence a waste of resources, but it may also reflect a backlog of health problems as well as a more cautious position among physicians in their diagnoses. In any event, comprehensive health care certainly increases the quantity and probably the quality of health care which goes to the lower-income groups with a resulting very high economic yield. It is only in recent years that attention has been given to the economics of health services; and while it is an extremely complex subject, as Kenneth J. Arrow has recently shown,[59] it is also unquestionably a very profitable social investment.[60] The high pay-

58. M. G. Taylor, *Financial Aspects of Health Insurance*, Canadian Tax Paper No. 12 (Toronto, 1957).

59. "Uncertainty and the Welfare Economics of Medical Care," *American Economic Review*, LIII (Dec., 1963), 941–973.

60. See, for example, R. Fein, *Economics of Mental Illness* (New York, 1958), and B. A. Weisbrod, *Economics of Public Health* (Philadelphia, 1961).

off could be a strong efficiency argument for increased resource-use by the health industry.

We turn now to the final set of issues to be raised here—those dealing with stability and growth. During and immediately after World War II, before memories of the Great Depression had faded, a great deal of attention was paid to the formulation of counter-cyclical policy tools. Certain of the proposed social welfare programs were lauded because they were purported to possess this characteristic. Official statements concerning the demand-sustaining qualities of family allowances and old-age security benefits have previously been cited,[61] and certainly the same was believed to be true of the unemployment insurance programs. This sentiment was based on two assumptions: first, that these programs would redistribute income in the proper direction; second, that the size of these transfers would fluctuate inversely with the business cycle. To increase aggregate demand via redistribution, it must have been assumed that the various social welfare programs would transfer income from savers to non-savers and that there would be no resulting decline in any of the non-consumption spending components (or at least no decline of any significance). The facts remain, however, that the methods of financing some of the programs have reduced somewhat the extent of the desired redistribution and therefore the demand-sustaining properties of these programs. I do not mean to suggest that these programs have not contributed to the alleviation of the deficient demand problem, but only that they have not been as effective as anticipated.

What of the counter-cyclical automaticity of these programs? How sensitive are they to business cycle variations? At least one of these, the unemployment insurance program, shows a close correlation between its outpayments and the levels of unemployment, but even here there are important limitations, particularly if the unemployment is structural and hence of longer duration.[62] But when one considers the other major social welfare programs, there is a noticeable absence of cyclical movement. Instead, family allowances and old-age benefits exhibit a steady and upward

61. Nn. 34, 38, *supra.*
62. Goffman, *Some Fiscal Aspects of Public Welfare in Canada,* pp. 37–38.

secular trend, and though this may have been a welcome phenomenon when the predominant fear was secular stagnation, its business cycle asymmetry is conducive to inflation when aggregate demand is pressing productive capacity.

Along these lines, the new Canada Pension Plan may yield some ominous and unintended results. This admonition was clearly voiced by William C. Hood.[63] For the first time there is to be a very large funded welfare program which is certain to replace a sizable portion of private pension plans and hence will absorb a significant portion of private savings. The basic question this raises is concerned with the channeling of these new government funds to investment purposes, for it is imperative that the savings be directed to the most productive uses. While there is no basis for an a priori argument that only the private sector is capable of efficient investment, there may be some basis for arguing that the provincial governments, who will have command over the pension plan reserves, are not at present sufficiently prepared to make the capital formation decision which will be theirs. Moreover, the reductions in the size of the stock of savings available to the private sector will reduce the possibility of some large-scale private investment projects which are so necessary to increased productivity. As a result there are some fears that this major structural change in savings in Canada could lead to a less than optimum growth rate in total output, so that Canadians will fail to realize the standard of living which is warranted by the magnitude of their saving. Instead there would likely be increased inflationary pressures and/or increased importation of goods and services from abroad with all its international financial implications.

Conclusion

This essay has been concerned with the development of Canadian social welfare policy and particularly with the nature of that policy area and the issues surrounding it as Canada enters its

63. "Economic Policy in our Federal State," paper presented at the Canadian Political Science Association meetings, June, 1964.

second century. It has been shown that a steady evolutionary and pragmatic approach has been applied in expressing the concern of the society over the well-being of its members. There has been an obvious absence of anything which appears to be doctrinaire, and this undoubtedly led to the relatively peaceful though dramatic changes in social arrangements which have in fact taken place, even though the period of change has been a most trying one in Canadian history.

The programs in existence may not be the best ones for attaining the national goals, and modifications will continue in the future. But within the past two decades, there appears to have been a coalition composed of a broad sweep of the political spectrum, which is firmly committed to social welfare policy of the type which makes some minimum level of need-satisfaction the birthright of all Canadians.

10

The Military Policies of Contemporary Canada: Principles, problems, precepts, prospects

James Eayrs

Preliminary Notions

Military policy concerns decisions of governments of members of the state system about their military establishment, including the decision whether or not to maintain a military establishment. Military policy is an inescapable function. To be a member of the state system is to have a military policy.

While a government of a state has to have a military policy, it does not have to have a military establishment. It confronts, instead, a choice among four possible courses of action: (1) to maintain its own military establishment for some or all of the purposes to which it may be put; (2) to rely on some other government's military establishment for some of the purposes to which it may be put, primarily the purpose of defense against external aggression; (3) to rely on non-military methods for some of the purposes to which a military establishment may be put; and (4) to dispense entirely with its own military establishment and with reliance upon any other.

The contemporary state system comprises approximately 140 members. None of these has chosen option four. A very few governments have considered option three and one or two have chosen it. Tanganyika on first attaining independence considered it.[1] Costa Rica chose it; her government has no military establish-

1. William Gutteridge, *Armed Forces in New States* (London, 1962), p. 6.

ment at its beck and call, preferring to repose responsibility for the maintenance of internal law and order in a sizable and well-trained civil police, and, even more basically, in the kind of social and political institutions which, it hopes, will keep the peace without police assistance.

A few governments have chosen option two. It is an obvious, and sensible, choice for those political communities preferring to become "associated states" rather than fully sovereign members of the state system. (Associated statehood is the status which has been devised for the tiniest and poorest of the remnants of empire—the so-called rocks and islands—for which full independence neither is desired nor can be afforded. Typically, an associated state entrusts the conduct of its affairs, excepting local administration, to a protecting power, always with the option of exchanging this arrangement for some other, including full independence, at any time and for any reason.) Antigua, on attaining associated statehood, thus continues to rely on the military establishment of the United Kingdom, having none of its own. Western Samoa, a fully independent member of the state system, maintains no military establishment, relying instead upon the protection extended to it by New Zealand.

Iceland is the only member of the state system whose people, in the words of the Secretary-General of her Ministry for Foreign Affairs, "are and have been for centuries . . . without arms."[2] In 1940 Icelanders paid a price for their defenselessness in the form of occupation, against their will, by Canadian and British forces. A year later, by inviting the United States to take over their defense from the British, they exercised option two. They did so again in 1949, by entrusting their protection to their allies in NATO. Unlike Luxembourg (the other tiny member of the alliance), Iceland has made no military contribution—not even a token contribution—to the common defense.

The overwhelming majority of the members of the state system have chosen option one. Nearly all governments maintain a military establishment. It is true that the force which these military

2. Agnar Kl. Jonsson, "The Foreign Policy of Iceland," *NATO Letter*, Jan. 1966, p. 10.

establishments are able to deploy ranges over a scale of destruction whose extremes are as far apart as lower and upper limits could possibly be—from the pikestaffs of the Papal Zouaves to the multimegaton bombs and intercontinental ballistic missiles of the American Strategic Air Command. But practically no member of the state system has felt able to dispense with a military establishment of some kind, capable of exerting force on some scale.

Why should this be so? The simple answer to the question why more states do not try to get along without a military establishment is that their governments feel themselves to live in a dangerous world. And dangerous it is.

And yet, hostile as is the international environment for many of them, it is not very hostile for some of them; for a fortunate few it is hardly hostile at all. Some may have enemies who are out of range. Some may have enemies whose weapons are non-military. Some may have no enemies at all. The number of states who require military establishments for the purpose of warding off military aggression comprise a minority of the membership of the state system.

The less simple answer to the question why more states do not try to get along without a military establishment is that warding off military aggression is only one of several functions that military establishments may and do perform. There are five others, making six functions in all.

Six Functions of Military Force

1. Inflicting military defeat upon the enemy of the state constitutes the *strategic function* of the military establishment. The enemy may be an aggressor. Or the enemy may be the aggressor's victim. Usually the enemy is another state. Occasionally the enemy is an alien ideology.

2. To function in a strategic role, the military establishment must have an enemy. But there are often periods in a country's history when there are no enemies in sight, when the international environment ceases to be hostile and appears to be hospitable.

But this does not necessarily make the maintenance of military power a foolish project. For if the international environment is friendly, it is also fluid. Everything flows. Today's ally may be tomorrow's adversary. Protection conferred by geography may be wiped out by technology. One may mistake one's foe for friend.

To guard against these contingencies, the maintenance of military power is justified. A military establishment may perform an *insurance function*. It is not needed now. It may be needed in the future. One keeps it just in case. One never knows.

In primitive societies, the insurance function of military power can be provided by training citizens in the arts of war, which are also primitive. The provision of military insurance in modern societies requires the maintenance of a force in being.

3. Military establishments may be required not so much for protection from without as for protection from within. They have a *law and order function*, known, in military parlance, as "aiding the civil power." In this role, the military establishment reinforces, or takes the place of, police.

Aiding the civil power is a commonplace task of military establishments in empire states. Between the two world wars it was the prime preoccupation of the British Army[3] as, between 1945 and 1954, it was the prime preoccupation of the French Army. It was invoked by Stalin as a justification for building up the Soviet armed forces in defiance of the doctrine of the disappearance of state power. It is the remedy for regional and tribal disorders in newly independent countries. Even the most stable and settled society may require the military to keep order during periods of exceptional malaise and unrest.

4. The military establishment may also serve the state as an *instrument of modernization and development*. In this role the military may be retained not to combat an enemy but to improve the environment, a task sometimes called "civic action." The civic

3. "To minds trained to think in terms of the events of the Great War," a British general wrote in 1933, "the police duties of the Army, even when they take the form of small wars, may appear of insignificant importance." His thesis suggests the opposite state of affairs: they are of "vital importance . . . [especially] when applied to the British Empire, affected as it is by all the currents and eddies of racial, religious, and political interests" (Major-General Sir Charles W. Gwynn, *Imperial Policing*, 2nd ed.; London, 1939, pp. 7–8).

action army builds roads, plows fields, digs wells, erects dams. In more economically developed countries, these are specialized tasks for a specialized force. The United States Army Corps of Engineers is a celebrated example. In less-developed countries, civic action is part of the normal duty of the military, as in, most notably, Israel, Pakistan, Thailand, Peru, Colombia, and Guatemala.

Even where not formally engaged in civic action duty, the military establishment can scarcely evade its modernizing role. A military establishment is a training establishment. It imparts attitudes and skills to people who might not otherwise acquire them. In newly independent and economically underdeveloped societies the swiftest and surest way of creating the rudiments of a labor force may be to conscript for service in the armed forces. Snatched from village or tribal life, the new member of the military learns how to read and write, how to use a wrench or hammer, how to drive a truck or train. He learns that it is possible to get ahead in the world. He learns that it is desirable to get ahead in the world. He learns how to get ahead in the world. Only when thus instructed is he of any value to his country.

And when nature, not a nation, is the aggressor, the military establishment is called upon in every country to help clean up in the wake of fire, famine, flood, pestilence, or earthquake.

5. Not to be overlooked is the *ceremonial function* of military power. A military establishment is invariably a status symbol. It can be kept and groomed not so much for protection as for prestige. It lends dignity to the image of the state. It is a symbol of sovereignty. Since most states have them, most states want them, especially newly independent states. There, an authority has written, the military establishment is a "symbol of national prestige and of the apparent need to assert a community's standing in the eyes of the world. In contemporary Africa in particular, inability to mount a professional guard of honour and at the same time to make a contribution, however small, to the U. N. force in the Congo would amount to more than a blow to national pride."[4]

4. Gutteridge, *Armed Forces in New States*, p. 7.

So strong is the urge to display the military as an ornament of statehood that governments have succumbed to the temptation to create armed forces, knowing that they were thereby creating rivals to their own authority and possible usurpers of their power.

Maintaining a military establishment for prestige purposes can be cheap or costly. It depends on the ceremonial. One can spend a little or a lot on getting married or getting buried. So, too, with military ceremonial. A color guard, pleasing to the eye of the tourist and flattering to the foreign dignitary, lies within the purse of almost any state; the main expense (apart from pay and pensions) is dry cleaning. But with states, as with individuals, buying status can get out of hand. The nuclear ceremonial is especially expensive, particularly if delivery systems are thought to be among those items necessary though optional at extra cost.

6. Finally, the military establishment may be used as an adjunct to various non-military techniques of statecraft. Arms are a means to influence. An army can be as much a political argument as an instrument of combat, a valuable adjunct to negotiation. And not an army only. Nelson displayed a natural occupational bias in describing a man-o'-war as "the best negotiator in Europe," but the Fleet did Castlereagh (and his successors) little harm. Nor need it always be deployed at these outer limits of coercion. It was "the friendly influence" that carrier forces were capable of spreading around the world which Vice-Admiral Donald Gibson, flag officer, R. N. Naval Air Command, stressed when publicly deploring the emphasis of the British White Paper on Defence for 1966 upon air power at the expense of sea power. "A bomber," he declared, "can drop a bomb. The Fleet Air Arm can also drop a bomb but can give a cocktail party or play a football game, which is better than dropping bombs."[5] And so, for winning friends, it is.

It can be, as well, an instrument of propaganda. Here the gradation of persuasion extends across a wide scale. At one extreme a Great White Fleet conveys an image of the power of its

5. *The Times* (London), Feb. 25, 1966, p. 3.

proud possessor by friendly visits to foreign ports. (The mid-twentieth-century equivalent of this favorite device of Rooseveltian diplomacy is the British Vulcan bomber, also painted white, for years now the star attraction at the Canadian National Exhibition.) At the other, a fifty-megaton bomb is defiantly detonated on the eve of an Afro-Asian conference.

It is also part of the apparatus of economic warfare. Without a military establishment of some sort, blockades are difficult to mount and impossible to run. Boycotts and embargoes are only slightly less provocative—sanctions, as someone has said, mean war—and states deficient in military power exploit them at their peril.

As an adjunct to these non-military techniques of statecraft, the military establishment may be used on a variety of non-military assignments. It may be used to acquire access to sources of intelligence or to locales of decision-making, from which its controlling authority would otherwise be excluded. The cost of armed forces retained for this purpose resembles the price of admission to some private entertainment, the dues of membership in some exclusive club. It may also be used to purchase high esteem from those who might otherwise think less well of the purchaser. The cost of armed forces retained for this purpose resembles the depositing of funds in a bank; the object is to create a kind of diplomatic credit, a balance of favorable regard, upon which the depositor may draw at some later date, or on some rainier day.

One may note that for this purpose it frequently does not matter to what use the military establishment is put, just so long as it is used; or of what it is composed, just so long as it is composed of something; or how much it costs, just so long as it costs enough. The object is to convince one's friends and allies that one is pulling one's weight, that one is not a parasite or freeloader, that one is bearing fair shares of sacrifice. This being so, what matters is that one is spending x per cent of gross national product, y per cent of the annual budget. Defense expenditure under these circumstances may often resemble the pot-latch ceremony practiced by the Kwakiutl Indians of the Northwest Pacific Coast of North America—a ceremony familiar enough to anthropologists but with which defense analysts might with profit become better acquainted.[6]

Finally, a military establishment may be used to catalyze friends and allies into making a more energetic commitment to the common defense than they might otherwise make. A classic example is the decision of the government of the Grand Duchy of Luxembourg, NATO's second smallest member, to maintain, despite a hostile public, its miniscule contribution to the land forces of the alliance, namely, one battalion of 105 mm. howitzers. The object was not to defend Luxembourg but to serve as an example to more powerful members of the alliance.

This discussion of the six functions of military force is intended to suggest the inadequacy of any analysis of defense policy which confines itself, as many do, to the strategic uses of a military establishment. In the case of Canadian defense policy, so restricted a view is particularly misleading for, as will be contended in what follows, the Canadian military establishment is currently deprived of adequate strategic justification.

The Strategic Role of the Canadian Military

Throughout Canada's peacetime history, two countries only have been thought to pose a threat of the kind which enabled the military establishment to function in its strategic role. These are the United States and the Soviet Union.

It was only natural that at the outset of the formation of the

6. The most celebrated account of the potlatch is, of course, Ruth Benedict's: "The whole economic system of the Northwest Coast was bent to the service of this obsession. There were two means by which a chief could achieve the victory he sought. One was by shaming his rival by presenting him with more property than he could return with the required interest. The other was by destroying property. In both cases the offering called for return, though in the first case the giver's wealth was augmented, and in the second he stripped himself of goods. The consequence of the two methods seem to us at the opposite poles. To the Kwakiutl they were merely complementary means of subduing a rival, and the highest glory of life was the act of complete destruction. It was a challenge, exactly like the selling of a copper, and it was always done in opposition to a rival who must then, in order to save himself from shame, destroy an equal amount of valuable goods" (*Patterns of Culture*, New York, 1946, p. 178).

Dominion of Canada the United States should have been regarded as a potential enemy. All previous international experience suggested that when a great and powerful nation exists
alongside a small and weak nation, at once inviting aggression
and vulnerable to aggression, the greater power will eventually
attack the weaker. Nor did Sir John A. Macdonald ignore the
lessons of history. "A great future would await our country," he
wrote privately in 1867, "were it not for those wretched Yankees,
who hunger and thirst after Naboth's vineyard. War will come
some day between England and the United States, and you in
India could do us yeoman service by sending an expeditionary
force of Ghurkas, Beluchis, etc., to attack San Francisco, and hold
that beautiful and unusual city and the surrounding California as
hostages for Montreal and Canada."[7] In the event, a less dramatic
strategy was employed. No Indian troops invaded California. But
British troops remained in Canada.

Today's observer, accustomed to the spectacle of newly independent nations attempting with varying success to rid themselves of the military presence of their former rulers, might conclude that the objective of the Canadian government in the
immediately post-Confederation years was to expel the British
Army from its territory. In that he would be wrong. It was the
British government, stretched then as now too thinly along its vast
defense perimeter in Europe and in the empire, which wanted to
withdraw. The Canadian government no less firmly wanted it to
stay. "It will be a century," Macdonald remarked in 1869, "before
we are strong enough to walk alone." The British government did
not intend to wait a century or even a twentieth of a century. By
the end of 1871, British garrisons remained only at Halifax. These,
and other British troops established later at Esquimalt, were withdrawn for good in 1905. "The basis of our decision," the Colonial
Secretary informed the Governor-General, "is that for the only
enemy who is in the remotest sense to be feared—& thank God it
is the remotest sense—the existing defences [are] wholly inade-

7. Quoted in Blair Fraser, "Canada: Mediator or Busybody?" in J. King Gordon,
ed., *Canada's Role as a Middle Power* (Toronto, 1966), p. 3.

quate, & yet they are very costly to us & divest the Canadians of all responsibility for what is after all their affair."[8]

To the intelligence operatives advising the Canadian government, the threat posed by the United States to the security of the Dominion did not then, nor for many years afterward, appear so remote. "The United States is and always must be a dangerous enemy to Canada," a Canadian naval officer wrote in 1912. "Although at the present time both Federal and Imperial relations with her are cordial, that they will not necessarily always be so is shown by the existence of the Canadian Militia, which would seem to be of little use except as a defence against the United States."[9] That conclusion was not exactly logically unassailable. An alternative, and no less valid, conclusion was that the Canadian Militia was not required even for that purpose.

By 1920, a number of Canadian politicians had arrived at the alternative conclusion. "The Government says this expenditure is needed for the defence of Canada," cried the Leader of the Opposition during the debate of that year on the militia estimates. "Defence against whom? There is no answer; there is no answer to be made."[10] But the Canadian military had an answer. The General Staff was already engaged upon a priority project of the postwar years—the formulation of what was to become Defence Scheme No. 1, a war plan the central assumption of which was that there existed a clear and present danger of attack upon the Dominion of Canada by the armed forces of the United States.[11]

In 1938, Mackenzie King, then prime minister, repeated what, as leader of the opposition, he had affirmed in 1920: that Canada faced no enemy of a kind which constituted a strategic threat to her security. "At present," he declared, "the danger of attack upon Canada is minor in degree and second-hand in origin." The Gen-

8. Alfred Lyttleton to Lord Grey, Jan. 26, 1905, Grey Papers (Public Archives of Canada).

9. R. M. Stephens, "Defence of Canada with Reference to Naval Control on Great Lakes," Feb. 1912, N. S. 1005-3-1, Vol. I (Office of the Naval Historian of Canada).

10. Canada, *House of Commons Debates, 1920,* IV, 3646.

11. The history of Defence Scheme No. 1, from its inception in 1920 to its destruction in 1933, is recounted in James Eayrs, *In Defence of Canada,* Vol. I: *From the Great War to the Great Depression* (Toronto, 1964), pp. 70–78; extracts from the plan will be found in Document 1, pp. 323–328.

eral Staff, however, did not share his view. "The liability of direct attack on Canada by Japanese forces," wrote its Director of Military Operations and Intelligence in September, 1936, "has become a matter requiring urgent consideration and action. . . . The prospect of war breaking out at some not distant date between some, or all, of the Anglo-Saxon communities which have important interests in the Pacific, and Japan, are apparent. Under such circumstances the Western Coast of Canada will be within the area of hostilities and is likely to be attacked not only by Japanese naval and air forces, but in the case of important shore objectives, by Japanese landing parties operating in some strength."[12] Colonel H. D. G. Crerar (as he then was) was right about the prospect of war, but wrong about the scales of attack. The most the Japanese could do was to dispatch balloons made of mulberry bark and armed with smallish charges of incendiary explosive. Some of these fell as far inland as Manitoba and may have singed a few sections of wheat. But this was not what people had by then learned to call *blitzkrieg*.

The overwhelming majority of the roughly 100,000 Canadians killed and wounded in World War II were casualties of the conflict with Nazi Germany. How did Germany become Canada's enemy? In what cause were such sacrifices made? Not for King and country. "The fate of a single city, the preservation of the independence of a particular nation, are the occasion, not the real cause of the present conflict. The forces of evil have been loosed in the world. . . . That is why the present war is for the Allied Forces a crusade."[13] In these words the Prime Minister of Canada described, on September 3, 1939, the reason for his country's impending belligerency. The words were true, but they expressed only part of the truth. After all, the forces of evil had been loosed in the world long before the Canadian Parliament declared a state of war between the Dominion and the Reich on September 10, 1939. What made the difference was that the United Kingdom had entered the fray. To the British government, and to the

12. Quoted in *ibid.*, Vol. II: *Appeasement and Rearmament* (Toronto, 1965), pp. 217–218.
13. Quoted in *ibid.*, p. 154.

Canadian public, Mackenzie King had been careful to make clear that the fact of British belligerency, even against Germany, would not necessarily cause Canada to enter the war. But in June, 1937, he told Hitler a different story.[14]

Germany thus became Canada's enemy in September, 1939, by becoming Britain's enemy. History is hard enough without going in for hypothetical history. But one may venture the hypothesis that Germany would not have become Canada's enemy by anything it did to Eastern Europe, or by anything it did to the Jews of Europe. "Our destiny," wrote a Canadian cabinet minister in 1937, "is on the North American continent. If Europe is going to insist on destroying itself, it is no part of our mission to destroy ourselves in attempting to prevent it."[15]

During the years immediately following Confederation, the enemy had been the United States, deterred by the might of the United Kingdom. In the years immediately following World War II, the enemy was the Soviet Union, deterred by the might of the United States. For the first time since the nineteenth century, the security of Canada was directly threatened by a foreign power.

Few if any members of the Canadian policy community entertained doubts about the nature of Soviet intentions by the end of 1947. These were perceived to be malign. For it had been in Ottawa, rather than in some other Western capital, that the Soviet Union had converted its embassy into a full-scale espionage operation and had, moreover, been apprehended in the act. The reaction in Canada was one of shock and dismay. "The Soviet Union," the Minister of National Defence remarked grimly in the House of Commons in June, 1948,

has flouted its war-won friendships, obstinately obstructed every move to arrive at understanding, and prompted chaos and disorder and the darkness of the iron curtain. . . . It has produced an attitude in Canada towards defence which is quite different from any that we ever had before in peacetime. Of one thing I am sure, and that is the deter-

---

14. See the memorandum prepared by Mackenzie King on his interview with Hitler, June 29, 1937, reproduced as Document 3 in *ibid.*, pp. 226–231.

15. Quoted in James Eayrs, " 'A Low Dishonest Decade': Aspects of Canadian External Policy, 1931–1939," in H. L. Keenleyside *et al.*, *The Growth of Canadian Policies in External Affairs* (Durham, N. C., 1960), p. 65.

mination of the Canadian people to defend our country against attack.[16]

That determination was not immediately forthcoming.

Early in 1946, on instructions from their respective governments, the senior military officers of Canada and the United States drafted a joint appreciation of the requirements for defending North America from direct attack. Hitherto, they noted, North America had been virtually immune to such attack, enjoying the protection of the oceans and the Arctic. (The joint appreciation naturally did not refer to the historic possibilities of direct attack by one North American nation upon the other.) That immunity, conferred by geography, was now being whittled away by technology. New weapons of destruction—the atomic bomb, chemical and biological instruments—and new delivery systems—the long-range aircraft, guided missiles, and improved techniques of submarine warfare—combined to bring North America within the range of aggression by a hostile European or Asian power. By about 1950, the planners estimated, the enemy would be capable of inflicting long-range air bombardment of vulnerable areas in the United States and Canada, possibly with atomic weapons, shorter-range bombardment by guided missiles, rockets, or aircraft launched from submarines, and seizure of objectives in the subarctic regions of Canada, Alaska, and Labrador as *points d'appui* from which further follow-up raids might be attempted. As a combined deterrent and operational defense against this contingency, the planners recommended that Canada and the United States co-operate in the construction of an effective air defense system including early warning, meteorological, and communications apparatus, a network of air bases deployed as far forward as possible from probable targets, sufficient numbers of fighter interceptor aircraft to inflict unacceptable damage upon the attacker, and adequate anti-aircraft defenses suitably deployed. In addition to the air defense system, the requirements for North American defense were said to include: (1) a program of air mapping and photography; (2) air and surface surveillance

16. Canada, *House of Commons Debates, 1948*, V, 5779.

to give warning of infiltration or attack; (3) anti-submarine patrol and naval patrol of the sea approaches; (4) garrison and mobile forces to defend against lodgments; and (5) a command structure suitable to the needs of joint Canadian-American defense of the continent. All these, the planners considered to be essential, but the most urgent measure was the air defense system.

Although the joint planners' appreciation of the threat to the security of North America only confirmed the Canadian government's own appreciation, it was unprepared for the sweeping nature of their recommendations. These the cabinet found gravely disconcerting. The implementation of the measures proposed, particularly of the priority air defense proposals, would be very costly, perhaps fantastically costly. They would in any case involve a degree of intrusion of the United States into Canadian territory and upon Canadian sovereignty that could not be easily accepted and which might make for all sorts of political troubles. Some of the countermeasures proposed to deter enemy action in the Arctic might only incite it.

Joined to these initial disquieting reflections, and reinforcing them, were second thoughts of a more far-reaching nature. What if the intelligence, furnished largely by the United States authorities, were too alarmist? One could not blame the United States for that: a nation which had lost its navy in a matter of hours through surprise attack might be excused for taking excessive precautions five years later. But that did not alter the fact that the recommended precautions could be excessive. And was there, after all, no realistic approach to this matter, other than the desperate remedy of rearmament, leading, as it had always done, to an arms race which so often led to war?

Reinforced by advice from the British to proceed cautiously, the Canadian government rejected the United States proposals for an immediate start on the air defense system. It proposed, instead, a much more modest, wholly unprovocative, and infinitely less costly program of Arctic reconnaissance and research. With this alternative the United States government necessarily had to be content, for short of forcible occupation of Canadian territory, the implementation of its own plans depended on Canadian co-operation. The policy was announced by the Prime Minister on February 12, 1947, in a statement to Parliament somewhat lacking in candor:

I should like [he said] to comment briefly on the problems of northern defence. . . . Some quite unfounded suggestions have been put forward. There is a persistent rumour, for example, that the United States Government has asked for bases in the Canadian North. This is a rumour I should like to deny emphatically.[17] There has been talk of Maginot lines, of large scale defence projects, all of which is unwarranted and much of it fantastic. It is apparent to anyone who has reflected on the technological advances of recent years that new geographic factors have been brought into play. The polar regions assume new importance as the shortest routes between North America and the principal centres of population of the world. Our defence forces must, of course, have experience in the conditions of these regions, but it is clear that most of the things that should be done are required apart altogether from considerations of defence. . . . Our primary objective should be to expand our knowledge of the North, and of the conditions necessary for work and life there, with the object of developing its resources.[18]

Just as when, at the turn of the century, the Canadians had responded to a British request for a contribution to the Grand Fleet by promising to develop the Canadian Pacific Railway system, so, a half century later, they responded to an American request for northern defense by promising to develop cold-temperature research.

By 1950 the matter could not be so lightly turned aside. The Soviet threat to Western Europe, resulting in the formation of NATO, the Korean War, the confirmation that the Soviet Union now possessed, in the shape of nuclear weapons and the Tu-4 long-range bomber, the means of striking at North America—all combined to invest the problems of continental defense with new and unprecedented urgency.

The solution sought by the United States was distant early warning of impending Soviet attack. Given the two or three hours'

17. It was not, however, wholly without foundation: the American military had proposed greatly enlarging the number of United States servicemen at Goose Bay, Labrador (which, as part of Newfoundland, was then under British jurisdiction); and President Truman had supported this project in talks with Mackenzie King in Washington in October, 1946.
18. Canada, *House of Commons Debates, 1947,* I, 345–347.

grace which such warning would provide, people might take cover and—much more important from the strategic point of view—the retaliatory United States bombers would have a chance to operate. Studies carried out in 1951 and 1952—Projects Charles and Lincoln—demonstrated the technical feasibility of the concept, and in 1953 the Canadian government gave its permission for the United States to conduct, under conditions of the utmost secrecy, further feasibility tests at a site near Herschell Island in the Arctic. These studies led to a United States decision to build a chain of radar stations, fifty-eight in all, extending from Alaska across the Canadian Arctic through Baffin Island and thence to Greenland, following the 70th parallel.

This decision might be taken, but it could not be implemented, without Canadian concurrence. In Canada, as in the United States, there were doubts and misgivings about the wisdom of proceeding with the project. But, unlike 1946, when the Canadian government had turned down American proposals for the defense of North America as being what a senior Canadian defense official subsequently described as "excessive and inopportune,"[19] in 1953 the Canadians felt that they had no choice but to acquiesce in what the Americans might wish to do. "It may be very difficult indeed," the Canadian Minister for National Defence wrote privately in October, 1953, "for the Canadian Government to reject any major defence proposal which the United States Government presents with conviction as essential for the security of North America." So it proved. The agreement eventually signed in Washington on May 5, 1955, provided that the United States was to bear the full cost of the construction and operation of the Distant Early Warning (DEW) System.

"If the aggressor's weapon is the ICBM," a senior United States Air Force officer told a congressional committee in 1956, "the continent stands almost as naked today as it did in 1946, for I have no radar to detect missiles and no defense against them."[20] That was a dispiriting reflection in view of the $400 million or so

19. R. J. Sutherland, "The Strategic Significance of the Canadian Arctic," in R. St. J. Macdonald, ed., *The Arctic Frontier* (Toronto, 1966), p. 263.
20. Quoted by Hanson W. Baldwin, "Nuclear Repellents," New York *Times*, Jan. 22, 1958, p. 26.

already spent on development and construction of the DEW Line. It became more dispiriting still a year later, with the historic announcement by TASS on August 26, 1957, that "a super long distance intercontinental ballistic missile rocket has been released," covering "a huge distance in a brief time" and landing "in the set area." Delphic as that Soviet announcement might have been, there was no doubt about its significance a year later. The ballistic missile was now part of the Russian armory. Not long afterward, Nikita Khrushchev boasted that it was coming off the production line "like sausages."

Military reaction in America was twofold. There was the enormous expansion of strategic retaliatory capability, moving relentlessly through the stages of air-borne bomber alert, first and second generation ballistic missiles with intercontinental range (the latter invulnerably sited and instantaneously fired), and missile submarines. Then there was the development and construction of the Ballistic Missile Early Warning System (BMEWS).

For the first time in the postwar history of continental defense, Canadian co-operation was not essential. It is true that during the panicky search for a second-strike capability during the period immediately following the development of Soviet long-range missile capability, operational researchers could make their case for disposition of United States retaliatory forces in Canadian territory. But these were marginal dispositions only: if there were good political reasons for refraining from towing missile-firing barges about the Great Lakes, or shunting missile-firing flatcars about the Canadian railway systems—as indeed there were—other devices for invulnerability could be, and were, contrived. As to BMEWS, it was sited for technical reasons entirely outside Canadian territory—in Alaska, in Greenland, in Northern England. "On military grounds," a Canadian defense official has written, "a case can be made for the siting of additional [BMEWS] warning radars in northern Canada, but it seems clear that these would not be worth the cost."[21]

Is there then no strategic role for Canada in the defense of

21. Sutherland, "The Strategic Significance of the Canadian Arctic," p. 272.

North America against attack by the Soviet Union under present and future conditions of weaponry, technology, and doctrine?

None of Canada's present military efforts contributes significantly to the defense of North America. Neither the two squadrons of Bomarc-B interceptor guided missiles sited at North Bay, Ontario, and LaMacaza, Quebec, nor the interceptor fighter aircraft assigned to the North American Air Defence Command are useful in the event of missile attack. They are meant to be useful in the event of bomber attack. Yet it is evident that any bomber attack from the Soviet Union will occur only in the wake of a missile attack which must be presumed to have destroyed the important anti-bomber defenses. Canada's contributions to continental defense no longer have strategic significance. Their continued deployment must therefore be justified on other grounds; these, as argued below, are ceremonial and diplomatic rather than strategic.

If, however, the United States decided to meet the threat of Soviet missile attack by means of some system of anti-ballistic missile defense (BMD), the possibility would exist of Canada's once again playing a strategic role in the defense of North America.

This possibility could arise in three different ways. First, the type of BMD selected by the United States might require Canadian facilities for its deployment. The defense of major United States cities near the Canadian border (Seattle and Detroit are the obvious targets) could involve the siting of Spartan and Sprint defensive missiles on Canadian territory, as well as the location in Canada of the essential Multi-Function Array Radar (MAR) complexes used for the detection of incoming missiles and for the discrimination of warheads among decoys. Methods other than this so-called terminal defensive system (on which alone so far development has reached an advanced stage)—destruction of missiles during their launching or in that period of their trajectory spent outside the atmosphere (the so-called mid-course regime)— could conceivably require Canadian participation of some kind.

Second, the installation of a BMD system of demonstrated operational efficiency to defend major United States cities might lead to a demand in Canada that the same system be provided for major Canadian cities as well. Even if the cost of a Canadian BMD system were considered prohibitive by a Canadian government, its installation might be made possible by a decision of the United States to make the system available to Canadians at a fraction of its cost, perhaps in exchange for some needed defense facility or only for the added increment of deterrence it might be thought to provide the United States.

Third, the development and installation of a BMD system might, by reducing the effectiveness of a missile strike, cause a renewed emphasis on attack by other methods—for example, by bombers or by submarines operating in Canadian Arctic waters—which would once again create a strategic role for Canada in the defense of North America against Soviet attack.

On October 16, 1964, a nuclear device was set off in the People's Republic of China. On this event, the United States Secretary of Defense commented as follows in testimony before the House Armed Services Committee on February 18, 1965:

The nuclear explosion last October provided confirmation that the Chinese Communist leaders are determined to produce modern armaments even though the cost be great. That the nuclear program was able to continue in spite of a very severe economic crisis is testimony to the determination of the Chinese to produce modern weapons. Although results may be slow in coming, there is no reason to suppose that the Chinese cannot in time produce medium range and even long range ballistic missile systems and arm them with thermonuclear warheads. Given the hostility the regime has shown, this is a most disturbing prospect.[22]

Subsequently, McNamara and other leading United States defense officials have indicated that the principal utility of an investment in a BMD system would be to limit the damage that could be done to the United States by a Chinese nuclear missile attack, which they have estimated to be within China's capabilities by the 1970's.

Should the United States deploy some form of terminal defensive system to protect major West Coast and midwestern American cities from a Chinese missile assault, it is conceivable that

22. New York *Times*, Feb. 19, 1965, p. 17.

Canadian co-operation of the kind discussed above would be desirable from the United States point of view. It could, however, turn out that Canadian co-operation in the defense of North America against a possible Chinese missile attack would be less forthcoming than Canadian co-operation in the defense of North America against a possible Soviet missile attack. Canadians have never regarded Peking as an enemy in the sense in which they have regarded the Soviet Union as an enemy. "That an aggressive Communist China threatens Canadian interests," a Canadian authority has written, "is assumed by the vast majority and by the Government, but this threat is viewed in terms of long-range shifts in the balance of power rather than in the context of bases and military movements."[23] The acquisition by Peking of a crude nuclear strike capability is not going to change their assessment. Their attitude, and that of their government, toward any BMD deployment against China by the United States would probably resemble that of Western Europeans, as predicted by a Norwegian defense expert:

> In guesstimating European reactions to such a development it should be emphasized that the official American view of China is not widely shared in Europe. A decision as indicated might be interpreted as another proof of the American obsession with China. The threat from China in the ballistic missile sector is still several years in the future. It might well be argued in Europe that the Americans can afford to wait and watch where China intends to go as far as strategic delivery vehicles are concerned. . . . Those who fear American withdrawal from Europe may, furthermore, interpret an American BMD deployment ostensibly against China as another proof of the Asian priority in U. S. foreign policy. Others might focus on the marginal utility of such a system . . . and raise the question whether the embryo is not going to grow into a full-fledged system against the Soviet Union. . . .[24]

The Insurance Function of the Canadian Military

Canadians ought to be able to understand the insurance function of military power; they purchase more life insurance per

23. John W. Holmes, "Canada and China: The Dilemmas of a Middle Power," in A. M. Halpern, ed., *Policies Towards China: Views from Six Continents* (New York, 1965), p. 109.

24. Johan J. Holst, "BML and Western Europe: Some Preliminary Guesses," Hudson Institute Discussion Paper (mimeo.), HI-681-DP, April 8, 1966.

capita than any other people in the world. Possibly for this reason, the insurance metaphor figures prominently in their discussion of Canada's place in international affairs. In 1924, the Canadian representative to the Fifth Assembly of the League of Nations described that organization as "an association of mutual insurance against fire"; he went on to argue that "the risks assumed by the different states are not equal" and that Canada, being "a fire-proof house, far from inflammable materials," ought to pay lesser premiums than those exposed to greater risk.[25] In 1948, the Canadian Minister of Justice (soon to become prime minister) invoked the metaphor of insurance to argue the opposite case. "When I ask you," Louis St. Laurent told his Canadian audience, "to support a North Atlantic Treaty, I am simply asking you to pay an insurance premium which will be far, far less costly than the losses we would face if a new conflagration devastated the world."[26]

Two relevant points about the insurance function of military power may be noted. First, in order sensibly to justify the cost of insurance, it is not necessary for disaster to have struck or even to have threatened. An individual does not, and should not, wait until his house is on fire, or his car a crumpled wreck, or he has had a heart attack, before purchasing the appropriate policy. Similarly, governments do not, or should not, wait until their countries are attacked, or threatened by attack, before insuring against such contingencies by purchasing some degree of military power. Second, for governments, as for individuals, it is possible to be overinsured. There are other things to be done with the nation's resources besides putting them into a military establishment as a safeguard against a contingency that may never arise. "How much is enough?" is a question just as properly raised about a military establishment maintained for insurance as about a military establishment maintained for any other reason.

The insurance function of the Canadian military establishment is discussed, though briefly and none too clearly, in the government's White Paper on Defence, published in March, 1964. A conclusion to the paper acknowledges the inscrutability of the

25. League of Nations, Plenary Meetings, 5th Assembly, Oct. 2, 1924.
26. Department of External Affairs, Information Division, *Statements and Speeches*, No. 48/59.

future and cautions against accepting its own recommendations as the final solution:

The Paper is a charter, a guide, not a detailed and final blueprint. The policy outlined in it is not immutable. It can be altered or adapted to meet the requirements of changing circumstances, national and international.

What those circumstances will be in the future no one can foretell. It is certain, however, that force is not the solution to the problems of the peace and security in the world. . . . Nevertheless, and regrettably, it is essential to maintain force on our side as a deterrent against attack from potential foes who are themselves heavily armed. . . .[27]

The White Paper confines its discussion to the period of the next ten years, that is, until 1974. Beyond that it does not attempt to peer. Within the period are discerned two potential enemies: the Soviet Union and Communist China. For the former, as one "of the more affluent European Communist states," a "possible adoption of less militant external policies" is cautiously predicted. Communist China, on the other hand, "will grow in power, and unless its national objectives change, it may also grow in menace." Failure to check the spread of nuclear weapons "could fundamentally and dangerously alter the world security situation and render invalid many current defence assumptions." Such are the dangers of the state-system as foreseen by the White Paper over the next ten years. As a member of such a system, the government believes, Canada requires "adequate and flexible military forces . . . to be ready for crises should they arise."

Canada is allied and friendly with three nuclear powers. All are capable of mounting a devastating attack upon her. All are assumed by the White Paper to have no intention of doing so. Two of them—the United Kingdom and France—would in any case be deterred from attacking Canada (assuming the improbable contingency of their wishing to do so) by fear of retaliation by the United States. No comparable fear of retaliation by the United Kingdom or France deters the United States from attacking Canada. For the foreseeable future, any military preparations under-

27. White Paper on Defence (Ottawa, 1964), p. 30.

taken by Canada to insure against so bizarre and remote a possibility—for example, investment in a small store of thermonuclear weapons and their delivery systems (which, targeted against Detroit, need a range of no more than half a mile)—may confidently be described as an extreme form of overinsurance.

But what of the more distant future, twenty years rather than ten years on? Ten years brought the White Paper to 1974; twenty years brings it to 1984. Is Orwell's scenario (or some variation thereof) really so wildly improbable that no Canadian strategist need seriously concern himself with the contingency of Canada's becoming Airstrip Two (or Airstrip Nine) in Oceania's alternating wars with Eurasia and Eastasia, by her leave or without her leave?

This question will seem rhetorical to that majority of analysts of Canadian-American relations which assumes that the two states of North America have entered irrevocably into what has been called a "security community"—a grouping of governments no longer disposed to pursue their relations with each other by force of arms.[28] For the short and intermediate terms, its assumption is doubtless correct. For the longer term—1984 and beyond—it may be in error.

Nothing in the Canadian-American relationship requires the student of international politics to exempt its parties from the pitiless laws of the international state system. It is a relationship between two members of that system, each technically foreign to the other, of greatly discrepant power, geographically propinquent, economically and socially interconnected, whose policies toward each other are presently characterized by avoidance of those techniques of statecraft employing a high degree of coercion. There is nothing in the relationship to suggest that it evermore shall be so.[29]

---

28. See, for example, Arnold J. Heeney and Livingston T. Merchant, *Canada and the United States: Principles for Partnership* (Ottawa, 1965); Stanley R. Tupper *et al., United States–Canadian Relations* (mimeo.), Sept. 27, 1965; Robert S. McNamara's speech in Montreal, May 18, 1966 (Ottawa: USIA, mimeo.); and indeed any politician's utterance on the subject.

29. I develop this point further in "Canada and the United States: The Politics of Disparate Power," *The Centennial Review* (Michigan State University), X, 4 (Fall, 1966), 415–429.

The Law and Order Function of the Canadian Military

Historically, the Canadian military establishment has been kept busy at aiding the civil power. Between 1867 and 1914, two of the four occasions on which the Dominion government resorted to military force involved the restoration of law and order within the confines of the country—the dispatch to the Red River of a force of 1,000 men in 1870 and the expedition sent out in 1885 to put down the Riel Rebellion.

After the Great War, the law and order function was thought by some members of the General Staff to be the prime duty of the armed forces. An army memorandum of 1919 asserted that "the principal peril confronting us at the present moment is the danger of the overthrow of Law and Order in our own country."[30] Such was the conclusion of those who feared that the Bolshevik Revolution, which had already swept through Russia and threatened Europe, was bearing down upon Vancouver and Winnipeg, Toronto and Montreal.

Not everyone shared the view of the General Staff that military force was needed to guard against the Red menace. "I say to this Government," cried a Prairie Member of Parliament in 1920, "trust the people! The heart of the Canadian people is as sound as our No. 1 Hard Manitoba wheat."[31] (That is, very sound indeed.)

The small Permanent Force army was nonetheless used in aid of the civil power several times during the early 1920's, usually to keep order when strike action threatened to become violent. Its deployment for this purpose grated on the Prime Minister's sensibility: "I am unable to understand," Mackenzie King wrote typically in 1923, "wherein it has been necessary to send to Cape Breton the numbers of troops that are there at the present time."[32] His successor found the enterprise more congenial;[33] and during

30. Quoted in Eayrs, *In Defence of Canada*, I, 62.
31. Canada, *House of Commons Debates, 1919*, IV, 3969–3970.
32. Mackenzie King to George P. Graham, July 20, 1923, King Papers.
33. "A convention of unemployed labourers which met in Ottawa during the session of 1932 had seemed [like a] threat of revolution. . . . The staid citizens

the Great Depression coinciding with R. B. Bennett's prime-ministership there were only too many opportunities to use the military establishment to keep law and order in a troubled Canada.

During World War II, Mackenzie King's aversion to using the military in its role of aiding the civil power was evident during the emergency caused by the strike at the Arvida, Quebec, plant of the Aluminium Company of Canada. Troops were eventually used to restore order and the flow of aluminium for the war effort, but not before C. D. Howe, the minister responsible for munitions production, had threatened to resign from the government if they were not.[34]

Not since the Arvida strike of July, 1941, has the military been called out in any strength to deal with civil disorders within the Dominion. There have been at least two occasions when it might have been so deployed, but was not. During the strike in 1946 at the Steel Company of Canada's plant at Hamilton, Ontario, resort was had not to the army but to the Royal Canadian Mounted Police. Quartered at a nearby naval base, the R.C.M.P. served as a deterrent against mob violence but did not engage in any kind of physical combat. Again during the Royal visit to Quebec City in the summer of 1964, the role of preserving law and order among a hostile group of demonstrators was left to the Quebec Provincial Police. Some of its members performed their task with gusto verging upon sadism; they brought no credit upon their unit, and it was as well for the reputation of the Canadian military that none of the armed forces was involved.

To derive the benefits of the enforcement of law and order, it is not necessary that the military establishment be actually engaged

---

of Ottawa had never before witnessed such elaborate preparations for receiving a delegation. An armoured car appeared on Parliament Hill that morning; city policemen paraded up and down Wellington Street in front of the Parliament buildings; armed detachments of the Royal Canadian Mounted Police were posted in front of the East and West Blocks; another detachment, on horseback, was hidden in reserve. . . . It was an anticlimax when the delegation listened quietly to the Prime Minister's statement and then as quietly dispersed" (H. Blair Neatby, *William Lyon Mackenzie King*, Vol. II: *The Lonely Heights, 1924–1932*, Toronto, 1963, p. 401).

34. See J. W. Pickersgill, *The Mackenzie King Record*, vol. I, 1939–1944 (Toronto, 1960), pp. 228–233.

in policing. Its very existence contributes to stability. Even the most mature and responsible political community might not function so reliably, particularly in times of stress, if there were no armed force of any kind.

Granting that much, one may still be justified in concluding that contemporary Canada does not require a military establishment for the purpose of preserving law and order within the Canadian community. As a general rule, it is preferable in reasonably mature societies to use police forces for para-military duties than military forces for para-police duties.[35] This is all the more cogent where, as in Canada, the government has at its disposal a specially trained force, neither wholly police nor wholly military, but capable of functioning as either. If, as the White Paper on Defence of March, 1964, suggests, there are still "certain national tasks of a military or quasi-military nature" which need to be performed—the paper specifies "survival operations; search and rescue; communications; and aid to the civil power"—these may be done as well by a Royal Canadian Mounted Police force trained and equipped for air and sea operations. These duties might all the more expeditiously be assumed by the R.C.M.P. in view of the curtailment of its traditional role on horseback.

The Preliminary Report of the Royal Commission on Bilingualism and Biculturalism expressed the view that "Canada is in the most critical period of its history," and that "Canada has come to a time when decisions must be taken and developments must occur leading either to its break-up or to a new set of conditions for its future existence."[36] The possibility that Quebec might separate from the rest of Canada, taking its place in the state system as an independent political community, is real, if remote; and it has been argued that the maintenance of a military establishment at

35. This principle was recognized by those in charge of the international force responsible for the maintenance of law and order during the plebiscite in the Saarland in 1934/35. One of Its officers, Colonel A. II. Burne of the British Army, wrote that the force was guided throughout by three precepts, of which the second was "to keep the troops hidden away during the actual period of tension, leaving the maintenance of order, in the first instance, to the Police" (quoted in Gabriella Rosner, *The United Nations Emergency Force*, New York, 1963, p. 210).

36. A *Preliminary Report of the Royal Commission on Bilingualism and Biculturalism* (Ottawa, 1965), p. 133.

the disposal of the central government is needed to meet the threat of so mortal a blow to the Canadian body politic.

I would argue the opposite. Should the tensions of Confederation become so acute as to cause French Canada to wish to secede from the rest of Canada, it would be best to have no military establishment at the disposal of the central government lest it yield to the temptation, to which a panicky and rattled ministry might be prone, to send it out to fight in what would surely become the most futile and tragic of modern civil wars. If the government of Quebec should ever decide to issue a unilateral declaration of independence, it should be ushered into the state system with the assistance and support of the rest of Canada, not opposed by a show of force.

Much more scope for functioning in support of law and order lies outside the frontiers of the Dominion. Units of Canada's armed forces have participated in all of what, for want of a better term, have come to be called United Nations peace-keeping operations. To three of these operations—the United Nations Emergency Force in the Middle East (UNEF), the United Nations Operation in the Congo (UNOC), the United Nations Force in Cyprus (UNFICYP)—the Canadian contribution has been substantial and, in the case of UNEF and UNFICYP, critical.

What these operations have in common, distinguishing them from Allied operations during World War II and United Nations operations in the Korean War, is that they are not, or were not intended to be, combatant operations. Whatever the purposes of the forces dispatched under United Nations auspices to the scenes of disorder where their intervention was felt to be required, they were not to defeat an army in the field. Peace-keeping forces are not fighting forces. Often, being lightly armed, they are not equipped to fight. More often, being subject to confusing and even conflicting operational direction, they are not allowed to fight. If their tasks must be more positively defined, they are the tasks of interposition and of observation, investigation, and report.

In their investigatory role, peace-keepers, whether under United Nations auspices (as in Kashmir, Palestine, Lebanon,

Yemen) or not (as in Indochina), can usually keep clear of combat. Their numbers are small; perhaps fifty or sixty in all, half a dozen on a patrol; their equipment is modest: binoculars, a typewriter or two, radio, a service revolver. They are in no position to attack anybody; they are hardly in a position to defend themselves if attacked by anybody.

In their interpository role, peace-keepers have found it more difficult to maintain their noncombatant status. This was particularly difficult to maintain in the Congo. There, the anarchy of the local environment, the feebleness of the military forces challenging the United Nations, the contrasting size and power of the United Nations forces, the uncertainty of the mandate, and the lack of firm political direction from headquarters, all combined to lure UNOC across the blurred line between interposition and combat. Peace-keepers and peace-keeping suffered as a consequence.

It may not seem to matter much whether, as in the White Paper on Defence of March, 1964, peace-keeping is described as a strategic function of the military or whether, as here contended, it is better described as a law and order function. Both descriptions can be justified. On the one hand, peace-keeping even on the smallest scale in the most remote regions may, by preventing local disorders from spreading and becoming more violent, contribute indirectly to the peace and security of the international arena, upon which Canada's own peace and security ultimately depend. On the other hand, peace-keeping may be as legitimately regarded as a form of aid to the civil power, where the civil power in question is not one's own government but a foreign government.

The case for regarding peace-keeping as aiding the civil power in accordance with the principle of international concern rests upon the consideration that when it is so regarded, there is, or ought to be, less of a temptation to train, equip and deploy national contributions to peace-keeping forces as if they were on a combatant mission. When their role is conceived to be that of *gendarmerie* rather than that of battlefront soldiers, they are likely to perform their mission more successfully. The principles of aiding the civil power do not alter merely because the locale of peace-keeping is international rather than national; in foreign countries, as in one's own country, it is better to use police on para-military assignments than to use troops on para-police assignments, as the experience of police units from Australia used for peace-keeping operations on Cyprus demonstrates.

The present emphasis of Canadian policy is upon the interchangeability of personnel and equipment between the combatant and peace-keeping roles. Thus, the two brigades proposed in the White Paper as a mobile force and now on duty are "equipped to permit their effective deployment in circumstances ranging from service in the European theatre to United Nations peace-keeping operations." The consequence of this doctrine (itself the product of an admirable drive for economy and efficiency in the armed forces and of a less admirable unwillingness to face the fact that there is no longer any strategic role for Canada to play in the European theater) is that the mobile force is too lightly equipped and too small in numbers to be of much use to NATO, too heavily equipped and too large in numbers to be of much use to United Nations peace-keeping.

A case in point is the F-5, a fighter aircraft built by the Northrop Corporation, of which 115 have been purchased by the Canadian government at a cost of about $215 million. This is the machine prefigured in the White Paper, where it is described as "a high performance aircraft [which] will . . . provide sufficient flexibility for any task we might undertake from ground attack to air surveillance." So versatile an instrument, capable of functioning with equal effectiveness in the defense of North America, or of Western Europe, or of some country whose government has requested assistance of the United Nations, might well be a defense minister's dream (and a finance minister's dream). But the F-5 is not that versatile. It is unlikely to bring much joy into the lives of officers commanding NORAD, NATO, or UNFICYP. It is said to have brought some joy into the lives of American airmen in Vietnam. But Vietnam is not a theater of war for the Canadian military, and the Prime Minister of Canada has stated that it will never become a theater of war for the Canadian military.

"If our role is going to be nothing more than a purely peace-keeping one, I think that there would be a waste of time in having an air force at all."[37] This testimony by a former air marshal of the R.C.A.F. is indicative of the frustration that understandably afflicts a fighting service suddenly deprived of strategic justification. But there is still the insurance function of military power. It is this that provides the real justification for the decision to acquire the F-5 for Canadian service (together with the fact that, of the three types of aircraft under consideration, the F-5 was the cheapest). It is a means of keeping some fighter aircraft capability in being, for use at some distant date against some unknown enemy.

The Role of the Canadian Military as an Agency for Modernization and Development

Modern Canada owes its enviable position as one of the world's wealthiest and most highly industrialized powers to the demands on its potential resources of two great wars and of preparations made to deter a third.

During the Great War, the stimulus to modernization and development was experienced mainly on the home front. On the battle front, the arts of war were not such as greatly to improve the skills of the more than 300,000 Canadians who fought in the trenches. Nor could the more than 60,000 who died be easily reckoned as an economic asset, nor the wounded who returned:

> He sat in a wheeled chair, waiting for dark,
> And shivered in his ghastly suit of grey,
> Legless, sewn short at elbow. . . .

But for those who did not march away it was very different. A year after the government's Shell Committee was formed, a Canadian officer paid it the following tribute, richly deserved: "The result has been nearly 400 million dollars worth of business for Canada; one hundred thousand Canadian workmen trained to be

---

37. House of Commons, Special Committee on Defence, *Minutes of Proceedings and Evidence*, No. 6 (June 9, 1964), p. 169.

skilled; millions of shells to the front; the furnishing of an example and model for all lands; prosperity to Canada; and not one law suit."[38]

It was not just the economy that prospered; so did the nation's sense of nationhood. "From the viewpoint of power politics," a Canadian historian has commented, "Canada's contribution to the war was the strongest possible argument for its obtaining separate representation at the Peace Conference and in the League of Nations. . . . Industrialism and military power . . . made possible a Canadian national foreign policy."[39]

World War II was no less beneficial. The economy took another great leap forward. "It was during the war years [1939–45]," an official paper of the Department of Defence Production points out, "that this country emerged from its traditional position as a supplier of basic materials to become an industrialized state."[40] And once again Canada's military contribution to the war effort was used by her prime minister as an argument for a more prominent role in the United Nations. With good reason might a Canadian nationalist repeat the cynic's prayer: "Lord grant us a good harvest and a bloody war in Europe." Without two bloody European wars, Canada might still be an economically underdeveloped country, a recipient, not a donor, of foreign aid, a supplicant society, not a Samaritan state.

Between two bloody wars lay the Great Depression. During the depression, the Canadian military establishment was used in a form of civic action. It had the task of relieving the unemployed, training and putting to work on various public projects those victims of the depression who were able-bodied, single, and homeless. Much public outcry was raised against the experiment. Pacifists protested the "militarization" of young Canadians; humanitarians, their exploitation as "slave labor"; unionists, their exploitation as "scab labor." These protests were for a time ignored. But the work relief camps administered by the Depart-

38. Quoted in William Kilbourn, *The Elements Combined: A History of the Steel Company of Canada* (Toronto, 1960), p. 107.
39. *Ibid.*, p. 108.
40. Reprinted in House of Commons, Special Committee on Defence, *Minutes of Proceedings and Evidence*, No. 22 (Nov. 24, 1964), p. 898.

ment of National Defence became a symbol of all that was thought hateful about the Bennett government, and, in the campaign preceding the general election of 1935, Mackenzie King promised to abolish the camps if returned to power. He was, and he did.

Since then, the military establishment has contributed to the modernization and development of Canada in indirect ways. Two may be singled out for comment. One way is by improving the skills and efficiency of the national labor force through the skills, experience, and education imparted to the members of the armed services during their period of enlistment. The training of a modern soldier, sailor, or airman is a complex business. It is no longer a matter of learning how to disembowel a sack of straw with a bayonet. Especially in the specialized sectors of soldiering—communications, for example—the acquisition of military competence involves the acquisition of skills and techniques which make their possessor far more valuable to his society. The modern military establishment thus functions as a national institute of technology, of which the nation is the ultimate beneficiary.

At the level of officer training, no attempt is made to hide the fact that trainees are participants in higher education. They gather by the computer, rather than around the sand-table; they are more likely to listen to disquisitions about "management skills" than about how Wolfe took Quebec. The National Defence College since 1948 has been offering year-long courses in "the training of senior officers of the Armed Services and civil departments of government in the principles of higher governmental administration and staff work, both in peace and war."[41] Its curriculum, being designed in part to steep the military mind in civilian modes of thought and aimed at future deputy ministers no less than at future commanding officers, is anything but narrowly technical. It is a kind of postgraduate center for the services, just as the Canadian Forces School is a kind of senior high school or junior college for the services.

41. Quoted from the National Defence College's "Handbook for Participants."

The value of these institutions is all the greater in a country like Canada, where constitutional and political inhibitions prevent the central government from directly assisting the institutions of higher education to the extent required by the needs of the nation. But valuable as they are, they cannot in themselves constitute a sufficient reason for the maintenance of a military establishment in the absence of any other reason. The training of man-power, with its beneficial consequences for modernization and development, is a by-product of the military establishment, not an end in itself. One aids higher education by aiding higher education.

The other way in which the military establishment contributes to the modernization and development of Canada is by serving as a stimulus to industry, and as a prop to the economy of backward regions. The dependence of significant sectors of Canadian industry upon purchases by the military establishment of Canada and of other countries is stressed in an official study, "Defence Expenditure and Its Influence on the Canadian Economy," prepared by the Department of Defence Production for the House of Commons Special Committee on Defence in 1964. As might be expected, this dependence is particularly pronounced in the aircraft and air-parts industry, in shipbuilding, and in electronics.[42]

From these facts, two very different conclusions may be drawn. One is that defense production is a national asset which ought to be encouraged. Not surprisingly, this is the conclusion urged upon the government by spokesmen for those industries which stand to profit most by its adoption.[43] The other is that to the extent that Canada's prosperity derives from defense production, it is a false prosperity resting on infirm foundations. It is dependent on the enlightened self-interest of allies, principally of the United States, which may not always be forthcoming. And it is

42. Department of Defence Production, "Defence Expenditure and Its Influence on the Canadian Economy," in House of Commons, Special Committee on Defence, *Minutes of Proceedings and Evidence*, No. 22, pp. 898–901.

43. See, for example, the statement and testimony of the president of the Air Industries Association of Canada before the House of Commons, Special Committee on Defence, Nov. 26, 1964 (*Minutes of Proceedings and Evidence*, No. 23).

dependent upon the perpetuation of political tension among the great powers, which it is (or ought to be) the purpose of Canadian policy to abate.

Present policy conforms more closely to the first of these conclusions than to the second, being concerned to encourage defense industry rather than to disengage the economy from dependence on defense. It ought to be made to conform more closely to the second than to the first.

A role exists for the Canadian military as an agency for modernization and development outside the frontiers of the Dominion. The kind of direct civic action undertaken by the Canadian Army at the time of the Great Depression might now be usefully extended in aid of the economic development of other countries. These do not, of course, require mere manpower; they require trained manpower, which the armed services can supply. A Canadian development and assistance corps, specially equipped and instructed to undertake the construction of needed facilities in backward communities throughout the world, could make a more constructive contribution to international peace and security than any of the roles which present policy has so far managed to contrive for the Canadian military establishment. The cost of such an organization, and of its operations abroad, ought to be borne by the Canadian people. The bill will be sizable, perhaps even as much as the $1.5 billion annually being spent on more conventional duties. It should be emphasized that this new role for the Canadian military—it might be described as international civic action—is meant to be a substitute for conventional military duties, not a complement to them.

The expense of an international civic action role for the Canadian military may be more cheerfully borne in the knowledge that, for once, a military establishment is being used to eradicate misery and suffering rather than to inflict them.

The Ceremonial Role of the Canadian Military

A military establishment maintained for strategic or insurance purposes, for keeping law and order, or for modernization and development, may justifiably be used in a ceremonial capacity when not engaged in its primary tasks. A military establishment may justifiably be maintained solely for ceremonial reasons provided that the national pride derived from its possession contributes to the national well-being in a constructive way, and provided, as well, that it is not purchased at too high a price. What is not justifiable is to maintain an elaborate and costly military establishment solely, or largely, for ceremonial purposes. In such a case it would be better to scale down the ceremony, investing the savings in ways and means of overcoming the national inferiority complex which made so large a ceremonial commitment seem necessary.

The White Paper on Defence of March, 1964, defines the defense of Canada as "those aspects of North American defence which must, *for reasons based upon Canadian national interests,* be subject to Canadian control." The phrase I have italicized is less than frank. Not national interest but national pride compels the government of Canada to undertake for itself, rather than entrusting to others, what the White Paper calls "the minimum requirements for the defence of Canada." Entrusting them to others is an option in no way inconsistent with conduct befitting a modern state, though it is certainly inconsistent with conduct befitting overly prideful and vainglorious communities.

"The minimum requirements for the defence of Canada" are listed in the White Paper as follows: "The ability to maintain surveillance of Canadian territory, airspace and territorial waters; the ability to deal with military incidents on Canadian territory; the ability to deal with incidents in the ocean areas off the Canadian coasts; and the ability to contribute, within the limits of our resources, to the defence of Canadian airspace." The qualification attached to the last of these tasks suggests that all but the last lie well within the capacity of Canada to finance and perform on her own. This is obviously true of some of them—for example, dealing with military incidents on Canadian territory or maintaining surveillance of Canadian territory. It is less obviously true of others—for example, maintaining surveillance of Canadian territorial waters or air space.

Surveillance of territorial waters is suggestive of traditional and modest maritime missions—chasing smugglers to their lair or warning foreign fishermen who venture too close to shore. These missions do not cost much and in their nature cannot be entrusted to a foreign jurisdiction. There is no case, therefore, for Canada devolving them on any navy (or air force) other than her own armed forces, although there is a case for devolving them upon non-military or para-military forces.

Today, however, surveillance of territorial waters involves, in addition to these traditional tasks, looking out for enemy submarines. This mission costs a good deal. To perform it, the Canadian government appropriated $213 million in 1964—$142 million to acquire four helicopter-carrying destroyers of new design (the so-called DDH program), $65 million to convert seven destroyer escort ships to anti-submarine warfare (ASW) ships, $8 million to purchase two operational support ships, and $8 million to refit and improve the aircraft carrier "Bonaventure."[44] (These were estimates only: it is the way with estimates to fall short of final costs, and Canada's 1964 ASW estimates have conformed to this rule.)

The motivation for Canada's commitment to a costly anti-submarine warfare role is mixed, as motives usually are. It is argued that the role has strategic significance, providing "defence against surface and air attacks which can be expected during this time period [i.e., until the 1970's]",[45] that it serves an insurance function, that the ships involved can be used "to support peace-keeping operations,"[46] that participation in ASW is as good a way as any other for Canada to demonstrate to her allies that she is prepared to assume a fair share of the burden of the common defense. Something may be said in justification of each of these contentions, most on behalf of the last, least on behalf of the first. The basic motive has to do with status and with stature. Not strategy, not safety, not security, but national self-respect causes the Canadian government to make its own provision for surveil-

44. House of Commons, Special Committee on Defence, *Minutes of Proceedings and Evidence*, No. 26 (March 25, 1965), p. 1058.
45. *Ibid.*, p. 1047.
46. *Ibid.*, p. 1049.

lance of its own territorial waters and of the ocean adjacent to its coastlines.

The element of pride is also discernible in the fact that the ships to be procured for the ASW role are to be of Canadian design, rather than of British or American design. This makes them more costly than if they were purchased from the United Kingdom or the United States. The extra cost has been justified by the Director-General, Ships, Royal Canadian Navy, in the following words:

I think a warship is very much a Canadian entity. It is much more representative of our national ethos than is an airplane. It represents a way of life, which is one thing in the destroyers we have designed ourselves and is a very different thing when you come to try it out in a vessel of another nation. . . . I subscribe to our doing our own design. . . .[47]

So does the Minister of National Defence, for slightly different reasons: "It does increase our costs," Hellyer conceded in March, 1965, "but, at the same time, . . . we are able to introduce Canadian concepts, improvements and adapt Canadian equipment, which has an industrial application as well."[48]

Surveillance of Canadian air space is a further aspect of North American defense which, in the words of the White Paper, "must, for reasons based upon Canadian national interests, be subject to Canadian control." To rely on United States aircraft to perform the vital mission of identification of unknown aircraft in Canadian air space has been considered to be incompatible with Canadian sovereignty and unbecoming to Canadian status.

Consequently, Canada has relied upon her own aircraft to perform the vital mission. Unhappily for its effective performance, there was a period of perhaps four years (1957 or so to 1961 or so) when Canada possessed no aircraft capable of keeping up with Air Canada airliners, let alone with Soviet jet bombers.[49] Despite this deficiency, no consideration was given to inviting the United States Air Force to do the job on Canada's behalf. Only when the CF-101 (Voodoo) interceptor replaced the slower

47. *Ibid.,* p. 1077.
48. *Ibid.,* p. 1076
49. House of Commons, Special Committee on Defence Expenditures, *Minutes of Proceedings and Evidence,* No. 4 (May 18, 1960), p. 102.

CF-100 in Canadian service was this gap in the defense of North America finally filled in. It was not the only gap for which the government of that day must bear some responsibility.

The White Paper concedes that there is one aspect of the defense of Canada which it may not be possible for Canadians to manage on their own. This is "the defence of Canadian airspace," for which the White Paper requires only that the armed forces "contribute, within the limit of our own resources." On August 1, 1957, the governments of Canada and the United States announced that they had agreed "to the setting up of a system of integrated operational control of the air defense forces in the Continental United States, Alaska and Canada under an integrated command responsible to the chiefs of staff of both countries."[50] This cryptic announcement concealed what may in retrospect be regarded as a crucial decision. But it may not have been so regarded at the time.

It is still far from certain exactly how the government of Canada took the decision. According to the then Prime Minister, John Diefenbaker, the agreement had been worked out by the preceding Liberal government.[51] According to the then senior military adviser to the government, General Charles Foulkes, the Liberal government had thought it unwise to implement the decision in view of an impending election campaign, telling him that it would be done after the election had been won.[52] It was fought and—for the Liberals—lost. It seems that the new Conservative government, having no very clear idea of what the draft agreement duly coming before them was all about, accepted it in the mistaken belief that its subject was of routine significance only. Certainly the faltering replies of ministers to questioning in Parliament once the terms of the agreement became known suggest an imperfect mastery of its implications. "I do not regard the command of NORAD as having actual command over either United States or

50. New York *Times*, Aug. 2, 1957, p. 1.
51. Canada, *House of Commons Debates, 1958*, I, 993.
52. Interview with the writer, Oct. 20, 1960. See also General Charles Foulkes, "The Complications of Continental Defence," in Livingston T. Merchant, ed., *Neighbors Taken for Granted* (New York and Toronto, 1966), pp. 115–116.

Canadian units," the Minister of National Defence stated in the House of Commons on June 11, 1958. He added: "However, I should like to have the time to explore the situation and find out about it more definitely, because it has not been brought to my attention."[53]

George Pearkes' initial reaction proved to be the correct reaction. That what was called "operational control," with which it was conceded that NORAD had been vested, was something very different from actual control became starkly evident in October, 1962. The Canadian interceptors assigned to NORAD remained in their usual status, in contrast to the United States component which had been alerted to the possibility of a Soviet attack on North America, until forty-two hours after President Kennedy's speech to the world disclosing that the Soviet Union had constructed intermediate-range ballistic missile bases in Cuba. A United States request for permission to move some interceptor squadrons to Canadian bases, and to arm R.C.A.F. interceptors with nuclear weapons, was refused by the Canadian government. When asked to explain the reason for his government's position, the Secretary of State for External Affairs remarked that the government was primarily concerned "with trying to keep the Canadian people from getting all excited about this business."[54] If that was the object of the enterprise, it did not succeed.

In April, 1966, a new operations center at NORAD headquarters in Colorado Springs, Colorado, built deep inside a mountain at a cost of $142.4 million, was formally inaugurated. To mark the event, United States and Canadian flags were raised at the main entrance to the underground complex. A ceremony planned in conjunction with the flag-raising had to be canceled because of snow and cold.

Canada's membership in NORAD has always been primarily of ceremonial and symbolic significance. It has cost the country a good deal to have its flag run up outside Cheyenne Mountain in

53. Canada, *House of Commons Debates, 1958,* (June 11), p. 1044.
54. Quoted in Denis Stairs, "Canada and Cuba" (unpublished paper).

Colorado. The opportunity to take it down will be presented in August, 1968, when, under the terms of notes exchanged by the member governments on May 12, 1958, the North American Air Defence Command is no longer to function. It may, of course, be renegotiated. It is to be hoped that, having done its ceremonial duty, it may be allowed to lapse.

The Diplomatic Role of the Canadian Military

"The objectives of Canadian defence policy, which cannot be distinguished from foreign policy, are to preserve the peace by supporting collective defence measures to deter military aggression; to support Canadian foreign policy including that arising out of our participation in international organizations; and to provide for the protection and surveillance of our territory, our air-space and our coastal waters." In these words, the White Paper on Defence of March, 1964, defines the purposes the military establishment of Canada is meant to serve.

Of these purposes, the diplomatic role of the Canadian military —the maintenance and deployment of armed forces as an adjunct to various non-military techniques of statecraft—is listed second. If the decisive criterion were that of importance, it should be listed first.

The principal justification for the retention, despite the current absence of any strategic role, of military forces of the scope and on the scale now contemplated is that so sizable a commitment assists Canadian diplomacy. One does not find this proposition so baldly stated in official policy pronouncements, but it is no less true for all of that. "The key decisions," an unofficial pronouncement observes, "which would determine our survival, are now made outside of Canada—in centers such as Washington, Moscow, New York, Paris and Peking. We want to be able to influence those decisions, and cannot do so effectively unless we are paying, in the form of armed force, our membership fees in a number of international organizations." And, "The overriding factors in determining the content of Canada's military policy can, and should, be the resolve to purchase influence. There is no other country for which this consideration is more compelling."[55] The compulsion of this consideration, more than any other, has determined Canada's unwavering military contribution to the North Atlantic Treaty Organization.

It has been noted previously that when the object of a military commitment is primarily political and diplomatic—to demonstrate good will to allies rather than to demonstrate strength to enemies—it may not matter too much what the nature of the commitment is, just so long as it is expensive. If the object is to convince one's friends that one is bearing fair shares of sacrifice, the important thing is the tangible evidence of sacrifice. Defense policy, under such conditions, may properly become a policy of *potlatch*.[56]

Examples are not hard to come by. The most conspicuous is the decision of the Diefenbaker government to accept what came to be known as a "strike-reconnaissance" role for the R.C.A.F., to be performed on NATO's behalf in Western Europe.[57] By this decision, Canada undertook to maintain eight squadrons of CF-104 Starfighters (eighteen aircraft to a squadron) at bases in France and Germany. It has been suggested that, as with the decision to sign the NORAD agreement, the inexperienced Diefenbaker government did not fully realize the implications of this commitment, being unaware that the strike-reconnaissance role was intended to be a nuclear role. Be that as it may, the government surely real-

55. Peyton V. Lyon, "Defence Policies Related to Foreign Policy," in *Special Studies Prepared for the Special Committee of the House of Commons on Matters Relating to Defence* (Ottawa, 1965), p. 26.

56. This notwithstanding the testimony of John Gellner before the House of Commons, Special Committee on Defence: "We simply cannot afford to take on commitments when we know that the equipment we are purchasing serves no military purpose. . . . To buy a merchant ship and to put in Polaris missiles only for political reasons would be a terrible waste of money" (*Minutes of Proceedings and Evidence*, No. 16, Oct. 24, 1963, p. 563).

57. Exactly when the government made up its mind to accept the strike-reconnaissance role has not been officially disclosed. According to the then chief of the air staff, Air Marshal C. R. Dunlap, it made its decision "in the spring of 1959 when General Norstad, who was then SACEUR, came to Ottawa and outlined the need for a strike role and suggested that perhaps Canada participate" (House of Commons, Special Committee on Defence, *Minutes of Proceedings and Evidence*, No. 18, Oct. 31, 1963, p. 649).

ized that, nuclear or non-nuclear, it would be a costly role. That was why it was undertaken.[58]

The military significance of this force has always been marginal, despite the fact that once equipped (after mid-1963) with nuclear weapons it constituted one of the most formidably destructive weapons systems in the world.[59] NATO already had so much megatonnage and kilotonnage at its disposal that the addition of Canadian capability only added to the overkill, while adding microscopically to the deterrent. But the force was not created for its military significance. It was created for its diplomatic significance. It is an illustration of the Luxembourg effect on a larger scale. Its purpose is exemplary and inspirational. It is intended to provide evidence of what Canada is prepared to do in defense of people and territory three thousand miles from the Canadian people and Canadian territory and, by so fine an example of sacrifice, encourage others to enter into and abide by comparable commitments.

58. The capital cost to Canada of the roughly two hundred aircraft involved, including extra engines, spare parts, tools, and twenty-two trainer aircraft, amounted to more than $420 million. The annual upkeep of the force constitutes by far the largest item in the bill for Canada's membership in NATO. Just how large that bill is the government has been unwilling to say:
> *Mr. Herridge*: . . . we ought to be able to save our present costs of maintaining our forces in NATO, which I understand amounts to $500 million a year. Is that correct, sir?
> *Mr. Hellyer*: I should not want to comment on the figure.
> *Mr. Herridge*: The Minister does not want to comment.
> *Mr. Hellyer*: It depends how you apportion it.

(Canada, *House of Commons Debates, 1966*, (Feb. 18), p. 1493)

59. Asked to comment on the destructive capability of one air division, its commanding officer offered the following information: "Let me give you a few parameters against which you can form your own answer. . . . War is an ugly business. . . . I was on the first thousand bomber raid . . . . It was comprised of four and two engined bombers and let us say there were 3000 engines thumping away carrying this force aloft . . . . The average weight of bombs . . . was probably in the neighborhood of two and a half tons . . . . We will say 2000 tons [total] just by way of loose figures. The time taken to complete this was an hour and a half over the target . . . . The target was Cologne . . . . According to the reports at that time, we burned up 935 acres, I don't know how many were killed or wounded or made homeless. Now, we get over here. I have got one engine, not 3000, I put one aircrew, I put one minute, if the distance is roughly the same, . . . I will put down, like Ivory Soap, 99.9 percent, and the damage he will do, I don't know but it will be ballpark for that. . . . It is a large destructive effect . . . . This is nuclear. . . ." "That," responded a member of his audience, "is the clearest answer we have had from anyone." The record does not disclose whether any irony was intended. (House of Commons, Special Committee on Defence, *Minutes of Proceedings and Evidence*, No. 20, Nov. 14, 1963, pp. 707–708.)

A similar purpose is intended, and served, by the infantry brigade group of approximately 6,000 officers and men maintained at Soest, West Germany. This force, it has been noted, "amounts numerically to one four-hundredths of the allied troops available in Europe."[60] What is its mission? If to roll back the Red Army, it is clearly too tiny. For that mission Canada should maintain two to three divisions in Western Europe, not a brigade group—50,000 to 60,000 troops, not 5,000 to 6,000. If, on the other hand, the force is composed not of soldiers of fortune but of hostages to fortune, it is probably too large. A regiment would do as well.[61] When Field Marshal Foch was asked in 1913 what he considered to be the smallest British unit that would be of practical assistance to France in the event of war with Germany, he is said to have replied: "A single private soldier, and we would take good care to see that he was killed."

When a military establishment is maintained primarily for diplomatic purposes, it is much more difficult to know how large it should be, what its composition should be, what its weaponry should be, than when it is maintained primarily for strategic purposes.

Canada's military establishment is maintained primarily for diplomatic purposes, Sweden's primarily for strategic purposes. The Swedish Parliament has thus described the armed forces it deems to be required for this role:

The armed forces are to work for the preservation of our peace and freedom. Therefore, the armed services are to have such strength, com-

60. Andrew Brewin, *Stand on Guard: The Search for a Canadian Defence Policy* (Toronto, 1965), pp. 49–50.
61. As hostages to fortune, the brigade group offers far more than its own personnel: the dependents of its own personnel are cast involuntarily in that unenviable role. The officer in charge of their well-being has thus described his task: "There are to look after . . . approximately 3,000 families. . . . We have 2,700 odd school children who attend in 113 classrooms and we have 151 teachers. . . . We have a gymnasium, we have four artifical ice rinks, bowling alleys, squash courts, theatres, Junior Ranks Club; . . . churches we have one each, Roman Catholic and Protestant. . . . We have tennis courts and the usual sports fields. . . . You will find . . . Boy Scouts, the Cubs, the Girl Guides, the Brownies, the Teacher Parent Home and School Association, the Teen-Age groups, Little League Hockey, Little League Baseball, the Cadet Corps. . . . We have three banks. . . . We have our own radio station. . . . We have our own newspaper . . ." (House of Commons, Special Committee on Defence, *Minutes of Proceedings and Evidence*, No. 20, Nov. 16, 1963, pp. 721–722).

position and state of preparedness that attacks against Sweden require such large resources and are so prolonged that the advantages which stand to be gained by the attack cannot be realistically evaluated as worth the costs.[62]

How can this formulation be adapted for the Canadian condition? One starts as follows: "The armed forces are to work for the maintenance and enhancement of our prestige and influence. Therefore, the armed services are to have such strength, composition, and state of preparedness that. . . ." That what? One begins easily enough. One cannot conclude.

When military outlays are used to purchase defense, rather than to purchase influence, the question "How much is enough?" becomes relatively easy to answer. "The military planning process," Charles Burton Marshall has written, "insofar as it relates to the ponderables of real or hypothetical campaigns, turns out tidy and complete answers. . . . The quotients are precise, the columns are even, and the conclusions concrete."[63] It is otherwise when military outlays are used to purchase influence rather than defense. The first assignment involves proportions of force, readily quantified by computers and cost accountants. The second involves intangibles of assessment, which even the most experienced foreign service officers (one might say especially the most experienced) do not dare to venture with any pretense at precision.

The rate of exchange between military outlay and influence is fluctuating and uncertain. But that is not all. Influence acquired in one capital may diminish influence in another. To the complexities of calculating the costs of influence one must add the complexities of calculating the ratios of power. The medium of exchange between military outlay and influence is by no means tried and true. Consider the following. Country *A* has two allies. Ally *B* is diligent in the performance of its duties; it pays its dues, it keeps its commitments, it does not complain, it does not criti-

62. Quoted in Kjell Goldmann, "An 'Isolated' Attack Against Sweden and Its World Political Preconditions," in *Co-operation and Conflict: Nordic Studies in International Politics*, No. II (1965), p. 18.

63. Charles Burton Marshall, "The Nature of Foreign Policy," in *The Exercise of Sovereignty* (Baltimore, 1965), p. 61.

cize. Ally *C* is far from diligent; it reneges, it defaults, it back-slides, it is outspoken in criticism. Who familiar with recent international history would dare to say which of the two allies is assured of greater consideration?

Finally, the concept of influence itself is not to be taken for granted. It should be analyzed, not assumed. Credit may not exist, or may exist only imperfectly, in international society. The state system may not resemble a banking system. It may be impossible, or difficult, to accumulate a balance of favorable regard. Governments may have no memory or their memory may be short.

To raise such questions is to challenge the whole set of assumptions on which Canadian defense policy has rested over the past ten years. It is hardly surprising that no minister of national defense has tried to raise them. It is enough that he should be preoccupied with the project of unifying the armed forces and with the host of administrative trivia to which this absorbing matter has in recent months given rise. What to call the unified force? How to designate its officers and men? What sort of uniforms should they wear? These questions are not so easily answered as one might suppose. They stir up vested interests, they arouse strong emotions, they consume in consequence time and energy better expended, perhaps, on other things. But troublesome as they are, they are not so toublesome as questions which lead to the conclusion that even a unified force contributes little to the Canadian national interest in the years to come.

11

Canadian External Relations at the Centennial of Confederation

Richard A. Preston

The nature of Canada's relations with other powers gives important clues to Canada's future and may be the crucial question in an investigation of the Canadian scene on the eve of the celebration of the centenary of Confederation. To explore this question it is necessary to study the situation that Canada faces externally, to uncover the underlying factors that have determined decisions in the past, and to note the degree of success obtained. When these things are understood it will be easier to assess the impact of current uncertainties and to attempt forecasts.

To understand Canadian foreign policy problems, a classical model of the control of foreign policy in the early part of this century must first be examined. It was a basic assumption that foreign policy was manipulated in the interests of the state; and the first duty of policy-makers was to guard against all external danger. Since any infringement of sovereignty was customarily regarded as a step toward the elimination of independence, its every aspect was guarded jealously. Adequate defense against future military threats had to be accompanied by care lest a rival or potential enemy, or even a nation that was currently friendly, gain an advantage in time of peace by securing strategic territory, by making hostile alliances with other powers, or by any other means.

The second interest that had to be satisfied was the maintenance of the well-being and the cultural identity of the people of the state. Every government, and especially every constitutional government, was (and still is) obliged to identify these interests and to secure them in order to retain public support. Its capacity to do this depends on many natural circumstances beyond its control; but of first importance in the conditions prevailing in international relations earlier in the century was the fact that almost the only ultimate arbiter in quarrels between states was war. Therefore foreign policy had to be backed by power and covered by alliances. Negotiation had to be from strength. Strength depended not merely on the size and condition of a nation's armed forces and on the steadfastness of its allies, but also on its strategic position, its natural resources, the number, temperament, ability, and orderliness of its people, the stability of its government, the efficiency and probity of its administration, and finally on the state of its economic development. Although in some cases there had to be a choice between guns and butter, prosperity was generally regarded as desirable in order to bolster national strength as well as to satisfy the inhabitants.

There were important factors qualifying this state of affairs. Where rival groups or interests or policies conflicted, it was the task of government to decide which contributed more to the general good. But since the interests and capacities of a state change only slowly, it followed that foreign policy continued to run along pretty much the same lines despite changes of government or of the personnel within a particular government: bipartisanship has been a noticeably common phenomenon in foreign policy.

In the past, resort to war to solve national problems was deterred by alternative peaceful ambitions, by fear of retaliation, and by power balances. But in this century, the classical concept of *Realpolitik*, in which war seemed the rule rather than the exception, became modified by certain forms of attempted restraint. One was the League of Nations, conceived as a result of the devastation of World War I. Aggression—if it could have been defined—would have been made impossible by the collective action of all other states—if that could have been organized effectively. Collective security failed dismally in the thirties; but it had become so much an accepted concept of the world state system that when World War II ended it was promptly revived—only to become blocked immediately by the cold war between the two greatest powers.

By the outset of the cold war a second restraint upon war had already appeared as a result of the development of the atom bomb. It became apparent, especially after fusion bombs supplemented fission bombs, that war might now possibly lead to the destruction of civilization or even to the extermination of man. Although not entirely ruled out in all its forms, war became a less satisfactory means of backing foreign policy because it might escalate into a total nuclear conflict that could not be contemplated with equanimity by any except madmen or fools. The full impact of this restraint became clear when the two rival major powers each obtained the capacity to destroy the other with a resultant deterrence in the form of a "balance of terror" brought about by mutual fear of an unacceptable nuclear attack that could not be resisted or prevented.

A third modification of the classical model of foreign policy manipulation came with the collapse of Western imperialism after World War II; but it had roots deep in the past. Subject peoples won their freedom because national independence had come to be regarded as a moral right which liberal imperial powers no longer wished or were able to deny. Many newly freed peoples lacked the economic and military strength that the seizure and maintenance of independence had previously required. But their emergence was facilitated by the existence of a partially effective system of collective security and also by the increase in their bargaining power due to the cold war. They came to exercise a collective influence in international affairs out of all proportion to their military and economic power.

In a speech delivered to the Council of the World Veterans Federation in May, 1966, Canadian Prime Minister Pearson outlined his view of the impact of these changes in the international scene. He spoke of the need for the subordination of national policy to international imperatives, including even the subordination of the ultimate national policy of survival itself. He said that full recognition of the interdependence of all peoples should have priority over the independence of each state. International imperatives require the recognition of the fact that no nation, not even the most powerful, can now guarantee its own security, let alone the security of others, by its own strength. They require the acceptance of the necessity of collective action for collective security. Pearson declared, "To fall back on nationalist policies and nationalist organization for defence and security in the nuclear and jet age is as foolish and archaic as a cavalry charge against a tank armed with nuclear cannon."[1] His statement that even the most powerful nation in the world cannot guarantee its own security by its own endeavors alone referred, of course, to the United States.

This expression of the Canadian Prime Minister's view of the current imperatives of international relations must be borne in mind when Canadian external policy is examined. It does not mean that the Canadian approach to foreign politics is entirely utopian. The occupants of the External Affairs offices in the East Block at Ottawa are hardheaded realists trained in the rough school of practical international politics; and the Prime Minister himself was originally one of them and is no starry-eyed amateur. But for historical and contemporary reasons Canadian policy is more flexible than that of the United States. Although compelled to accept the political implications of a continuing ethnic division, the Canadian founding fathers consciously rejected a constitution as loose as that which had plunged the United States into civil war. Furthermore, brought by the greater difficulties they faced in western expansion to rely more heavily on the central government, Canadians have developed an outlook on politics quite different from that of Americans. A Canadian scholar has recently suggested that these frustrating experiences in nation-building have had an effect on his country's attitudes in foreign policy. Canadians are less likely to see the world in hard shades of black and white or in terms of good and bad, they are less afraid of

1. Lester B. Pearson, to the Council of the World Veterans Federation, May 11, 1966, quoted in *CIIA Monthly Report*, V (May, 1966), 66.

state-centered economic systems which they have rejected for themselves, they are less prone to regard force as the ultimate solvent of international difficulties, and they are more pragmatic and more prepared to compromise.[2] They are thus in certain ways better able to adjust to a world that is different from the classical model of international politics than is the United States.

Hence although in general in agreement with the United States that resistance to Communist aggression is the most pressing problem of today, Canadians differ both about the degree of its paramountcy and about how to tackle it. They find Americans have been inclined at times to label as Communist almost any government that they dislike or which opposes them internationally. In particular Canadians think that the United States has been too quick to class as part of a worldwide Communist conspiracy revolutionary upheavals that are caused primarily by local poverty or by insurgent nationalism or by anticolonialism. They believe that force alone can be no solution to such problems and they lean more readily to policies that will check the spread of communism at its roots. They are quicker to see signs of a softening in Communist attitudes and also to attempt to enlarge any *détente* into a permanent state of coexistence. It must be noted in passing, however, that they are able to take a more tolerant view of the motives of certain other countries only because they have less immediate responsibility than a great power.

Prime Minister Pearson stated his position on relations with the Communist world categorically (and did not adopt the ambivalent approach of his predecessor in order to appeal to ethnic group voters) when he told Paris reporters in January, 1964, that he believed there could be no question of toppling regimes or of "rolling back Communism by armed might" in an age when a local incident at some critical point could escalate to a nuclear war between two superpowers, each of which has the power to annihilate the other.[3] Paul Martin, Secretary of State for External

2. Alastair M. Taylor, "Multi-relationship in American and Canadian Foreign Policies," *C.A.A.S. Bulletin*, I (Winter, 1966), 62–64.
3. Lester B. Pearson, to the press in Paris, Jan. 17, 1964, *CIIA Monthly Report*, III (Jan., 1964), 2.

Affairs, added later that the Canadian government believes that since Cuba, the U.S.S.R. has come to think much in the same way as Canada about the danger of nuclear war.[4] With regard to the Chinese menace, although careful not to offend the United States by recognition of a regime which has, indeed, given no evidence of a willingness to come half way, Canada braved American disapproval by selling the Communist regime huge quantities of wheat when it was plagued by a critical shortage and also took other steps designed to reduce its isolation by fostering press contacts.[5] Although these wheat deals were made to relieve Canada of embarrassing surpluses, they were in line with the frequently expressed Canadian belief that ostracism is not an effective answer to Chinese intransigence. In 1966 Canada proposed that the question of the presence of "two Chinas" in the United Nations should be considered by a committee and Paul Martin went to Moscow to explore the possibility of Russian co-operation in ending the war in Vietnam.

A preference for solutions based in this way on the international imperatives suggested by Pearson is a product of the Canadian outlook as well as of the fact that a smaller power inevitably hopes that morality may help to compensate for its relative weakness. It is also a product of the timing of the emergence of Canada as an independent state. Complete Canadian control of foreign policy was secured only after the birth of the concept of a system of international collective security: a fully independent Canada and the League of Nations were both progeny of the Treaty of Versailles in 1919. Hence the Canadian diplomatic machine never knew the pre-collective-security world and so may be less conditioned by it. In the twenties and thirties Canada lacked the diplomatic staff to pursue a distinctive policy of its own; and Prime Minister Mackenzie King was mainly concerned to strive—rather unnecessarily in his day—for independent status against a possible reassertion of British control. Canada

4. Paul Martin, at Wayne State University, June 18, 1964, *CIIA Monthly Report,* III (June, 1964), 64.
5. Paul Martin at Kitchener, Ont., press banquet, April 18, 1964, *CIIA Monthly Report,* III (April, 1964), 47.

was at the time strongly influenced by the American example of isolation from Europe's problems; and Canadians were absorbed first with national economic development and then with recovering from the Great Depression. Accordingly it was not until the traumatic and yet stimulating experience of involvement in World War II that Canada began to build a full-scale diplomatic corps and to develop a distinctive and constructive Canadian foreign policy.[6] Significantly these developments were contemporaneous with the emergence of the United States from isolation.

An early offspring of foreign policy fashioned in the new Canadian mold was the NATO alliance which both Canadians and Americans have claimed as their brainchild. There has never been any question about where Canada stands in the cold war struggle that made NATO necessary; but Canadian views about it differ in some respects from those of the United States. Although both countries agree upon the need for the co-operation of "like-minded" peoples to resist Russian Communist expansion in Europe, Canada's interest in the economic aspect of the NATO alliance can be seen in the fruitless insertion of Article II in the NATO pact. Furthermore, Canadians have been less prone to regard NATO as an exclusive alternative for an ineffective United Nations.

In part this different attitude came about because, once the United States accepted the burden of world leadership, aggressive communism became the single adversary to the defeat of which foreign policy was directed. Canadians, however, were not completely convinced. Although most of them believed that communism represents the greatest and most immediate challenge to Canada's security and to the Canadian way of life, many are also of the opinion that their identity and their prosperity might, in the long run, suffer at American hands. While Americans find it difficult to believe that Americanization, or American investment, are

6. For the growth of the Canadian Department of External Affairs, see Department of External Affairs, Information Division, Reference Paper 69, *The Department of External Affairs* (June, 1959; rev. Aug., 1961). The department aims at putting Canadian representatives in all major African and Middle Eastern capitals and at reducing the number of joint accreditations (Charles Taylor, "The Diplomats: The Generalist Slowly Gives Way to the Specialist," Toronto *Globe and Mail*, July 21, 1966).

evils, many Canadians fear them almost as much as they fear communism;[7] and the American presence is closer. Opposition to communism does not, therefore, claim undivided attention in Canada. Many Canadians are worried about the impact of the United States on their cultural, economic, and political identity.

This perverse attitude is perhaps easier to comprehend when it is recalled that Canada exists as a separate political entity only because the United States did not follow its manifest destiny to the north. It matters little whether the explanation of this omission is British protection, or American lack of appetite, or a combination of both things. What is important is that Canadians feel that they have created a form of society and government that is peculiarly their own, that is as free and democratic as that of the United States, but that is peculiarly Canadian and so is preferable. Many feel that this special Canadian polity and society is endangered in the future at least as much by peaceful American pressure as it was in the past by threat of militant American invasion, and as much as it is at present by the possibility of Communist aggression. They are afraid that an American obsession with the cold war menace, if made to seem a desperate emergency that requires all hands on deck, might lead to the neglect of long-term Canadian interests.

The result is that Canadian foreign policy cannot be considered apart from Canadian-American relations which are interwoven in every part of its fabric. Therefore, before exploring further the nature of Canadian policy in general, something must be said about certain features of those relations. Discussion of this one part of Canadian policy at this point is appropriate because, although for political reasons or as a result of national pride, official presentations and even some academic studies in Canada often seem to deny it tacitly, every aspect of Canadian foreign policy must in fact be considered against the background of the peculiar relations that Canada has with her neighbor to the south.

7. The latest expression of this fear is to be found in Walter Gordon, *A Choice for Canada* (Toronto, 1966). Gordon's successor as minister of revenue, Mitchell Sharp, is less afraid of American investment (Blair Fraser, "The Sharp/Gordon Debate," *Maclean's*, LXXIX, July 23, 1966, 8–9, 36–38).

The Canadian Secretary of State for External Affairs recently pointed out that for the U.S.S.R., the United States is the only non-Communist country worthy of attention. Canada, he said, was of interest to Russia less for what it is itself than because it is close to the United States, a position which gives its views more weight than if they had been uttered in isolation.[8] It is equally true, but for political reasons it is more difficult to put as bluntly in Canada, that a Canadian reaction to Russian policies cannot be indifferent to American views. Although they do not always care to admit it, Canadian policy-makers must always keep one eye on Washington—even if only to be able to deny promptly any suggestion that Canadian policy is made there.

No other two states have so many intimate and exclusive social and economic relationships with each other and have developed such a successful partnership. However, disparity in population in the proportion of ten to one creates problems for Canada that are exaggerated in their effect beyond that mathematical proportion by American acceptance of worldwide responsibilities and by Canada's loneliness in the American shadow. Even when the government in Washington realizes the desirability of preserving a special relationship with Canada, American private or local government interests can be less than sympathetic and may pursue policies that seem inimical to Canadian interests and cannot easily be brought in line with United States government policy. Furthermore, the American government is often so engrossed in other problems arising from its far-reaching responsibilities that it tends to take Canada's acquiescence for granted. Canadians, on the other hand, frequently overlook the fact that there is a great deal of American sympathy and respect for Canada and also that Americans do not want the relationship to seem like one of master and slave. Furthermore, although Livingston Merchant, who has twice been American ambassador in Ottawa, could claim in 1962, "I cannot think of another country in history that exerted as much

8. Paul Martin, "Canada's Role in East-West Relations," speech at Carleton University, March 11, 1966, in Department of External Affairs, Information Division, *Statements and Speeches*, No. 66/10, p. 9.

influence on a larger neighbor,"[9] that influence is often exercised by diplomacy and therefore without publicity. The result is that many Canadians believe that their interests are often either deliberately infringed or ignored.

Canadians often complain that Americans know far less about Canada than they themselves know about the United States. Examination of the newspapers in the two countries suggests that this is largely true; but the degree of informed and intelligent Canadian opinion on American relations is nevertheless also quite low and some of it is very prejudiced. Poor attendance at the infrequent foreign policy debates in the House of Commons, and even at the sessions of the blue-ribbon Committee on External Affairs,[10] and the excessive sniping of Members of Parliament and the press about American attitudes and encroachments is an indication of this state of affairs. Policy formation is in the hands of professional diplomats, but the politicians have their say at crucial points, and they are at times inclined to pander to cruder expressions of public opinion that are too often based on prejudices. Former Prime Minister Diefenbaker used to suggest that he was not anti-American, only pro-Canadian.[11] The distinction is not always clear. Nationalism tends to be a negative rather than a positive force, developed more often against foreigners rather than for constructive purposes. According to the frequently expressed opinion of Canadian nationalists, Canada lacks a clear identity. If this is true (and it is not entirely so), then the country must have less attraction as an idea upon which popular opinion can focus. Therefore, as Canada lies so close to the United States, and as it is abnormally subject to American influences, even though Canadians envy many aspects of American life, Canadian nationalism easily becomes anti-Americanism available for political exploitation.

9. Statement to the press in Montreal, Feb. 12, 1962, *CIIA Monthly Report,* I (Feb., 1962), 17–18.

10. Robert Spencer, "External Affairs and Defence," in *Canadian Annual Review for 1961* (Toronto, 1962), p. 131.

11. E.g., "Hemisphere and Global Problems," address to the Kiwanis Convention, Toronto, July 3, 1961, *Statements and Speeches,* No. 61/7, p. 2.

A long common border, closely intermeshed economies, shared waterways, far-reaching media of mass communication, and the North American habits of traveling often and for long distances and of thinking in wide horizons, have provided many points of contact at which bilateral difficulties can develop. The Canadian sense of being at a disadvantage means that Canadian feelings are quickly aroused. Even so, although the smaller degree of American interest and concern in the relationship makes it necessary for Canadians to be eternally vigilant, and although there have been many occasions on which Canadian fear of American encroachment has led to public outcry, the achievement of good Canadian-American relations on local problems of mutual concern has been extraordinarily successful. It has been achieved by effective diplomacy and has been marked by the growth of institutions for bilateral co-operation like the International Commission on Boundaries and Waterways, the Permanent Joint Board on Defense, the Canada–United States Inter-Parliamentary Group, the Canada–United States Ministerial Committee on Joint Defense, and the Joint United States–Canada Committee on Trade and Economic Affairs.

Although many Canadians believe that the preponderance of power on the American side of the bargaining table inevitably means that Canada gets the worse end of all deals and in all joint bodies, the United States has made many concessions by grace rather than by need. A case in point is the sharing of defense production when the building of the NORAD system led to large purchase of whole weapons systems in the United States for use in Canada and when the balance of defense-buying therefore moved heavily against Canada. By agreement between the two governments arrangements were made to facilitate defense subcontracting by Canadian firms, and this more than redressed the Canadian grievance about failure to share production. Yet, as the Minister of National Defence, Paul Hellyer, pointed out, there is still room for a greater Canadian share in development.[12]

12. "Canada—Neighbour not Satellite," address at Houghton College, N.Y., April 29, 1966, *CIIA Monthly Report*, V (April, 1966), 50; Richard A. Preston, *Canada in World Affairs 1959–1961* (Toronto, 1965), pp. 158–162.

The successful solution of many bilateral problems of this kind in Canadian-American relations is, however, a result rather than a cause of overall harmony. When Canadian-American relations deteriorated severely over nuclear weapons policy around 1960, and when personal antagonisms marred relations at a high level, some of the machinery that had been set up to promote Canadian-American co-operation and understanding slowed down or ground to a halt. The joint cabinet defense committee did not meet from 1960 until June, 1964, and the Inter-Parliamentary Group from March, 1962, to January, 1964.[13] These institutions, designed to further co-operation, are a product rather than a source of mutual good will which they cannot create. Furthermore, new problems are certain to arise and to require a continuance of the spirit of compromise that has been so effective hitherto. For instance, a critical scarcity of water in the United States is already leading to unofficial American proposals that the water of the continent should be shared and to Canadian protests against the permanent alienation of natural resources. As the late General McNaughton[14] insisted, the solution of this problem will probably require assurances that care is taken to insure that American water is not wasted and that adequate measures are taken in the United States against pollution. It will probably also need concessions in other spheres as a *quid pro quo*.[15] Such arrangements can only be reached if harmony continues.

The increasing interest of both Canada and the United States in world affairs has meant that bilateral problems are no longer the most important aspect of Canadian-American relations. Geography and technology have decreed that these two independent countries will share the same fate in the event of total nuclear war. American foreign policy can vitally affect Candian hopes for peace. Foreign policy and defense measures have therefore be-

13. The government was questioned about this in February, 1962, Canada, *House of Commons Debates, 1962,* I (Feb. 16), 928.
14. General Andrew McNaughton, commander-in-chief of the Canadian Army in Britain in World War II, was chairman of the Canadian Section of the Canada-United States Permanent Joint Board on Defense, 1945–49, and chairman of the Canadian Section of the Joint Commission, 1950–62.
15. *CIIA Monthly Report,* V (June, 1966), 81; *Maclean's,* LXXIX (Aug. 6, 1962), 4.

come vastly more important in both countries and are the major source of disagreements between them. Walton Butterworth, when appointed American ambassador to Ottawa in 1963, claimed that his country was fully conscious of the existence of a Canadian identity and called for equal understanding in the opposite direction. He said, "We hope that you will be mindful of the immensity and occasional urgency of the problems which confront us as a nation on which history has imposed unprecedented responsibilities and burdens."[16] If the United States is inadequately supported by Canada, American policy might possibly fail in its objectives. On the other hand, if American policy is mistaken, the United States would not suffer the consequences alone. Accordingly, the need for Canadian influence in Washington has become the more urgent.

Representations through diplomatic channels, as has been said, are often best kept secret even though this means that the Canadian opposition parties imply to the public that the government has been silent or has yielded to American pressure. Public criticism may, indeed, sometimes have more effect on United States policy than private communications; but Canadian criticism of American policy could obviously at times be very harmful. Although a Canadian failure to give adequate political and military support to the United States might not necessarily be fatal to the West's cause, it could seriously diminish Canadian influence in Washington. This would not merely harm Canadian immediate local interests but would also weaken future efforts to steer the Americans toward policies that Canada thinks wise. This was amply shown when Howard Green, the Secretary of State for External Affairs under Prime Minister Diefenbaker, was determined to make a stand for nuclear disarmament despite the fact that two successive ministers of national defence, George Pearkes and Douglas Harkness, wanted nuclear weapons to make Canadian forces more effective in NORAD and NATO. Prime Minister Diefenbaker's support for Green, and his subsequent equivoca-

16. Address to the Canadian Club, Ottawa, Jan. 23, 1963, *CIIA Monthly Report*, II (Jan., 1963), 11.

tions when trying to conceal the fissures in his cabinet, reduced Canadian influence in Washington. Diefenbaker eventually stung the State Department into making an unprecedented interference in Canadian affairs by issuing a statement explicitly contradicting what the Prime Minister had said.[17]

On the other hand, an all-out military effort in support of American policy would not merely diminish the value of Canadian efforts in other directions but would also be very unpopular in certain quarters in Canada and would stir up anti-Americanism. It would be alleged that the government had become a lackey of the United States and was no longer able to look after Canadian interests. The government of the day is thus inevitably torn between an appearance of silent acquiescence with American policies that are not popular in Canada or the advocacy of policies that the American government dislikes and that might therefore impair Canadian-American relations and reduce Canadian influence in Washington. This dilemma, although most apparent during the Progressive-Conservative regime, plagues its successors also. Pearson showed what he felt about it when he complained in 1965 that if he did not speak out against unpopular American policies he was accused of being a satellite, but that if he did, the opposition said he was interfering in the affairs of another country.[18]

In an effort to ease Canadian-American relations and to heal the wounds caused by earlier clashes during the Diefenbaker regime, two professional diplomats, Arnold Heeney of Canada and Livingston Merchant of the United States, were instructed in 1964 to examine the techniques of diplomatic and political cooperation. Their report was released on July 12, 1965. Amid many rational suggestions for facilitating the conduct of relations between the two countries, it was suggested that Canada should abstain from embarrassing the United States about questions in which Canada had no special interest. There was no clear definition what might constitute such questions, and the next sentence

17. *Canadian Annual Review for 1963* (Toronto, 1964).
18. Canada, *House of Commons Debates, 1965*, I (April 6), 35.

conceded Canada's right to an independent judgment and indicated the advantages of non-public representations.[19] However, the statement about Canadian restraint was widely interpreted as an attempt to "gag Canada." Pearson promptly, though mildly, suggested at a press conference that he thought the statement should have added that Canada had a "right of pronouncement,"[20] and at the Banff Conference on World Development in August he said that while the Canadian government must remain in close and friendly touch with its great allies, it was becoming "increasingly difficult to develop a satisfactory national identity and a profitable balance of national interest in that way alone."[21]

In March, 1966, Martin dealt extensively with this dilemma in an address at Carleton University. He was replying to many demands of Canadian intellectuals for an "independent" foreign policy. This demand arises because the peculiar relationship of Canada with the United States clearly reduces the latitude within which Canadian foreign policy can fluctuate. As a result, there are insistent calls from many sides for more boldness and imagination, there are complaints that Canadian external relations are overcautious, and there are requests for the adoption of alternatives, usually without any offer of constructive proposals by the critics themselves. Some of these stem directly from underlying Canadian anti-Americanism, and many Canadians ignore the practical problems involved and the consequences of alternative policies. However, others advance sound criticism of American policy and tender constructive advice to the Canadian government on how it should attempt to change it. Martin's opinion was that a solution for Canada's problem was possible because the bipolarity of recent years (in which, incidentally, Canadian diplomats have always hitherto professed not to believe) has gone and that "The smaller powers, including Canada . . . [now have] greater scope for the pursuit of their own national interests and

19. Arnold J. Heeney and Livingston T. Merchant, *Canada and the United States: Principles for Partnership* (Ottawa, 1965).
20. *CIIA Monthly Report*, IV (July–Aug., 1965), 81.
21. J. King Gordon, ed., *Canada's Role as a Middle Power* (Toronto, 1966).

. . . for the exercise of constructive initiative in the search for solutions to problems of concern to the world as a whole."[22]

This generalization might serve to attempt to disarm critics and to ward off the opposition, but it does not give a detailed answer to Canada's fundamental dilemma. It does not show the means by which a permanent solution for Canada's inordinate susceptibility to the American presence can be effected. Martin in his speech gave a hint of a way out when he spoke of the "growth of pluralism." If this does not simply mean the old multilateralism all over again, it points to some form of international co-operation in a form that is more than merely a temporary alliance to meet immediate dangers. This might be regional or, less likely in the immediate future, universal. The word "pluralism" was apparently used because it signifies a bundle of single entities and therefore permits the continued existence of the national unit.

A little earlier, Martin had said that the objective of Canadian policy was "to remain truly independent."[23] On this occasion he was talking to businessmen rather than students and professors, and the words may have been chosen to suit the audience. These concepts of pluralism and independence are, however, not necessarily incompatible unless they are regarded as absolutes. They indicate that the problem for Canadian policy-makers is not merely to evade American pressures but also to help to fashion international organizations that, while preserving national autonomy, will be effective within the spheres for which they were designed. Only through them can Canada retain an adequate degree of freedom of action. In Canadian opinion they would also be a means of ending the cold war.

Canada's care to protect her sovereignty against American encroachment, and the nationalist emotions that are so easily aroused by fear of American domination, contrast markedly with public expression about the need for pluralism and international organization. This dichotomy is not unusual. Indeed, it parallels a

---

22. *Statements and Speeches*, No. 66/10, p. 1.
23. Paul Martin, address to the Canadian Club, Toronto, Jan. 31, 1966, *Statements and Speeches*, No. 66/3, p. 6.

contradiction written into both the League of Nations Covenant and the United Nations Charter, each of which imposed limitations upon national sovereignty while at the same time claiming to preserve the sovereignty of member states. It is a feature of our age that nationalism is in certain respects growing stronger while international institutions and, even more, the need for them, are increasing. Middle powers like Canada are more perplexed by this contradiction than are either small powers, whose relative weakness and insignificance enable them to adopt contradictory positions with greater facility, or the great powers who have more confidence in their ability to stand alone. It is this dilemma, more than the problem of withstanding American influences or seeking to prevent Communist aggression, that is at the root of Canadian problems in external relations.

Traditionally, Canada offset the American pull by maintaining ties with Great Britain. Now, on the eve of celebration of the centenary of Confederation, a more palatable alternative to over-close identification with the United States must be found in international organizations. Within the Commonwealth, reversing an ancient policy, Canada supported African proposals for the creation of a Commonwealth Secretariat, led the opposition to Britain's effort to join the European Common Market, and accepted the concept of a multiracial Commonwealth more fully than any of the other older members, except perhaps Britain. The Commonwealth, however, cannot adequately supply the makeweight that Canada needs because it is too disparate an organization and too much disturbed by its own internal rivalries and antagonisms. The Commonwealth is therefore unable to satisfy Canada's need fully and adequately.

Hence Canada has turned also to other newer forms of international organization. NATO has provided a means by which Canada can support American policies while preserving Canadian identity. A transatlantic alliance is more comfortable for Canada than one that is purely North American or, indeed, one that is purely British. To remain comfortable Canada must be sure of retaining influence. Canadian spokesmen at NATO have therefore persistently demanded that there should be consultation of all members before the greater powers take action, they have resisted efforts to set up inner controlling groups, and they have preferred the idea of an Atlantic community to a dumbbell form of association with subdivision on each side of the ocean. NATO has thus provided Canada with security not only against the Russians but also against her own allies.

But it is in the United Nations that Canada finds the greatest hope for a permanent solution for her difficulties as well as for current cold war tensions. It is therefore not surprising that Canadian support for the world body has been remarkably consistent and persistent and that it can be said with truth that the United Nations is the cornerstone of Canadian policy.[24] Canada has been involved in more peace-keeping and supervisory operations within the United Nations than any other country; and because of early work on atomic energy as well as for other reasons, Canada has been a regular member of international arms-limitation committees. In the belief that certain middle and smaller countries are peculiarly able to contribute something to the easing of international tensions where great-power action would be dangerous or unacceptable, Canada wanted a permanent United Nations military peace-keeping staff to prepare to meet problems as they arise. When this idea did not gain immediate acceptance, Canada took it upon itself in 1964 to call a special conference of powers with peace-keeping experience to discuss the problems involved. Paul Martin was careful to make clear that there was no intention to create a new organization to replace the big-power-dominated Security Council which the charter charges with the duty of maintaining peace.[25] But the history of peace-keeping operations, successful and otherwise, suggests that Canada and similar powers can often step in when the Security Council is thwarted by its internal schisms.

Canadian initiative in peace-keeping, although not an integral part of the direct Western confrontation of communism, is in line with Western hopes and aspirations. Not only have the United

---

24. "Canada and the United Nations: The Record After Fourteen Years," *External Affairs*, XI (Sept., 1959), p. 253.
25. *Canadian Annual Review for 1964* (Toronto, 1965), pp. 219–220.

States and Britain borne the lion's share of the expenses, but on one occasion, in Cyprus, British troops formed part of the United Nations peace-keeping force. Canada would have found it difficult to do as much in this direction if the United States had disapproved, and Canada once acted at direct United States request. In March, 1964, President Johnson telephoned Prime Minister Pearson to ask Canada to send troops to Cyprus. He said that Canada was the only country that had any hope of preventing the situation from deteriorating into a war that would involve two members of NATO. Pearson's reply, without asking a favour in return, that troops would be on the way that night is said to have gained Canada considerable diplomatic credit with the President.[26] Although France and the U.S.S.R. refused to pay their share of the cost of these operations, their stand did not lead to the breakup of the United Nations as was feared. There seems hope, then, that Canadian activity in this area may have useful results. Peace-keeping appeals to Canadians because it satisfies an urge for the assumption of a leading constructive role in world affairs.

Latterly American policy in Vietnam has caused a deterioration of relations between Canada and the United States which shows that the Liberal government, though it has proved more capable of coping with them, is not immune from the problems that plagued its predecessor. On January 25, 1966, Martin told the Commons, "I must ask the House what such a defeat would mean by way of encouragement to an aggressive brand of action"; and he asserted that Canada supported the purposes and objectives of American policy "because no form of international violence could be permitted."[27] However, after the bombing program began on January 31 he stated that there were fundamental differences between Canada and the United States on Vietnam policy and pointed out that Canada had urged a cease-fire and peace negotiations and had maintained that the problem could not be solved by military means.[28] The Canadian government resisted public

26. *Ibid.*, p. 231.
27. Canada, *House of Commons Debates, 1966* (Jan. 25).
28. Canada, *House of Commons Debates, 1966* (Feb. 1); *CIIA Monthly Report,* V (Feb., 1966), 13.

demand that it should send a strong official protest against the American operations but, without first warning the United States well in advance (which seemed a deliberate departure from diplomatic protocol), the Prime Minister used a speech at Temple University on April 2 to propose a "pause" in the bombing program. It got a cool reception from the President.[29]

The Canadian government made it clear that, unlike the other dominions, it will not send troops to aid the United States against the Viet Cong. When private groups in Toronto proposed to establish a volunteer brigade to help the United States, a Canadian government spokesman said it would be against Canadian law.[30] Canada sent envoys to sound out the North Vietnamese about their readiness to come to the conference table,[31] though without any encouraging results. One explanation of the Canadian position and Canadian actions is that Canada has a special status in Southeast Asia as a result of membership in the International Control Commission which would be jeopardized by becoming a combatant. Canadian service personnel with the commission have therefore put maple leaf patches on their shoulders to distinguish them from Australian and New Zealand combatants whose uniforms are similar. No doubt the possibility that Canada can act in a mediatory capacity has some value for the United States. But the United States does not feel that the role of peace supervisor and mediator automatically gives Canada the same right of criticism as that enjoyed by a fully committed supporter.

The difficulties that beset the formulation of Canadian foreign policy are thus caused partly by the stubbornness of the cold war situation, partly by the fact that proximity to the United States gives a degree of security but at the risk of loss of freedom of action (though in some ways this also permits Canada to strike individual poses), but fundamentally by the contradictions found in the need for Canada to move toward interdependence yet

29. *CIIA Monthly Report*, IV (April, 1965), 30–32; Canada, *House of Commons Debates, 1965*, I (April 8), 94–96.

30. *CIIA Monthly Report*, V (Feb., 1966), 16; Canada, *House of Commons Debates, 1966* (Feb. 24).

31. E.g., Chester Ronning, Canada, *House of Commons Debates, 1966* (March 8).

retain national identity. However, according to the classical concept of foreign politics, success in meeting external problems depends in large degree on the absence of serious domestic divisions and especially of internal conflicts that destroy the unity of the state. Therefore, since 1962 Canada's relative success in international ventures has been threatened by the deterioration in the harmony between the two founding races. At the same time there has been a growth of provincialism in reaction to the centralizing tendencies that came with the wars and depression of this century. It remains to be seen how far these internal problems have affected, or are likely to affect, the Canadian role in world affairs.

The present strength of French-Canadian separatism must not be unduly exaggerated; for although the overall separatist vote in the last Quebec election was larger than its electoral successes, the separatist parties have as yet made little political headway. Daniel Johnson, the premier of Quebec, has said that the establishment of real equality between the races would strengthen Canada, not destroy it. But one federal party, the Creditistes, was for a time led by an avowed separatist; and most if not all French Canadians believe that the time has come to remove disadvantages which they have always endured. As these disadvantages are partly the result of the fact that numerically French-speaking Canadians are in a minority, especially in relation to the vast number of those who speak English in the whole of North America, and as they are also partly a result of the territorial distribution of the two races in Canada itself, any attempt to remedy the situation, to be successful, could require radical constitutional changes in the structure of Confederation. Changes of that order would seem almost certain to decrease the strength of the federal government and therefore would affect its influence in relations with other states.

Provincialism is, of course, not confined to Quebec. Indeed, Premier Bennett of British Columbia has on occasion made more extreme statements and claims about provincial claims to revenue than any Quebec premier. It may be indicative of the trend toward the growth of provincial powers and interest that, whereas the federal government was once the traditional protector of the natural resources of the country and provincial government tended to be lavish with concessions to foreign interest, the reverse is now sometimes the case. In the case of the Columbia River Treaty it was the provincial government of British Columbia that claimed to be concerned about Canada's future need for water resources which it alleged the federal government was prepared to alienate permanently without adequate compensation.[32] Similarly, whereas Duplessis's government maintained itself in Quebec by the aid of American concessionaires, Lesage's, which followed it, vigorously husbanded provincial natural resources. These trends may be straws in the wind marking the aspiration of the provinces for greater power and greater responsibility.

Nevertheless, Quebec's claims, being mixed with "national" sentiment based on language, "race," and culture, are much the most important. It is noticeable that although official designation is "province" (which is still to be seen on Quebec automobile license plates) some responsible Quebec leaders have begun to talk of "l'état de Québec." Moreover, on two occasions Quebec cabinet ministers have in effect challenged the right of the federal government to that exclusive control of foreign relations with which it is endowed by the British North American Act.

When, with federal approval, Quebec established a provincial agency in Paris like those which various provinces already have in London, Paul Gérin-Lajoie, the Minister of Education, then claimed the right to negotiate with the French government an agreement, which would not be a treaty, about matters that came within provincial jurisdiction by virtue of the British North America Act. In a spirit of "co-operative federalism" (the Liberal government's phrase to counter separatism), Ottawa was willing to agree that negotiations with foreign powers about matters in which the provinces had the exclusive right of implementation could best be negotiated directly by the provincial ministers concerned.[33] Quebec's negotiations with France were covered by an

32. Preston, *Canada in World Affairs*, p. 170.
33. Paul Martin, press release, "The Provinces and Treaty Making," *CIIA Monthly Report*, IV (April, 1965), 44, Appendix A; *ibid.*, IV, 15–16, 38–39, 117–118; Canada, *House of Commons Debates, 1965*, I, 628–630.

exchange of letters between the French and Canadian governments. It has been said that, according to the Montevideo Convention on the Rights and Duties of States of 1933, the definition
of a state in international law includes the capacity to enter into
relations with other states; and it has been suggested by an authority that this definition does not exclude those territories
which, though capable of conducting some or all of their external
relations, have those relations conducted by another state.[34] The
federal government claimed that Quebec's participation in negotiations introduced nothing new. But it resembles in some ways
the first step that Canada made on the road toward negotiations
independent of Great Britain. It is arguable therefore that Quebec
has moved a short distance down the road to possible independence.

More recently, Eric Kierans, when Acting Minister of Revenue
of Quebec, addressed letters directly to United States Secretary of
Commerce John T. Connor and to Secretary of the Treasury
Henry M. Fowler, to protest the balance-of-payments guidelines
laid down by Washington which called for a reduction of dollar
spending abroad by the foreign subsidiaries of American companies. Kierans knew that he was infringing federal prerogatives in
the field of foreign affairs but claimed that he had to do so
because Ottawa was "selling Canada down the drain." Washington did not reply to his letters, but copies of them were sent
through the State Department to the Canadian ambassador. The
Canadian government denounced the Quebec minister's action.
Nevertheless, he claimed that he had forced Ottawa to take a
stronger stand and that he "got results" when Washington made
exceptions in the case of United States subsidiaries in Canada.[35]

French-Canadian separatists believed that Paris would be more
favorable to Quebec's aspirations than Washington. They established an office in Paris and were received cordially everywhere. They were encouraged when De Gaulle said "the French-

34. J. E. S. Fawcett, *The British Commonwealth in International Law* (London,
1963), p. 92.
35. New York *Times*, Feb. 13, 1966; *CIIA Monthly Report*, IV (Feb., 1965)
12; V, 7–8, 23–24, 32–33.

Canadians are French in everything but sovereignty," when he publicly accepted a volume by a separatist, and when the French cultural attaché in Canada said, "We shall build the next civilization together." High-placed Gaullists were rumored to have promised the separatist movement money. Rumors spread that the Province of Quebec's new offices must be spacious because they would be needed by the Republic of Quebec. But De Gaulle's first reaction to the glamor of a prospective French state in North America, which may have never been as favorable as the Separatists believed, cooled rapidly when a succession of responsible Quebec leaders showed their disapproval and when De Gaulle came to realize that schism in Canada had no practical advantage for him.[36]

In the model of the classical functioning of international relations drawn earlier in this essay, a connection was made between the internal cohesion of a country and its external power and influence. That relationship has not been demonstrated positively in Canada's recent development. In the Diefenbaker years Canada's influence reached a low point not because of racial friction but because the external problems of the day proved to be too difficult for the government to surmount. The restoration of Canada's international reputation, which was partly a result of Pearson's international reputation, was accompanied by a growth of provincialism and of cultural schism, two elements which in the normal model would lead to weakness. Governments plagued by internal problems have often used foreign bogies to divert attention from domestic problems and to attempt to unite their people. In Canada's recent history a reverse causation seems to have occurred. Although it is not the only factor, separatism appears to have served to distract Canadian attention from the alleged danger of American domination. But it has not yet noticeably diminished Canadian prestige and influence, which has, in fact, revived.

There is, of course, the possibility that the weakening of Canada will come as a delayed reaction. In March, 1966, the Penta-

36. Bernard Kaplan, "How France Froze Out the Separatists," *Maclean's*, LXXIX (Aug. 6, 1966), 170.

gon, concerned about the defense of North America, is said to have considered setting up a commission to study the repercussions of Quebec separatism. But it dropped the idea when the State Department protested. When questioned about this story, the Prime Minister replied that he was not aware of any investigation of this kind but added typically, "I do not know what Americans have investigated what."[37] Even though an independent Quebec might assume the same international alignments as Canada,[38] the secession of French Canada and the partition of the continent into two, or perhaps even more, separate states would weaken Canada's capacity for resistance to American pressures at the same time as it decreased Canada's ability to contribute to the common defense and to earn diplomatic credit thereby in Washington. Even if the result of the present agitation is not rupture but an easing of the ties of Confederation—for instance, by the establishment of two "associated states" of Canada, with foreign policy controlled by Ottawa—resultant financial stringency could reduce defense-spending and could lessen Canada's influence in Washington and elsewhere. It would thus reduce Canada's ability to achieve the objectives of its foreign policy.

Paul Martin's answer to French-Canadian aspirations is that Canadian foreign policy must, like all other aspects of national policy, express the bilingual and bicultural nature of the country.[39] Presumably a bicultural Department of External Affairs would mean more opportunity for French Canadians (who have, however, been difficult to recruit) to rise to positions of influence, and would also place more emphasis upon English-speaking diplomats' learning to speak French. Linguistic ability would be a condition of promotion. Some English-speaking Canadians believe that this would lower the quality of the diplomatic service.

Of course, Canadian statesmen have, for political reasons, always been aware of the need to appeal to the Quebec vote. Thus,

37. *CIIA Monthly Report,* V (March, 1966), 33; Canada, *House of Commons Debates, 1966* (March 1).

38. A separatist suggested that an independent Quebec might stay in the Commonwealth (Marcel Chaput, *Why I Am a Separatist,* trans. Robert A. Taylor, Toronto, 1961, p. 49).

39. Paul Martin, to the International Relations Club of the University of Montreal, March 12, 1966, *CIIA Monthly Report,* V (March, 1966), 42.

to match financial aid given to African members of the Commonwealth, Canada aided former French colonies in Africa. Furthermore, French-speaking officers are usually selected for assignment to important posts in French-speaking countries and even to London.

But, although states find that the use of a common language can ease relations with another state, foreign policy does not necessarily reflect cultural or ethnic qualities. A bicultural foreign policy would presumably mean one that adequately reflects the wishes of both English-speaking and French-speaking Canadians. In the past, French-Canadian opinion on most international questions has not differed significantly from English-Canadian opinion, and French-speaking Canada has divided on roughly the same lines and in the same proportion as English-speaking Canada. There is, however, one important exception. Perhaps as a continuance of the more deeply intrenched French-Canadian tradition of isolationism, and much as Quebec took a firmer position against conscription during both world wars, so there is today a stronger opposition to nuclear weapons in French Canada than in English Canada. One must therefore conclude that what a bicultural foreign policy might mean for Canada would be an increase of French-Canadian influence by a greater recognition of what has been called "the French fact" to the point where, on certain important matters, French-Canadian opinion would exercise a complete veto. This situation would obviously put a halter on the conduct of Canadian foreign relations.

There may, however, be another and different development. The call for a bicultural policy may simply mean that the Canadian outlook on external problems should reflect more thoroughly what has been illustrated above, namely, that Canada, as a result of its history, is a land of tolerance and compromise. Presumably, under an ideal interpretation of biculturalism Canadian statesmen would strive more vigorously than ever for full opportunity for all peoples to develop in peace in an orderly world not dominated by any single great power or by any single concept of society. Although it is true that, inside Canada, French Canadians have not shown a great tolerance for the idea of equal rights for other ethnic groups, there is no reason to believe that outside Canada their influence would not be thrown toward the concept of general racial equality. Furthermore, although the Balkanization of North America might leave the former territory of Canada more open to external influences, especially from the south, than it has been in the past, less extreme readjustments would still leave room for the exercise of that skilled diplomacy and patient negotiation that has been Canada's strongest weapon.

It is possible to imagine that even if an independent Quebec were set up alongside the Dominion of Canada, this might in certain circumstances mean no diminution of, but perhaps even an increase in, the weight that Canada exerts internationally. The present separatists are apparently almost completely oblivious of international problems. But that could change overnight with independence and, like Eire in an earlier generation, they would probably seek to play a leading role. There is no reason to believe that that role would be opposed to the policy followed by Canada. It might actually mean that Canadiens and Canadians, aided by the memory of old associations and habits, would be seen working together in the committees and corridors of international organizations. This possibility could arise, however, only in the kind of world that Pearson postulated when he talked of the decline of national sovereignty and national interests and the growth of international co-operation. The future of Canada's international prestige thus depends not only on the course of events inside Canada but also on the development of a world in which the classical state system is modified and is replaced by an increasingly effective internationalism.

12

Contemporary Canada

Richard H. Leach

It is difficult to catch the mood and quality of contemporary Canada. As these essays make clear, Canada does not project a single, simple image, one easy to understand and describe. Rather, there are many Canadas, and each speaks with a different voice and seems to have something different to say. Most important, it is quite apparent that today Canada is in a state of flux, of transition; change is the dominant theme of this book. It must be equally apparent, however, that all the side effects of that change have not yet been felt. Thus, to describe contemporary Canada it is necessary in a sense to catch a bird on the wing, never an easy thing to do. Moreover, it is difficult to describe contemporary Canada because of the lack of data about it. Even the United States has not developed anything like complete data on its manifold aspects. The inadequacy of statistics is far greater in a country with a population the size of Canada's and with a proportionately smaller number of social scientists. All kinds of additional data are needed before thoroughly reliable predictions and projections can be made in virtually any field of Canadian life. Hopefully, the future will see a concerted effort to fill the information void and to establish a data bank which can be drawn on by future students of Canada. The science of data processing has now reached a level sophisticated enough to make the creation and use of such a bank entirely feasible. The benefits which would redound from it would be incalculable. But even if contemporary Canada is not wholly perceptible, one thing is certain: Canada at the century mark is very different than she was at the beginning of her national existence, and even from what she was at the end of World War II. The Canada of the future will very likely be different again from the Canada of today. A young and vibrant nation, flexing its muscles on the international scene even as it attempts to find its own identity at home, Canada has great potential. As it enters its second century of national existence, it demands and deserves attention and respect.

The essays in this book have served to give Canada attention, and one cannot read them through without developing respect. In a remarkably short span of time, Canada has triumphed over a list of formidable obstacles—physical, economic, social—and in the process has established a culture and an economy which have placed her favorably among the nations. The essays make clear, however, that Canada has not made achievements without encountering problems. Indeed, one cannot read the essays without becoming aware of the many difficult problems which still face Canada as she enters her second century.

Thus there are problems of government, particularly in the area of federalism but also in the need to create a viable party system; problems of economics, which are revealed most clearly in Canada's excessive dependence on American capital; social problems, which of course encompass the difficulties encountered in developing a society in which French Canadians can play a full and equal role as well as in finding ways to overcome the effects of a declining birth rate; problems in defense and foreign policy, which arise out of Canada's position as a middle power in a world divided by a cold war; and behind them all, psychological problems, in that Canada does not feel sure of her own identity and is struggling just now to establish and maintain it at the very time she is experiencing the strains which accompany rapid growth and development. Thus Prime Minister Pearson in his 1966 Year's End Message described "the great challenge to Canadianism" as being the necessity of answering the question

Whether we can live together in confidence and cohesion; with more faith and pride in ourselves and less of self-doubt and hesitation; strong in the conviction that the destiny of Canada is to unite, not divide;

sharing in cooperation, not in separation or in conflict; respecting our past and welcoming our future. . . .[1]

Some of Canada's problems would appear on the agenda for the future of any modern industrial nation. The problem of how to govern sprawling urban areas, for example, is no more pressing in Canada than it is in the United States, Great Britain, Australia, or France. Indeed, Canada is among the leaders in developing solutions to the metropolitan area problem (the Toronto and Winnipeg areas are particular cases in point); but the dimensions of the problem continue to grow. Similarly, Canada, like all nations, is faced with the necessity of adjusting to the impact of technological change, particularly to that of automation. And the problems posed in devising suitable methods of controlling the use of natural resources and by the appearance of depressed areas in the wake of that change are additional examples of problems Canada shares with other advanced countries. But Canada is different in many respects from other industrial nations. Certain problems she faces in the future arise out of her own peculiar history and circumstances. Although she may hope to benefit from the experiences of others in solving problems that are shared with other nations, she will have to rely largely on her own ingenuity and intelligence in solving problems that are unique to Canada. In this category of problems, at least five might be mentioned here.

1. The immediate problem of national leadership. Although the essay on parties and politics developed this point, it has become of even greater urgency than it seemed at the time the essay was written. Prime Minister Pearson has announced that he will retire from his position as prime minister and hence leader of the Liberal Party early in 1968. The state of Canadian political parties as described in that essay suggests grave doubt about the possibility of their functioning well enough to provide a successor who can be assured sufficient backing and a tenure in

1. Department of External Affairs, Information Division, *Canadian Weekly Bulletin*, Jan. 4, 1967, p. 1.

office long enough to develop a long-range program of action, much less implement one.

2. The need for parliamentary reform. In Canada, as in the United States, the handicap inefficient and outdated procedures place upon the effective functioning of the legislature has been increasingly recognized. The role of the Senate continues to be questioned. But unlike the United States Congress, which has before it recommendations for the improvement of its procedures, the Canadian Parliament has not yet acted to initiate the process, and pressure is mounting that it do so. Prime Minister Pearson recently set up a committee on parliamentary reform, however, and hopefully Parliament will accept its recommendations when they are made.

3. The problem of labor unrest. Canada has increasingly been plagued by strikes as workers demand continual wage adjustment as prices have climbed in recent years. So far the strikes have been settled on an *ad hoc* basis, rather than the basis of a long-term plan for equitable remuneration. Thus the August, 1966, railwaymen's strike was settled by a back-to-work law hurried through Parliament after the strike had begun to have serious economic effects on the nation, and the Quebec teachers' strike was ended by pushing through a provincial law that bans strikes by teachers only until July, 1968. The issues in the labor situation need to be faced squarely and on an across-the-board basis if labor agitation is to be alleviated.

4. The problem of markets. Canada's prosperity depends upon her export trade. Despite President De Gaulle's repeated opposition to the proposal, it is still possible that Britain may be able to enter the Common Market. Even if she does not, the growth of Common Market trade may have the effect of reducing the level of Canadian trade with Europe. More perhaps can be done to widen the American market,[2] but Canada must remain alert to the need to reduce tariffs to the end

2. The United States-Canada Automotive Products Agreement of 1965 was the first step in that direction. A joint undertaking, described in President Johnson's words as designed to "create a broader market for automotive parts, to liberalize automotive trade between the two countries, and to establish conditions conducive to the most efficient patterns of investment, production and trade in this

of providing greater opportunities, especially in Western Europe and Japan, for Canadian exports. Indeed, Canada's first trade-policy priority continues to be the implementation of the Kennedy Round.

5. The problem of an industrial development policy. Canada is at the stage of economic development where selective industrial development is highly desirable. She needs to devise a way to concentrate her economic efforts on those industries in which she can be assured of the greatest profit with the smallest investment and to abandon those which can be sustained only at the expense of high tariffs and other artifical props.

But if problems appear to dominate the essays in this book, it should have been equally obvious as one read that Canada is aware of them and has begun to act to solve a good many of them. For the essays also make it clear that Canada is willing to look at herself analytically ("reassessment" is a word frequently used in these essays) and to consider proposals for remedial action. Indeed, the overall impression to be derived from these essays is perhaps Canada's frankness in recognizing and discussing her problems on the one hand and the lack of any doctrinaire approach to their solution on the other—those, and a sense of confidence and faith that they will ultimately be solved and that Canada will have even richer years of national progress in the future.

For Canada simply has too much "going for it," as the expression goes, to permit any other conclusion. This is perhaps more evident from an actual visit to Canada than it is from merely reading about developments there. I had the opportunity to visit every province in Canada save Newfoundland during 1966 and to observe at firsthand some of the aspects of that complex nation. The impressions that remain with me bolster that conclusion. There is a buoyancy about Canada, especially in the West and in Alberta, which is remarkable; everywhere the Canadian presents

---

critical industry," it resulted in the first year of its operation in raising the value of total trade in automotive products between the United States and Canada from $1.1 billion in 1965 to in excess of $2 billion in 1966 (*Congressional Record*, 113:S4112, March 21, 1967). Even so, the agreement aroused much opposition in both the United States and Canada, and its future is far from certain.

a happy, confident, secure image of a free man. Moreover, despite all the Canadian talk about searching for an identity, the "Canadianness" of things impresses one. Canadians are not mere Americans north of the border, nor yet a sort of English-French hybrid. They are distinctly Canadian, a quality which is hard to describe but which is very evident upon contact. The very great strides Canada has made in twenty years (my last visit was in 1947) are equally impressive, not only in such immediately obvious things as the general excellence of the Trans-Canada Highway (there is a good deal to say for the assertion that the Trans-Canada Highway is the best illustration of the strength, vitality, and purposefulness of modern Canada) and of good accommodations nearly everywhere one goes, but in more significant things such as the literally new towns and cities in the West, massive renewal of the older cities in the East, extensive industrialization and mechanization of agriculture, and the marks of prosperity to be found everywhere in the stores, on the streets, and in Canadian homes. The prosperity of modern Canada shows itself equally in the cities and on the farms, and if it is not uniform all across the nation (parts of Saskatchewan, western Ontario, and the Maritimes still present a lean and hungry appearance to the observer), it is so vastly greater than it was twenty years ago that the overall impression of prosperity remains.

The internationalism of Canada is also impressive. It is evident in the variety of people and accents one encounters and in the tremendous selection of imported goods one can choose from in the stores (the traveler from the United States at least is intrigued with perfume from Cuba and the U.S.S.R., clothes from Yugoslavia, and sandalwood soap from Communist China so widely available and reasonable in cost). Canadians also appear to have accepted their responsibilities on the world stage and to be truly concerned about working for world peace. If Quebec's insistence on self-assertion in 1966 (one must speak French more often than one had to in 1947 to get service!) and the separateness of the Atlantic provinces are also obvious, they are the exceptions that prove the rule. The overwhelming single impression that remains

with me agrees exactly with the sentiments expressed by Prime
Minister Pearson at the end of 1966:

Economically, we have become a rich society and a great industrial
power. We have built new dimensions of progress and welfare into the
Canadian way of life. The boundaries of freedom and opportunity have
been expanded for every Canadian. . . . We have laid a strong foundation on which to build in our second century. If we have the will and
the good will, there is no limit to our progress.[3]

Figure 1. *Annual Growth in Real Gross National Product.*

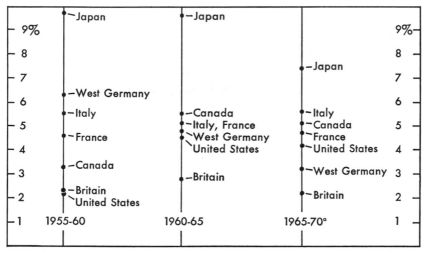

a. Likely growth except for Britain, where it is maximum permitted, in the
view of the National Institute of Economic and Social Research, by the balance
of payments.
Source: Economist, March 11, 1967, p. 940.

Another way to demonstrate the advantageous position in
which Canada finds herself today is to compare her with other
nations. Figure 1 illustrates Canada's average annual growth in
real gross national product for the five-year intervals 1955–60, and
1960–65, and the projected growth for the five-year interval 1965
to 1970. It is clear that Canada has not only improved her own
position but that she has also improved relative to the other major

3. *Canadian Weekly Bulletin,* Jan. 4, 1967, p. 1.

industrial nations of the world. Indeed, if the projected growth rate for 1965–70 turns out to be accurate, Canada will have increased her national output in the fifteen-year period proportionately more than any other nation except Japan. Recent action by the government suggests its determination to make the prediction come true. In a series of announcements in mid-March, 1967, it suspended the 5 per cent refundable tax on corporate cash profits which had been imposed in May, 1966, restored full depreciation allowances, and announced a cut in the tax on the sales of production machinery, all of which were intended to give the Canadian economy a significant boost upward. At the same time, the government announced that the 1966 current account deficit in trade in goods and services with other countries had been reduced from $1.08 billion in 1965 to $983 million in 1966. If all of these demonstrated Canada's concern to keep the nation on a healthy growth path, an even more significant assist in that direction may be forthcoming as a result of the consideration which will shortly be given by the Canadian government to the recommendations of the Royal Commission on Taxation to overhaul the country's tax structure. The aim of the commission's recommendations in general terms was to replace "the present jerry-built system with a much fairer and firmer base." If that aim is realized, it will provide, as the New York *Times* remarked editorially, "permanent benefit to the Canadian economy."[4] If its recommendations are adopted, domestic investment would become more attractive to Canadian investors and so Canada's long, heavy dependence on foreign, chiefly American, capital could be substantially reduced. "Carrying out the recommendations . . . may take some time," the *Times* concluded. "The Liberal Government is not committed to adopt the proposed reforms and it will come under attack from some quarters if it tries to do so. But, since the report [of the commission] has conclusively demonstrated the inequities and weaknesses in Canada's present tax structure, the Government will also be under pressure to initiate reform."[5] If it does so, it will

4. March 16, 1967, p. 46.
5. *Ibid.*

provide perhaps the soundest, most efficient and fairest tax structure of any major nation, a factor which will add still further to the strength and potential of the Canadian economy.

To disagree with the prediction one so often hears in the press that the Canadian federation will dissolve, because Canada is essentially too prosperous and content to permit it, is not to say that Canada will move on through the next hundred years over a smooth and straight road. There is on the contrary a good deal to suggest that that road instead will be a rocky one. For one thing, as Professor Beck has made quite clear, the federal system in Canada is in ferment. There is to be sure nothing particularly unique about that—it is in the nature of federal systems to undergo constant adjustment and adaptation. The American system is a good case in point; President Johnson's concern to establish a "creative federalism" is nothing more than a clever way to point to his recognition of the fact that great changes are taking place on the American scene and that the federal mechanism must be accommodated to them if it is to remain a viable part of the American system of government. So also as Canada has industrialized and has moved forward on the world's economic stage, her forward motion has created a number of problems of adjustment, one of the sorest of which is to bring Quebec into the same cycle of movement as the rest of the nation. Adjustment of this kind and dimension is never easy and in this case there has been more than the usual resistance. But Quebec *is* making the adjustment, and the federal fabric has not been torn asunder. It may instead have been strengthened. It is in any case not the same fabric that it was a short while ago. Perhaps inspired by Quebec, perhaps in tune with what may be an immutable law of politics which requires a certain amount of devolution to accompany the growth of the role of government in modern society, the provinces have come to play a larger role in Canadian government than they used to, a larger role in fact than is played by the subordinate units in any other federal system. "One has constantly to be reminded," Thomas Winship observed after studying present-day Canada, "that the central government . . . is not nearly so powerful as [the

American] Federal government; that the provinces are far stronger than [the] 50 [American] states."[6] It is clear from the essays in this book and from any acquaintance with the realities of contemporary Canadian life that to the provinces falls a large share of the responsibility for the practical realization of Canada's national goals of the future, whatever they may be. There, one finds the prime initiative and aggressive leadership in Canadian public affairs. The average Canadian citizen has come to look more to the provincial capitals and less to Ottawa for the satisfaction of his growing needs.

Even so, the provinces have not grown in strength evenly, and they are far from equal in their capacity to meet those needs. The names of certain of the provinces have featured more prominently in the preceding pages than the names of others, and this is very likely to continue to be the case. The several provinces were quite different from one another at the time of Confederation, and they have continued so—and perhaps have become even more so—since then. The Atlantic provinces, especially the three Maritime provinces, constitute perhaps an exception to the rule, but the slowness with which they have moved toward union, despite a long-sustained drive to that end, demonstrates that there are meaningful and important differences even there. These differences are to some extent by choice; but there are regional disparities in resources, power, and manpower that are not volitional. These were paid particular attention by the Economic Council of Canada in its Second Annual Review,[7] and if the recommendations it made under its mandate to suggest economic policies which can best foster the *balanced* economic development of all areas of Canada are adopted, the removal of those disparities will be a major objective of both the provinces and the national government in the years ahead. The point is, however, that as Canada enters its second century it does so more under provincial leadership than might have been expected, and because that is the case,

6. "Canada Today: A Report on the Confederation's 100th Birthday," Boston *Globe*, Feb. 27, 1966, quoted in *Congressional Record*, 112:A1079 (March 1, 1966).

7. Economic Council of Canada, *Second Annual Review: Towards Sustained and Balanced Growth* (Ottawa, 1965), esp. chap v.

it does so unevenly and to a large extent under relatively unknown leadership. Certainly one of the aspects of Canadian development that bears close watching in the immediate future is the success of attempts to achieve a better balance among the provinces.

Quite as important as action to bring the provinces more closely into balance is need for agreement about federal and provincial responsibilities. For the shift to the provinces has by no means been accompanied by shunting the federal government entirely off the stage. The federal government's role has changed to that of financier for provincial activities. In many cases it is a standard-setter as well. Beginning with the tax-rental agreements during World War II through the postwar tax-sharing agreements, to the equalization grants of the late fifties, Ottawa has used its superior fiscal resources to help the provinces carry out their expanding programs. Obviously, problems arise as Ottawa's willingness to support one program over another varies and as federal tax policy seems to inhibit or encourage certain program activities. Moreover, there is a certain awkwardness in having continually to renegotiate a financial agreement between the federal government and the provinces. To get around these difficulties, some of the provinces, led by Quebec, have begun to demand full provincial control over taxes and have asserted their right to opt out of federally supported programs at their pleasure. By early 1967, however, it had begun to seem likely that the federal government would foreclose such a possibility. New York *Times* correspondent Jay Walz found "significant signs" that the Dominion government was planning "to take a dominant role in directing the national economy."[8] If so, it received an assist from the report of the Royal Commission on Taxation, released on February 26, 1967. The chairman of that commission, which had devoted four years to its task, reported that one of the commission's central aims was to provide ways to strengthen the federal government. It sought to accomplish that objective by giving greater tax control powers to the national government in the belief that it is primarily responsible for maintaining economic stability. Thus,

8. "Pearson Seeking Dominant Role," New York *Times,* Jan. 23, 1967, p. 48.

the commission recommended that the national government continue to collect personal and corporate income taxes and that no further increases in tax abatements be granted to the provinces. The commission's six-volume report will take a long time to be fully digested and understood and even longer to be acted upon. However, it is apparent already that "its implementation would have sweeping effects on Canadian economic life"[9] and especially on federal-provincial relations within the federal system. It is not too much to predict that adopting all the reforms proposed by the commission would amount to a revolution in Canadian federalism. Needless to say, political realities will very likely force a good deal of compromise in the actual event, but the next few years should in any case be particularly significant ones in the evolution of Canadian federalism as the questions raised by the commission are discussed across the nation and brought to a vote in Parliament.

If contemporary Canada's major internal problem is related to needed adjustments in the federal system, Canada's major external problem for the period just ahead may be related to finding ways of blunting the sharp corners of international tensions on the one hand and of preserving and enhancing her own independence on the other. Several of the essays in this book have touched upon the difficulties Canada has encountered in steering a course which takes into account both her own distinctive characteristics and needs and her very close social, economic, cultural, and defense ties with the United States. Prime Minister Pearson commented on those ties in a 1966 speech:

It is neither ingratitude nor unneighborliness that makes us worry about the [fact that] today, a greater proportion of Canada's resources and industrial production come under foreign—largely American—control than is the case with any other industrial country in the world. . . . nonresident interests—almost entirely in the United States—control almost 60 per cent of our manufacturing. Naturally, this—and other facts about [America's] share in our progress—worry us because of the effect it could have on our economic and . . . political development as a

9. New York *Times*, Feb. 27, 1967, p. 1; see also *Economist*, March 4, 1967, p. 856.

separate, independent state—and we want to preserve that. Our anxiety in these matters is perfectly natural. It is also increasing.[10]

At some point Canada can be expected to act to relieve that anxiety. The next few years, indeed, may well be marked by a concerted attempt to effect an adjustment in Canadian–United States relations. For as Pearson went on to note in the same speech,

it is the first responsibility of the Government of Canada, as of any government, to ensure that *our* national purposes are achieved, that *our* economic and material progress is continued, that its benefits are spread as widely and as equitably as possible among all our people and that our economy does not fall under external (by which we mean American) control.

One of the potential points of friction in Canadian-American relations which may provide an early test of Prime Minister Pearson's determination is the projected North American Water and Power Alliance. Pushed especially by Americans from the arid West and Southwest, the NAWAPA concept of continental water management involves Canadian-American co-operation in the conservation, development, and utilization of the continent's water resources as a whole. To date, all the pressure to adopt the scheme has emanated from the American side, with Canada so far taking no official stand but generally resisting the idea. Its American sponsors are diligent in its behalf,[11] however, and it can be expected to become a major issue between the two countries, especially as the United States becomes increasingly plagued by the pollution of her own waters.

Along with her relationship with the United States, Canada's relationship with the Soviet Union poses equally portentous problems for Canadian independence. As Minister of Finance Mitchell Sharp pointed out in 1966, Canada must understand that her independence is limited by the fact that not only does she "live in

10. Lester B. Pearson, "The Identity of Canada in North America," an address to the American Society of Newspaper Editors, Montreal, May 19, 1966, Department of External Affairs, Information Division, *Statements and Speeches,* No. 66/22.

11. See, for example, the remarks of Senators Montoya and Moss in the United States Senate, *Congressional Record,* 113:S4149 (March 21, 1967).

a world dominated by the changing relations between the two superpowers," but that both of them are "our next door neighbors."[12] Thus Canada is limited like most other nations by the bipolarization of world power and must adjust her own actions accordingly as the two great powers react to each other and as each reacts to the emerging power of China. But because of Canada's geographical location those limitations and adjustments are more sharply felt in Canada than in most other nations. The implications of the long border between Canada and the United States have long been felt and accepted by both countries. The fact is, however, that Canada also has a long border in common with the U.S.S.R., a border whose existence is just beginning to be realized and whose significance has yet to be fully explored or understood. Canadian cities and industrial centers are within easy range of modern aircraft from Russia over the polar ice cap, and as the air and rocket age develops, and as ways are found to exploit the frozen Arctic wastes, the space between the two countries will narrow still further and also become more important. And there is no long tradition of friendship and tolerance between Canada and the U.S.S.R., as there is between Canada and the United States, to help in the adjustment.

It is not, however, merely the dawning possibility of a Canadian confrontation with the Soviet Union which poses problems for Canada's future independence. More immediately, Canada is fearful of being caught in the middle of a nuclear holocaust, unleashed by design or accident by forces beyond her control. Canada is a nation, Minister for External Affairs Paul Martin observed not long ago, which "would be in the front line of another ghastly bloodletting that might bring western civilization down in ruins."[13] Recognizing that acting on her own there is little she can do to prevent it, Canada has been concerned from the beginning with the success of the United Nations and has been active in its programs. To speak only of the period since 1959,

12. "Strengthening Canada's Independence," an address delivered to the Association of Canadian Advertisers, Toronto, May 4, 1966, *Statements and Speeches*, No. 66/20.

13. "The National Interest," an address delivered to the Graduation Ceremony, Osgoode Hall, Toronto, March 25, 1966, *Statements and Speeches*, No. 66/13.

Canada has participated in United Nations peace forces in the Congo and Cyprus, has helped provide air support for observers in Yemen and for a Pakistan contingent in West New Guinea, and has provided the commander of an observations mission on the border of India and Pakistan. In 1967, Canada assumed a seat on the Security Council for the third time, which alone serves to indicate the contribution she has made to United Nations activities over the years. Since its establishment in 1949, Canada has also been concerned with the strength and success of the North Atlantic Treaty Organization and with the possibilities it offers for a stable and powerful Atlantic community. And in recent years especially, Canada has assumed a larger burden of responsibility for the underdeveloped countries. Finance Minister Sharp recently declared that it was his government's intention to boost Canadian aid to those nations to the minimum level recommended by the United Nations by the early seventies. The Caribbean member states of the Commonwealth have been of particular concern to Canada. She has begun to feel a special responsibility for them as Britain has found it necessary to abdicate her former imperial role. Finally, Canadian foreign policy goes beyond even these commitments to a broader involvement looking toward the eventual elimination of the forces which might lead to a nuclear war. As Martin put it,

We have chosen as the focal point of our policy in a universal sense the "diplomacy of reconciliation" which Dag Hammarskjold saw as the main task of the United Nations. . . . In all the varied initiatives of diplomacy in political, economic or social matters, we . . . [act] out of the conviction so eloquently expressed by an American judge on the International Court of Justice that "there will be general international realization of the common interest and that the timeless tide will still flow toward uniformity in the law of nations."[14]

Acting on this conviction, Canada has already become a major force in the world for peace, and her commitment can be counted on to lead her into a still more active role in the years ahead.

Thus Canada finds herself today occupied with both domestic and external problems of major proportions. Perhaps she might

14. *Ibid.*

have more time and energy to devote to their solution if she were less concerned about her own identity. The "identity crisis" may be largely a figment of the imagination of journalists and academics. Certainly as I moved across Canada in 1966 it seemed to me that the people *felt* Canadian and acted Canadian in a way that suggested they already have a sense of national pride and of national identity. But concern over finding herself has become so much a part of today's Canadian folklore that it cannot easily be dismissed. In part, the problem—to the extent there is a problem—arises out of the similarity between Americans and Canadians and out of the latter's insistence on making uncomplimentary comparisons between life in Canada and in the United States. Thus Minister of Finance Mitchell Sharp observed that

as I see it, it is the task of the rising generation of Canadians to create a new confidence and a new sense of cultural and civic identity in Canada. Unless we achieve some success on this front—and I believe we are beginning to do so—the very real attractions of the vigorous society to the south of us may attract too many of our able people. Then the human resources and skills required to shape and direct a complex industrial economy will simply not be available to us in Canada.[15]

This is not a black and white situation, with the United States having all the assets and Canada none. In the economic and social spheres, as the essays in this book have demonstrated, Canada is in some ways more advanced than the United States. And certainly, though none of the essays touched upon it, the cultural fabric in Canada is increasingly richly textured and able to attract and hold people because of its own qualities. It is no doubt true that in the early years of Canadian development, even as in the United States, a busy frontier people had little time to devote to the creation of a distinctive Canadian culture. However, especially since World War II, Canada has evolved a style and approach of its own in art, literature, music, and drama, and in the process Canadian nationalism has been encouraged and enhanced. The Canada Council, which was created by Parliament in 1957, has done a great deal to help in the evolution through its

15. *Statements and Speeches,* No. 66/20.

program of grants. Indeed, an essay might very well have been devoted to the Canada Council; at least, on the surface it would appear that its efforts have gone a good ways toward providing the very cultural identity Sharp felt was needed. Similarly, the Dominion Drama Festival gives expression to the Canadian spirit. Significantly, it has been bicultural from the first, with plays in both languages being judged by bilingual judges. The National Shakespeare Theatre at Stratford and the development of a vigorous national system of radio and television have also served to focus attention on Canada and so to help give it an identity.

It may be that the so-called identity crisis grows out of the fact that, as Edwin C. Hargrove recently asserted, unlike the United States, which was the product of a revolution and so from the beginning had a "charter myth," Canadian "political culture does not have in it the dynamics of a 'Canadian dream.' " The founding fathers of Confederation, Hargrove argues, were not the sponsors of a "democratic myth but [were] anti-revolutionary. . . . The transition to democrat[ic government] was made within the framework of the Crown's authority. Canada had no Jefferson or Jackson [as America did. Thus] Americans are messianic about their nation, and this causes dynamic, creative politics and programs, [while] Canadians are not messianic about their nation and this fact breeds a politics that is so pragmatic that it is often uninspired."[16] If Hargrove is correct, the lack of a satisfactory Canadian image will be difficult to remedy. On the other hand, Canadian history since Confederation has brought forth a number of eminent men who have served to inspire and direct Canadian life, and with time these may come to provide the kind of inspiration Hargrove finds missing in Canada today. Accompanying this development should be a resolution of the Canadian identity problem.

Finally, the "identity crisis" may arise out of a failure on the part of the Canadians to understand themselves and what is happening in their country. If this is so, Canada is not alone in her plight. Nor is it surprising. Canada, though still a developing

16. "On Canadian and American Political Culture," *Canadian Journal of Economics*, XXXIII (Feb., 1967), 107–109, 111.

nation, has come so far so fast that it would not be strange if her citizens were bewildered. Moreover, like most of her democratic counterparts, Canada has not developed according to an overall master plan against which the people could check the nation's progress at regular intervals. Rather, Canada has moved on both the domestic and international fronts in response to those demands and needs which had the support of the most powerful pressure groups. Like other democratic governments, the Canadian government has for the most part reacted to events after they have taken place rather than in anticipation of them. Canadian parties and candidates generally have operated on an *ad hoc* basis, presenting no clear-cut picture or program for the future to enable the people to see clearly where they are going.

Only with the establishment of the Economic Council of Canada in 1964 did Canada move "to develop special procedures and machinery designed to facilitate attainment of . . . widely accepted social and economic objectives," and even then, those objectives—full employment, a high rate of economic growth, reasonable stability of prices, a viable balance of payments, and an equitable distribution of rising incomes—were limited to the economic field and so failed to provide any overall agenda for the future. "Prosperity for What?" New York *Times* correspondent James Reston asked of the United States, a question he might equally well have asked of Canada. "What are the ends to which [this] accumulation of wealth is to be directed?"[17] Obviously, mere economic prosperity and stability are not ends in themselves; a productive economy is desirable only because it enables a nation better to achieve other objectives.

What are those objectives for Canada? The diffidence of the Canadian people which has received so much attention may, in sum, be rooted in their uncertainty about how that question will be answered. Perhaps one way to help alleviate the strain would be to utilize the new techniques of program analysis and prediction and on the basis of the data derived therefrom to formulate both short-term and long-term goals for national development.

17. New York *Times*, Oct. 13, 1965, p. 46.

Perhaps a Canadian counterpart to the Commission on National Goals, appointed by President Eisenhower in 1960, could at one and the same time initiate a process of goal establishment in Canada and, by giving the people a better understanding of themselves and their direction, solve the "identity crisis."

In any case, the problem of self-identification seems to have been overstated in Canada. It would seem to be time now to turn full attention to the solution of more pressing problems, even as Premier Louis Robichaud of New Brunswick urged early in 1967. "If Canada should perish," the Premier was reported as saying, "it will mark the first time in history that a nation died from an overdose of diagnosis. If many commentators are to be believed, the spirit of Canada is neuroticism tied to a death wish. In Canada today we should spend less time taking our own pulse and more time taking hold of our opportunities."[18] Those opportunities are so many and so varied that the outside observer is inclined to agree with Premier Robichaud.

One other aspect of the Canadian future deserves at least some attention before a volume on contemporary Canada can properly be brought to a close. One glance at a map showing population distribution and density in Canada will suffice to suggest the problem of Canada's tremendous land mass, much of which remains uninhabited and remote from the vital currents of Canadian life, but for all of that exerting a continuing fascination on the Canadian mind and spirit. The fascination is not merely an infatuation with a mysteriously beckoning unknown, although that is part of it. Much more to the point here are the deposits of gold, silver, nickel, lead, zinc, iron ore, and natural gas which lie in still unestimated quantities all over the North, but in especially large amounts in the Canadian Shield which surrounds Hudson Bay. There is an increasing number of mines on the Shield's edge, and other developments have been started on Baffin Island and in the Yukon Territory. So far, most of the exploration and development has been undertaken by private companies. Canadian federal investment in the Northwest and Yukon territories

18. *Globe and Mail* (Toronto), Feb. 10, 1967, p. 2.

amounts to only about 2 per cent of the national budget, and Quebec, which administers her own northern areas, devotes about the same percentage to them. So far, none of the political parties nor any important combination of pressure groups have taken on the cause of a larger governmental role in the North. But it would seem to be both inevitable and necessary that the North be developed and thus that the government's role must be increased. Certainly part of the answer to American domination would be supplied by greater production in that area. In any case,

Developed or not, the North remains all important to the Canadians' self-image. It makes their country the second largest on earth. Its promise of riches is a lottery in which every Canadian holds a ticket, yet at the same time it is a reminder of the frontier past, of a simpler and purer world into which he may still escape. Above all, its brooding physical presence over the land is a warning that Canadians have not yet conquered their universe.[19]

As indeed they have not. One hundred years of Confederation, and two hundred years before that of colonization and settlement, have succeeded for the most part in taming only the southernmost strip of the Canadian land mass. If there is a high degree of sophistication and urbanity there, these run out fast as one goes north. There is still a frontier in Canada—to be sure, a largely frozen and inaccessible one—but one of even more possibilities than the American frontier of a century ago. Canada cannot help but be affected by its constant presence and challenge.

To what extent the development of the North will occupy the Canadian people is problematical. They are moving in so many other directions at the same time that in the last analysis there may be little time or money left for extensive exploration and exploitation there. Not only is Canadian manufacturing carrying Canada to a new level of industrial sophistication and her involvement in world affairs requiring greater investments of resources and energy, but the development of the arts and sciences, particularly of medicine, also competes for attention. These too are frontiers for Canada, and only she can choose among them.

19. Brian Moore, *Canada* (New York, 1963), p. 109.

The exciting thing is that Canada is able to choose, a luxury denied to many nations. For on the one hand, Canada is blessed with prosperity and a literate and energetic people; on the other, she is a middle power and so is not forced to devote a major portion of her resources to achieving solutions to world problems, as is the United States, for example. Canada still retains, in other words, freedom of choice and is in the fortunate position of having sufficient wealth and talent to sustain her on whatever course she may decide to take.

Indeed, as the second century of Canadian national life begins, the options are many. "There is abroad in the country today a feeling comparable to that of a younger America," Brian Moore observed, "a feeling that parties and institutions are not securely entrenched . . . that anything [could] happen. . . . [A] new and heady uncertainty . . . has gripped Canadians."[20] Their second century may well be devoted to developing a variety of possible answers to the question, "Which way, Canada?"

❖   ❖   ❖

It was said at the outset that centennials are fundamentally causes for celebration. As the reader moved through this volume, he perhaps came to a contrary opinion, as have many students of modern Canada, that instead of celebration the condition of contemporary Canada warrants commiseration and sympathy. Certainly as the essays in this book have all pointed to problems, the reader could not be blamed for assuming that the country was in perilous straits. Such a conclusion is totally wrong. The reverse is in fact the case. Few nations are as fortunate as Canada as they face the future in the mid-twentieth century. If the "French Fact" includes a remote possibility of the secession of Quebec, and the resultant destruction of the Confederation as it stands, the same set of circumstances can be read as an indication of the remarkable tolerance and diversity which exist in Canada and of the success that two very different racial groups have had in their

20. *Ibid.*, p. 148.

experiment in international living, a success which by itself would seem to guarantee the continuation of the framework that has permitted it. If the Canadian economy is marked by structural problems and by other weaknesses, not the least of which is the very real threat of American domination and control, it is nevertheless a prosperous economy which has provided Canadians with a remarkably high standard of living and promises to continue to do so in the future. If Canadian education is at a crossroads, none of the alternate routes seems to lead backward to ignorance and oppression. Rather, the several choices all suggest a continued emphasis on both quality and service to the Canadian people. If there are problems in the area of military policy and international relations, some of them truly of serious proportions, none of them would seem to lead Canada toward destruction. Her position on the international stage is an enviable one which has enhanced her image around the world. And if there are problems of government and politics, they are not the kinds of problems which involve the dissolution of the nation. In a word, though the essays herein reflect a variety of concerns about the Canadian future, they should not be read as portents of doom. The problems Canada faces today are the problems that a new age and new opportunities bring along with them. Canada is alert to their presence and concerned to find timely answers and solutions for them. Thus, as Prime Minister Pearson put it:

As we enter our centennial year we are still a young nation, very much in the formative stages. Our national condition is still flexible enough that we can make almost anything we wish of our nation. No other country is in a better position than Canada to go ahead with the evolution of a national purpose devoted to all that is good and noble and excellent in the human spirit. . . . The record gives us good reason for optimism about the progress we can make in our second century. As we can look back with pride, so we can look forward with hope and with confidence.[21]

No better send-off could be given to a nation as it enters its second century of national existence, and no better cause could exist for national celebration.

21. *Canadian Weekly Bulletin,* Jan. 4, 1967, p. 1.

Index